Economic Development and Governance in Small Town America

Who governs? And why? How do they govern? These remain vital questions in the politics of our small cities and towns. In this new book, author Daniel Bliss takes issue with those who believe that small towns and cities are fatally vulnerable to the pressures of a global economy. Based on in-depth analyses of small town America, this book demonstrates how political agency can address and solve real problems affecting US towns, including capital flight, industrial closures, and job losses. Bliss illustrates how small localities exercise choices – such as nurturing local businesses and developing infrastructure rather than engaging in a "race to the bottom," and heavily mortgaging tax revenues to attract large box retailers and small box call centers while passively watching more productive firms and better-paying jobs slip away.

Taking careful account of comparative literature as well as variations in city governments, their planning agencies, and their relations with state authorities, this book explores the ways in which local politicians and public planning bodies can mobilize local constituencies to weather global challenges and common structural problems such as unfavorable demographics, skill shortages, and out-migration. *Economic Development and Governance in Small Town America* holds out the promise of meaningful democratic change even in unfavorable political and economic circumstances.

Daniel Bliss is Assistant Professor of Political Science at the Illinois Institute of Technology, USA.

"Daniel Bliss presents a remarkably timely and thoughtful analysis of small town governance in the United States. In contrast to the uncritical romanticism and victimization narratives often drawn on to depict rural and small towns, Bliss makes a powerful empirical case for how local institutional capacity and citizen involvement shape differences in effective local problem solving."

– **Susan Clarke,** *University of Colorado at Boulder, USA*

Economic Development and Governance in Small Town America
Paths to Growth

Daniel Bliss

NEW YORK AND LONDON

First published 2018
by Routledge
711 Third Avenue, New York, NY 10017

and by Routledge
2 Park Square, Milton Park, Abingdon, Oxon, OX14 4RN

Routledge is an imprint of the Taylor & Francis Group, an informa business

© 2018 Taylor & Francis

The right of Daniel Bliss to be identified as author of this work has been asserted by him in accordance with sections 77 and 78 of the Copyright, Designs and Patents Act 1988.

All rights reserved. No part of this book may be reprinted or reproduced or utilised in any form or by any electronic, mechanical, or other means, now known or hereafter invented, including photocopying and recording, or in any information storage or retrieval system, without permission in writing from the publishers.

Trademark notice: Product or corporate names may be trademarks or registered trademarks, and are used only for identification and explanation without intent to infringe.

Library of Congress Cataloging-in-Publication Data
Names: Bliss, Daniel, 1970– author.
Title: Economic development and governance in small town
America : paths to growth / Daniel Bliss.
Description: 1 Edition. | New York : Routledge, 2018. |
Includes bibliographical references and index.
Identifiers: LCCN 2017045371 | ISBN 9780815393719 (hardback : alk. paper) |
ISBN 9780815393726 (pbk. : alk. paper) | ISBN 9781351188036 (ebook)
Subjects: LCSH: Cities and towns–United States. | Cities and towns–Growth. |
Economic development–Government policy–United States.
Classification: LCC HT384.U5 B55 2018 | DDC 307.760973–dc23
LC record available at https://lccn.loc.gov/2017045371

ISBN: 978-0-815-39371-9 (hbk)
ISBN: 978-0-815-39372-6 (pbk)
ISBN: 978-1-351-18803-6 (ebk)

Typeset in Times New Roman
by Out of House Publishing

Contents

Preface	vii
Introduction	1
1 A Theory of Institutional Capacity and Governance for Economic Development	18
2 The Economic Context of Municipalities	43
3 Institutional Frameworks: Intergovernmental Support and Bureaucratic Organization	64
4 Ely: Infrastructure Delivered, Governance Contested	83
5 Hibbing, Minnesota: The Evolution of Activist Development	122
6 Sterling and Rock Falls, Illinois: Reform and Recovery?	153
7 Comparing Governance of Economic Development	180
8 Conclusion	197
Appendix: Survey Questionnaire	210
Index	213

Preface

This book grew out of the interaction of a liking for small towns with a life experience that friends have compared to a plot line from the TV show *Northern Exposure* but seemed natural to me at the time. I grew up in a small town in England, and regularly came back to the United States to visit my relatives in similarly small communities in the Midwest. The more relevant life experience (in terms of this project) was a "flyer" I took early in my career on a small but visionary independent newspaper in northern Minnesota, *The Timberjay*. I was looking for a journalism job that would let me cover state and local government, and, with the role that *Timberjay* owners Marshall Helmberger and Jodi Summit gave me, I had an immersive experience in reporting and occasionally editorializing on small town government and planning. My subsequent switch to academia was a chance to gain a more analytical appreciation of the subject, and to take a broader look at the structural limitations in which local governments operate.

Observing city, township, school, county and state government first as a journalist and then as an academic has given me a great appreciation for their work. I saw a struggle to recover from a globally driven recession in the steel industry; and I saw the extent to which state aid to these communities provided a valuable leg-up and a desperately needed safety margin, but often came accompanied by awkward conditions and a startling indifference to places that didn't "fit" the perspective of state politicians. These observations were reminiscent of what I'd seen a few years earlier on an internship in the United Kingdom studying the local government response to the Channel Tunnel, a situation in which, at least on the English side of the channel, municipalities ("district councils" in English parlance) and counties were operating without the tools they needed.

Both my return to graduate school in political science and this project were an effort on my part to learn more and be in a position to say more in a way, I hope, will be helpful to private citizens and policy-makers alike. Small towns can, and often do, provide better access to public officials and business leaders than larger cities. They are functional examples of policies and institutional forms of governance that are applicable to communities of all viii *Preface*

sizes. In particular, I saw the project as a useful opportunity to refine the methods of urban policy and politics research and apply them to places even non-urbanists would identify with.

There is a long list of people to thank. First of all, I am indebted to the more than 100 survey respondents across the four communities, ranging from elected officials to staff at local and state agencies to business leaders and activists, whose interviews, some of them as long as three hours, several of them on multiple occasions, provided crucial insight into these towns over a course of a decade, through doctoral research and then the development and expansion of this project into a book.

I would like to thank people who have supported the project in additional ways, helping out with feedback on the manuscript, special insights into the communities, places to stay, access to records and facilities, and other forms of advice and/or support. These include Sterling, Ill. mayor Skip Lee and his family in Sterling, Marshall Helmberger at the Timberjay Newspapers in Tower and Ely, Minn., Barb Berglund, the Sterling Public Library, the Sterling-Rock Falls, Ely-Winton and Hibbing Historical Societies, the *Hibbing Daily Tribune*, the city governments of Ely and Hibbing, Minn., and Sterling and Rock Falls, Ill., Minnesota Discovery Center in Chisholm, Minn., staff at the Iron Range Resources and Rehabilitation Board, St. Louis County, Minn., and Whiteside County, Ill., and colleagues at the University of Illinois at Chicago and Illinois Institute of Technology. I would especially like to thank my PhD adviser, Dennis Judd at the University of Illinois at Chicago, as well as others, including Michael Pagano, Lyn Ragsdale, Sultan Tepe, Larry Bennett, Dick Simpson and Evan McKenzie, for their phenomenal support and feedback during the early stages of the project, helping me develop an idea into an award-winning dissertation, as well as advice since then on developing the book from these and other colleagues in the field, including Jonathan Davies, Zachary Taylor and Maureen Flanagan.

This book is for all those who work in, with and/or volunteer for local and state institutions of governance – the people who serve city councils, chambers of commerce, joint powers boards, school boards, parent–teacher organizations and a myriad of other groups and causes, and the state and higher-level government agencies and elected bodies that work with local government. You make your communities tick, and I hope you will find this book useful and helpful.

Finally, I would like to dedicate this to my family, who have supported this project emotionally, materially and editorially: my parents Bob and Paulette Bliss and sister Greta Bliss, my aunt and uncle Don and Mary Ellen Mackaman and family in Ely, and cousin Sandra Rasmussen. You all have helped me through good times and bad, and it counts so much.

Introduction

This book poses two simple questions. Are our politics so bound by the "imperatives" of the free market that we have lost democratic control over our ability as neighborhoods, municipalities and states to shape community and economic development? Or can citizens find institutional and organizational means to deliver local outcomes that meet public preferences and provide meaningful improvements? The questions arise because of the extent to which economies have globalized and shifted from manufacturing to services, while the national governments that are best placed to at least manage such trends have downloaded many responsibilities to states and local governments, which are financially stressed as a result. Thus, footloose capital plays one place against another, inciting often desperate bidding wars that compromise the distinctiveness of local places, harm the ability of people and communities to help themselves and threaten the effectiveness of democracy itself. Positive answers to these questions would suggest that local places may have far more opportunities than they think for self-help even on a limited budget, whether to effect long-term improvements or respond to momentary public preferences.

The idea of placing the community's desires or needs alongside, in conjunction with or even instead of bidding for outside capital is an enticing prospect for people of all ideological stripes, who might share interests in boosting business development, improving local infrastructures or just making a place better to live in. It raises the prospect of substantively improving even the smallest of communities through local individual or collective action, public policy and democracy. And finding such evidence in some of the most financially constrained communities of all – small municipalities beyond major metropolitan areas – would hint at universal possibilities.

Small towns such as the four Midwestern US communities in this book provide a political setting that, in the conventional economic wisdom of the past 40 years, should be close to a worst-case scenario in terms of local influence over economic development. These are places that are inherently short of the resources bigger cities or higher levels of government can use to entice businesses or build infrastructure and public services. The

2   Introduction

implication is these communities may find that efforts at economic development impose unaffordable taxes, require extensive financial inducements to business or are doomed to failure because of a lack of amenities that prospective business owners and employees alike want to have.

However, this picture of local impotence omits crucial facts. For one, small towns, particularly in states that share a relatively high proportion of their revenue with local government, can and do choose to prioritize social needs, community amenities and general infrastructure over business tax breaks and subsidies – a line of action often appreciated by business owners, and sometimes the only option in situations in which voters or special interests within the community fear favoritism of one business or business sector over another. But positive results can also arise from business subsidies or tax breaks, and some small as well as big cities have crafted procedures and institutions for adopting policies that insulate economic development from political opposition. And so much the better if their efforts come in varied political guises, such as the broad-based approach to community development often idealized by liberals and favored by skeptics of business subsidies, the approach of targeted capital and other assistance to business favored by many economic development professionals or the laissez-faire approach of libertarian conservatives.

This is an optimistic scenario for the future of local communities and their prospects for democracy and democratic control. After all, these are political and policy choices we may not have fully appreciated. Such meaningful choices as these legitimize local government and governance as processes through which citizens can operate to achieve their goals or gain redress of grievances. And they demonstrate that, even in financially stressed situations or under heavy pressure from outside capital, municipalities can support their existing residential and commercial taxpayers to effect favorable results.

This book asks how municipalities deliver on economic and community development, whether on behalf of capital, their citizens or both. Through building a theoretical framework applicable to most local governments and a detailed study of a representative selection of small communities facing the challenges of deindustrialization and aging, all of them well away from the economic interactions and pull of major urban centers, we see many examples of political choices and policy goals that may not dovetail with perceptions of economic vulnerability yet meet locally shared perceptions of community need. Through spreading the sample across state lines, we also get some idea of the influence of state government that, in the United States, is responsible for the framework of local government affairs. This includes a view of the effect of state-level choices on how much to micromanage local government, or whether to financially backstop municipalities with revenue-sharing, need-based assistance or other forms of compensation for a weak tax base.

Introduction 3

Local governments can serve as an effective intermediary between the individual and the state in both economics and politics by providing a venue in which individuals can organize collectively to make their lives better. At their best, they enable the free exercise of political choices in accordance with local preferences, whether they are enabled through favorable treatment from the state, community action within, individuals sharing common goals, or multiple cities working effectively together as peers as opposed to under higher supervision (Frug, 1999). If locally chosen and driven action is possible even in an unfavorable economic and political climate, even poorer communities may be able to meaningfully improve themselves without outside support beyond their control.

This is potentially a very different reality from the basic assumption of the race to the bottom, which goes roughly like this: to land a business, a city provides a subsidy, usually one or a combination of tax breaks, assistance with infrastructure, discounted or free land and buildings, venture capital, aid for worker training, and other incentives, and then keeps taxes and other costs of doing business as low as possible for it to stay there. If it fails in this endeavor, the business will seek other communities bidding to be the most attractive suitor. This theory grows out of the idealized world of consumers freely choosing their place of residence on the basis of packages of services and benefits between competing municipalities presented by Charles Tiebout, a strong advocate for the idea of tax competitiveness, in the 1950s (Tiebout, 1956); later on, it would be somewhat supported in far more pessimistic discussions of the topic from the likes of Paul Peterson (Peterson, 1981; 1995) and Saskia Sassen in the 1980s and 1990s (Sassen, 1991). Either way, the theory of a race to the bottom in practice places municipalities, states and even countries in intense competition with one another to be a business's cheapest and most compliant prospective partner.

In the way in which this assumption has been applied, political agency (Smith, 2001; O'Brien, 2015) – which I define as the freedom to individually or collectively effect change through politically exercised choices between different courses of actions – is often perceived as limited even at the federal level and profoundly weak at lower levels of government. In a system in which such a concept is a foundational part of both democracy and economics (Downs, 1957), this is a serious problem. The main role of a local government in this scenario is to seek outside capital through a balance of the lowest possible taxes with the best possible services within that constrained base of revenue, whether or not that reflects local public preferences. The attractiveness of a city to potential residents and therefore labor (Nevarez, 2003; Paulsen, 2004) is not as extensively considered. Cities that overspend, overtax or underserve will inevitably lose per this theory; cities short of resources to begin with may find themselves having to withdraw entirely from what might commonly be viewed as "essential" services and

4   *Introduction*

infrastructure, simply to keep taxes and borrowing low enough and economic development support high enough to attract investment.

Local governments are also vulnerable in many countries, notably those with legal systems derived from English law, because of their weak constitutional standing. In the United States, municipalities have no written constitutional standing at the federal level, although Supreme Court case law has reserved for them certain rights derived from English common law, such as power over zoning and land use. At the state level, circumstances vary significantly, depending on the application of Dillon's Rule (Frug, 1980; Frug, Ford & Barron, 2006), the rulings of Iowa Supreme Court Justice and later federal judge John Forrest Dillon. His Iowa Supreme Court opinion from 1868 remains a legal benchmark for American and Canadian local government's status with its words that "municipal corporations owe their origin to, and derive their powers and rights wholly from, the legislature. It breathes into them the breath of life, without which they cannot exist."[1]

The Dillon decision is a fact of life for municipalities in the English-speaking world, especially in North America. It is constitutionally deeply entrenched by precedent. This is because it upholds a deeply grounded tradition in English common law, dating back at least to King Charles II's *quo warranto* writ against the City of London in 1682,[2] that the sovereign body alone – in the American case, state government – issues the warrants by which local government operates. Furthermore, it is inherently limiting to local government, to the point that it has been roundly criticized as causing a "democratic deficit" (Frug, 1980), a limitation upon political agency that would normally be implied in basic social relations among people and institutions (Smith, 2001). However, this has not wholly abrogated local political power (Wolman & Goldsmith, 1990); when handling policy areas explicitly granted to it or not explicitly excluded from it, a local government has considerable authority, for example on land use (Wolf, 2008),[3] and more power still when states operate with a weaker implementation of Dillon's Rule. So, the degree of state devolution of power to local government is a significant influence. A state can proscribe power or grant it; it can alter the relationship of municipal government with the free market. In the United States, many different combinations of these powers and proscriptions are represented among the 50 states; the same applies to Canadian provinces, and even EU countries in which limitations on local government have evolved through other legal traditions.

Economic inequality is a case in point; it makes the provision of a typical suite of municipal services vary enormously in cost from one jurisdiction to the next, a situation that is difficult to remedy without state or federal government intervention to manage it. For example, if the state government does not equalize – or, in other words, top up on the basis of need – the local revenue that funds these costs, then communities that are poorer to start with, more in need of economic development and more

Introduction 5

adversely affected by trade and globalization stand at an inherent resource disadvantage (Feler & Senses, 2016), and therefore a potential bargaining disadvantage with private capital (Savitch & Kantor, 2002). This situation also needs to be considered in the context of emerging evidence that municipalities with high income inequality tend to "bite the bullet" and spend more on public services (Boustan, Ferreira, Winkler & Zolt, 2012). But, whatever a local government sees fit for economic and community development, it must still navigate state limitations, such as the lack of taxing power, restrictions on borrowing, or financial and fiscal structures that discourage cooperation among municipalities or encourage fragmentation of government.

This is why so much discussion of economic development focuses on constraints. Cities are described as facing "economic imperatives" (Harvey, 1990) to aggressively seek outside capital (Peterson, 1981), keep tax rates to a minimum and reduce spending on programs whose cost may interfere with lower taxes (Peterson, 1995). The perception is that increasing taxes to fund municipal improvements or even routine services risks driving holders of capital to invest elsewhere.

Nonetheless, there are opportunities for local governments to take economic and community development matters into their own hands, whether choosing to adhere to American traditions of privatism and boosterism (Barnekov, Boyle & Rich, 1989; Weaver, 2016; Molotch, 1976) or pursuing an agenda for community improvement that may be broader and costlier than the conventional wisdom would allow. The success or failure of these policies often rides on factors beyond economics or tax rates, such as local or state political will, or the configuration or rules of local institutions of governance that influence economic and community development. Political actors generally operate within limits (Simon, 1997), making choices within parameters set by the economic and political circumstances of the moment, building institutional capacity (Savitch, 1998) and making use of globalization's possibilities (Cerny, 2000) to help expand the scope of "bounded rationality"; in other words, to expand the scope of choices realistically available to community leaders. Cities of all sizes clearly exercise choices that fall outside the scope painted by those who suggest decisions driven by economic "imperatives"; for example, we see economically vibrant cities consciously choosing fast growth, as in Los Angeles (Abu-Lughod, 2000), or slow growth, as in San Francisco (DeLeon, 1992); and in some cases economically weak small towns choosing the path of no growth, as in small towns on Maryland's eastern shore resisting being drawn in to Baltimore's suburban ring (Ramsay, 1996).

This study aims, through the prism of small towns in two Midwestern states with differing approaches to local governance, to test that theory by observing how local governments handle these structural challenges. It analyzes how policies are chosen, produced and delivered at the local level,

6   *Introduction*

and how they succeed or fail, given the municipal institutions, politicians and other local elites involved in the process. The range of solutions is broad, on economic, institutional and political fronts. Much hinges upon the nature of local political support for or opposition to activist economic development, as well as demand for general services, infrastructure and social welfare. Economic development strategies (Leigh & Blakely, 2013) include, just among the four cases analyzed in detail here, grants of land; tax breaks; transportation, telecommunications and utility infrastructure; coordination between local schools, colleges and employers on worker training; market analysis studies; the provision of public amenities, such as parks; the pursuit of private amenities, such as retailing and services; boosting tourism; promoting the arts; direct recruitment of businesses; business development loans or grants; and strategies for retaining existing businesses.

Institutional reforms in these communities have included the appointment of city administrators to oversee department heads in mayor-council governments; reassigning authority over economic development policy within the local government, whether to the city council, a subcommittee or even semi-independent development corporations; or simply coordinating "steering functions," such as policy analysis, development and brainstorming, with "driving functions" including the power to fund, implement and mandate solutions. In this challenging, but potentially hopeful environment, we see in detail how specific towns, over a decade that has seen serious degradation of their traditional manufacturing base as well as the worst recession in more than 70 years, have chosen to upgrade or reform their response to today's economy.

Governance and Economic Development in the Case Study Cities

The four cases in this study – Ely and Hibbing, Minnesota, and Sterling and Rock Falls, Illinois (see Table I.1)[4] – demonstrate a wide range of conditions for governance and policy, with differing plans of government, levels of state financial support and approaches to developing and implementing economic development projects. But they share in common the challenging trends in economics and demographics of deindustrializing communities. In the face of these trends, they have adopted a wide variety of policies and processes in their pursuit of solutions for their problems, at each stage influenced by the governing institutions they have to work with, their leadership and even political traditions.

At the local level, the analysis considers differences between more reformed governments and less reformed governments. But a clear dichotomy does not appear between the two, on account of the variety of different approaches of configuring local government. In this study, at a minimum, one should compare also for the difference between state governments, and there are other major factors such as local politics, institutions and

Table I.1 Descriptive statistics of the case studies (2010 census data)

	Population (2010 census)	Population change (2000–2010)	Median age	Per capita general revenue (2008)	Per capita general revenue (2016)
Hibbing	16,361	−5%	41.0	$967	$1,128
Ely	3,460	−5%	44.1	$997	$1,260
Minnesota			35.4		
Sterling	15,370	−2.1%	36.3	$970	$1,008
Rock Falls	9,266	−2.8%	36.1	$713	$729
Illinois			34.7		
US average			36.7		

Note: Data are for central cities only. However, Ely population rises to around 7,400 when including Morse, Fall Lake, Eagles Nest and Stony River Townships and the cities of Babbitt and Winton. See Table 1.1 in Chapter 1 for median income and 2016 census estimates.
Sources: Illinois Office of the Comptroller; Minnesota Department of Revenue; city financial statements.

culture. In Minnesota, Hibbing's local government is more reformed by the standards of municipal administration than Ely's, with a city administrator, an economic development authority that sits separately from the city council, and large-scale annexation of surrounding territory, forming what almost amounts to a regional authority. Hibbing's political geography is thus relatively unified, city departments are overseen under a single administrator, and the day-to-day management of economic development, such as technical negotiations of deals with businesses, is delegated away from the elected authority – an insulation from public scrutiny that businesses often appreciate – even as the council has the final say over deals that involve general revenue and city resources. Ely, by contrast, maintains a weak mayor/strong council system, direct council control over economic development, and minimal annexation of territory over the past two generations despite a broad annexation agreement with neighboring Morse Township in 1974, though a recent innovation, a director of operations, combines some of the authoritative functions of a city administrator. It is the least reformed of the cases under study.

In Illinois, Sterling stands out as an archetypal reformed government; a council-manager system since the 1970s, delegation by the council on the technical aspects of economic development, and continuity in public policy, administrative procedure and personnel exceeding any of the other cases. This situation has played out in terms of financial stability; for most of the 2000s the city maintained a rare AAA bond rating until the pension underfunding widespread in Illinois started to take it down. Rock Falls reorganized its governance and administration in 2001, replacing a commissioner system in which council members themselves served as department heads with a strong mayor-council system that delegates much day-to-day running of city government to a city administrator.

8 *Introduction*

However, governmental reform also assures neither failure nor positive outcomes, with other variables playing an important role. Ely, the smallest of the communities in this study, illustrates this especially well. For example, cooperation among neighboring local governments is weak. Arrangements for such a basic service as fire protection are fragmented between Ely and its neighboring townships, a result of failure to develop either a regional fire authority or a stable contractual arrangement. The only shared emergency service at present is an ambulance district funded by a regional property tax levy. There are also strong disagreements on annexation, the divide between the city of Ely and Morse Township giving an indication of what might have happened had Hibbing and Stuntz remained separate entities, and even a generational gap between the city and the townships, with their higher proportion of retirees. The resulting difficulty of achieving local consensus makes the community more dependent on influence and help from higher levels of government for economic development. Yet Ely's city government has proved adroit over the years at financial management and developing public infrastructure, often with the assistance of higher levels of government, occasionally also through partnerships with neighbors or with county government. The city government has undertaken major new construction or reconstruction of facilities for water treatment, sewage, the public library, city administration, public works services, arterial streets and major utility lines, all since 1990. With a very different approach from Sterling but a more favorable state framework from the point of providing public service amenities, Ely has also maintained similar financial performance, currently running a AA– bond rating,[5] a step higher than Sterling's current A+ rating.[6]

All four cases are also interesting from a geographical perspective. They are far from major cities and therefore far from some of the strongest and most vibrant drivers of the global economy; Hibbing and Ely are on Minnesota's Iron Range, three to four hours' drive from the Twin Cities of Minneapolis and St. Paul, and Sterling and Rock Falls two hours' drive from Chicago. Additionally, these communities all participate in regional economic development arrangements: Rock Falls and Sterling in the Whiteside/Carroll County Enterprise Zone, a state-sponsored but locally run body for regionally assigning parcels of developable land to tax-preferred business zones; and Ely and Hibbing under the jurisdiction of the Iron Range Resources and Rehabilitation Board (IRRRB), a regionwide state agency whose official remit since its 1941 foundation has been the diversification of the mining-oriented economy in the area. All four communities, in particular the two in Minnesota, also face the challenge of balancing amenities and the natural environment with the often strong political and economic pull of resource-intensive industry – a challenge that creates a more complicated local debate than often appreciated by people who assume the primacy of the "race to the bottom."

Geography also manifests itself in the relationship of municipalities with their state governments. Minnesota and Illinois provide a sharp

Introduction 9

contrast in regimes of financial support for municipalities and approaches to coordinating the activities of local government. Minnesota has had a strong statewide regime of fiscal equalization in local government since the 1971–76 governorship of Wendell Anderson and the "Minnesota Miracle" tax reform (Berg, 2012), which provided large-scale need-based support for schools to offset property taxes and was accompanied by similar reforms to municipal finance. Originally this took the form of Local Government Aid (LGA), a need-based subsidy to mostly financially strained rural and inner city municipalities, and a similar program for supporting schools. In practice, this means that a safety net exists for basic public services, lessening the intensity of the link between economic development and tax revenue for local governments. The broadest change since the original reform was the move by Governor Jesse Ventura in 2001, backed by narrow margins in the legislature,[7] to have the state take over the general education levy for K-12 education. This decision, costing the state $2.7 billion in the 2003–5 biennium alone,[8] sharply reduced property taxes, especially in wealthier suburban districts that had previously little eligibility for need-based state support for the general education levy (Thorson & Anderson, 2006). However, it had the net effect of weakening finances for general purpose local government, as Ventura's successor, Tim Pawlenty, opted to close the resulting budget deficit in part by sharply reducing LGA, a decision that disproportionately hit rural Minnesota. Only with increases in income tax on high-income taxpayers under Pawlenty's successor, Mark Dayton, were the frequent deficits closed and a substantial portion of the LGA cuts reversed.

This becomes relevant for municipal finance because of the pressures that unequalized spending, whether for municipalities or schools, put on local tax bases. Illinois does not equalize municipal finance on the basis of need; rather, it shares revenue with local government, typically 10 percent of the income tax distributed on the basis of population, and revenue from a 1.25 percent sales tax (out of the state's 6.25 percent overall rate) on the basis of where transactions occurred. This means ongoing pressure on communities to maintain and expand their retail shopping base. The implication in terms of comparison with communities in Minnesota is that LGA is generally a more stable base of support for tax-poor communities. Ely, for example, could never have maintained its level of infrastructural spending under Illinois rules in the early 2000s considering the sharp drop in retail spending in the community during the first half of that decade.[9] Conversely, Rock Falls, Illinois, would likely see an improvement in state funds under Minnesota rules on the grounds that it would compensate for its relatively small retail base rather than simply reflecting it. Considering school finance makes the difference in financial pressure on municipalities in the state even more evident. Illinois has the highest local share of spending on schools of any of the 50 states, at 66.9 percent, while Minnesota ranks 46th for local share of spending, at 24 percent,[10] even though per

10 *Introduction*

student spending in schools in both states is very similar. This, in practice, means a heavy property tax burden on Illinois taxpayers that municipalities have to be mindful of when setting levies.

Nonetheless, Illinois municipalities have an alternative opportunity to raise revenue: they have wide latitude to raise local sales taxes – home-rule cities by a vote of the council, non-home-rule cities with a council vote and a local referendum. Their Minnesota counterparts must receive legislative permission for local sales taxes even when they are subjected to a sunset clause. That permission is usually not forthcoming without a specific policy goal and clear evidence of a strong local consensus for the tax. If a local priority cannot be funded from local revenues, and is declined for support by the state, an Illinois municipality can potentially raise sales taxes fairly easily; a Minnesota municipality likely must borrow or shelve the project.

The ability and flexibility of these communities to support economic development and fund local government and public services is also significant given the extent to which they are typical of the demographic and economic stagnation of the rural Upper Midwest region. As we analyze this question, it is worth considering the political and cultural dimensions of this. All these cities are in areas in which Democratic primary and caucus voters in 2016 tilted toward Vermont senator Bernie Sanders (see Figure I.1), and general election voters in a majority of precincts swung sharply toward Republican presidential nominee Donald Trump. Ely and Hibbing were both carried by Trump – Ely by a seven percent margin compared to a 16.7-point Democratic margin in 2012, Hibbing by a mere seven votes out of almost 8,100 compared to almost 33 percent for President Barack Obama in 2012 – in a first for a Republican presidential candidate in both cities since the 1928 election. And, while Rock Falls, Illinois, continued its long-time pattern of supporting Democrats, it did so by a sharply reduced margin: Hillary Clinton's nine-point win here contrasted unfavorably with Obama's 39 percent margin in 2012. Yet Sterling, with relatively similar demographics and economics to the other case study cities, shifted far less, from a 25 percent Democratic margin in 2012 to a 13 percent one in 2016, with several mostly middle-income precincts shifting in Clinton's favor and most switchers away from the Democrats opting for third parties rather than the Republican ticket.[11] A middle-income precinct just outside Ely, Fall Lake Township, also swung toward Clinton, producing a five-point Democratic margin, even as every other rural township in the area swung toward Trump. Down-ballot, the formerly safely Democratic 8th Congressional District in Minnesota has joined Illinois' 17th, the home of Sterling and Rock Falls, as a perennially competitive district, yet Sanders-endorsing Congressman Rick Nolan narrowly secured re-election to the 8th thanks to Iron Range votes – many of which split for Trump.

While this book does not delve deeply into the cultural explanations for such differences, the institutional and organizational differences among

Figure I.1 People stand in line for a Bernie Sanders rally at Hibbing High School, March 2, 2016. Economic populism is evident in the politics of all four communities in this study

Source: Hibbing Historical Society/Jace Tramontin.

these communities directly addresses the question of local powerlessness that helps play into political resentment. For all four of these cities, industrial history centered around manufacturing and mining is central to the cultural identity, especially of longer-term and older residents. The sense of loss of the past 20 years from the declining employment of these industries is palpable, and affects each community's goals for economic development. Where resentment and a sense of being beaten down enter into the political culture as well, the swings to Trump were dramatic, especially in Rock Falls, which shifted from overwhelmingly Democratic to a near-even split. On the other hand, Sterling has noticeably more consensual and less

12 *Introduction*

resentment-driven politics than the other communities, and a government that has been far more reformed along the lines of what professionals in public administration would regard as "best practice." Here the process for developing and delivering economic development has been more clearly defined, structured and organized in a way to promote rapid response and minimize political disputes. But, even here, the 2017 election of a populist to the city council demonstrates a sense of dispossession among voters sufficient to strongly question the status quo.

Organization of the Book

The introduction has made a case for the study of smaller towns because they exhibit some of the most adverse examples of the problems of economic pressure, outside competition, capital flight risk and fiscal crisis that face municipalities of all sizes in the United States and beyond (see Figures I.2 and I.3). Success in the realm of economic and community development in such towns would demonstrate enticing possibilities for

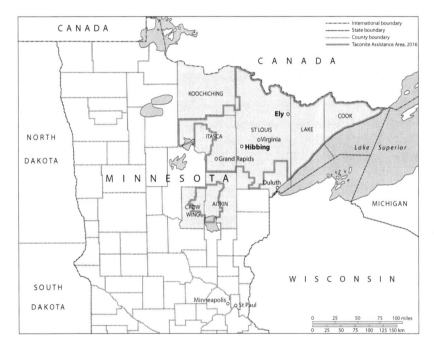

Figure I.2 Map showing the location of the Minnesota case study cities, Ely and Hibbing, within the Taconite Assistance Area, in relation to other northeastern Minnesota cities and Minneapolis/St. Paul. The TAA is the service area of the Iron Range Resources and Rehabilitation Board, a Cabinet-level state agency and the leading funder of economic and community development projects for the region

Introduction 13

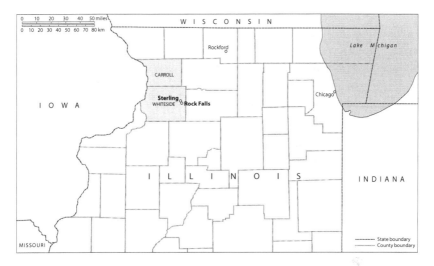

Figure I.3 Map showing the location of the Illinois case study cities, Rock Falls and Sterling, within Whiteside County. The map also shows neighboring Carroll County, whose municipalities, like those in Whiteside, also participate in the enterprise zone board that administers tax breaks for economic development

cities of all sizes. The rest of the book lays out theories for how economic and community development policy develops in local government; explains how power is accessed and exercised locally in the implementation of policy; sets the economic and political context in which this policy-making is taking place; and describes, compares and analyzes cases.

Chapter 1 introduces the theory of institutional capacity and discusses how organization within or among governments or intergovernmental relations between states and local government might impact the development and selection of economic policy. This includes discussion of the extent to which the configuration of local governance and intergovernmental relationships plays a vital role in enabling successful economic development, selecting public policies and bridging the political conflict that envelops economic development policy more than many other areas. The crucial point is that cities have more choices in negotiating terms with businesses than many scholars and practitioners in economic development and urban politics have acknowledged; these choices are influenced by differences in how local governments organizationally handle public policy and how much of a financial safety net they receive from state government. This chapter also explains the methods of the project, a survey-based, multi-level study using similar communities in two US states with a sharply differing approach to their relations with local municipalities. Chapters 2 and 3 address the evidence of continuing local "political agency," the exercise

14 *Introduction*

of independent political choice both for and against economic and community development amid the context of broader economic trends and institutional frameworks. Chapter 2 describes the context of recent and current trends in economics and globalization and related national policies, discussing and reviewing data and literature on the effect of all of these on local government policies on economic development. Chapter 3 reviews the state-level institutional and organizational framework facing local governments, and the prevailing literature on these topics, taking a close look at the decline in intergovernmental support for municipal government and providing a broad grounding especially for people new to the topic of economic development or its connections with politics and policy-making. It sets this in the context of the case communities – Rock Falls and Sterling, two neighboring cities in northwestern Illinois known in the past for their hardware manufacturing, and Hibbing and Ely, on northeastern Minnesota's Iron Range – which are representative of blue-collar-dominated, demographically stagnant communities in the United States and beyond.

Chapters 4 through 6 review the communities' recent histories with economy and community development through the eyes of local and regional community leaders. Chapter 4 discusses Ely, Minnesota, which provided the "template" for the project and has the most fragmented local government despite having the smallest population of the four. It operates within a strong state safety net for local government and in an environment in which policy-making over economic development is heavily influenced by a regional, state-run agency. But, within this context, Ely retains the "traditional" plan of US local government, with a weak mayor/strong council system, relatively little formal or institutionalized cooperation with neighboring local governments, and power over economic development policy concentrated on the elected city council rather than being delegated to a separate board or commission. Decision-making in Ely is highly politicized. And, for this study, it adds interest, with the striking contrast between its consistently successful delivery of major public and business-related infrastructure and sound financial management and its struggles with more finely targeted business assistance.

Chapter 5 moves across the Iron Range to Hibbing, Minnesota, which embarked on a different path of governance from Ely in the late 1970s by annexing a surrounding area roughly 15 times its size, reorganizing its local government by adding a strong city administrator to its own mayor-council system and delegating much of its economic development policy to a separate economic development authority. Hibbing's continuity in policy masks an ongoing split in local politics between a "pro-business" group, consisting mostly of leading local business owners as well as educators and public officials who have long emphasized business-targeted, "supply-side" economic development, and a looser alignment of local politicians and

Introduction 15

citizens, who have expressed considerable skepticism about much of the business community's ability to deliver effective results.

Chapter 6 reviews the two Illinois cases, Sterling and Rock Falls, together. A single urban area divided by a shallow river and a deep-seated political and cultural boundary, these two municipalities had sharply different approaches to economic and community development throughout the 1980s and 1990s, but both have seen government institutions play key roles in response to economic crisis since then. Sterling has a near-textbook example of council-manager government and delegates much of its economic development implementation to private bodies. Rock Falls' strong mayor-council system – the only one among the four cities studied here – for over a decade funded a community development corporation (CDC); while the city subsidy to the CDC it created has ended, the more activist policies and political culture developed over the past 15 years continue through the mayor's office, with some of the recruiting efforts farmed out to consultants, and what used to be the CDC's funding has been reassigned to other economic development initiatives.

Chapter 7 compares the findings of these case studies on the variables and dimensions of institutional governance and process, leadership and policy results. This includes a review of the impact of the communities' differences in governance, such as regional government bodies, devolution and the effectiveness of city institutions, and their effect on policy outcomes. It discusses how the institutional and resource differences interact and differently influence private-sector economic development deals and public-sector community development. Lastly, the conclusion in Chapter 8 reviews the importance of institutional capacity and its implications both for reform of governance within communities and the relationship between states and local governments on matters of economic and community development.

Notes

1 City of Clinton *v.* Cedar Rapids and Missouri River Railroad Company, 24 Iowa 455 (1868).

2 "*Quo warranto*" (literally, "by what warrant?") denotes the state's limitations on the ability of a local government to exercise authority – namely, that authority, whether exercised by the state or the locality, depends ultimately upon the warrant of the state.

3 This discusses in extensive detail the historic US Supreme Court zoning case of Village of Euclid, Ohio *v.* Ambler Realty Co., 272 U.S. 365 (1926), which affirmed local government's constitutional right to exercise power over land use.

4 The cases are compared with state and national statistics. Measured area for Hibbing, Rock Falls and Sterling is city limits; measured area for Ely includes full and observer members of the Community Economic Development Joint Powers Board (cities of Ely, Winton and Babbitt; and Morse Township) plus

16 *Introduction*

the neighboring town of Fall Lake. Per capita revenue in all cases is only for the central municipality. Sources: US Census Bureau and Citydata.com for 2008.

5 See T. Coombe, S&P: Ely economy "weak": Notation comes as part of bond rating, amid mining debate". *Ely Echo*, September 9, 2016.

6 Source: City of Sterling, Annual financial report: April 30, 2016; available at www.sterling-il.gov/docs/SterlingAuditFinal20162017.pdf.

7 H.F.2, the Education Omnibus Finance Bill, passed 69–62 in the House and 38–36 in the Senate, with voting breakdown more by region (high-tax-base metro suburbs in favor, rural Minnesota against) than by party.

8 Source: *A fiscal review of the 2001 legislative session*: Minnesota State Senate Office of Senate Counsel and Research, January 2002; available at www.leg. state.mn.us/docs/pre2003/other/020088.pdf.

9 See Minnesota Department of Revenue, Sales and use tax revenue by city.

10 National Education Association (2017); see in particular Table F-3, Percentage of revenue from local government.

11 Sterling and Rock Falls election returns are based on townships; Sterling Township, most of which is occupied by the city of Sterling, and Coloma Charter Township, most of which is occupied by the city of Rock Falls. Hibbing and Ely results are based on municipal boundaries. Sources: Whiteside County, Illinois; Minnesota Secretary of State.

References

Abu-Lughod, J. L. (2000). *New York, Chicago, Los Angeles: America's global cities*. Minneapolis: University of Minnesota Press.

Barnekov, T. K., Boyle, R., & Rich, D. (1989). *Privatism and urban policy in Britain and the United States*. New York: Oxford University Press.

Berg, T. (2012). *Minnesota's miracle: Learning from the government that worked*. Minneapolis: University of Minnesota Press.

Boustan, L., Ferreira, F., Winkler, H., & Zolt, E. M. (2012). The effect of rising income inequality on taxation and public expenditures: Evidence from US municipalities and school districts, 1970–2000. *Review of Economics and Statistics*, *95*(4), 1291–1302.

Cerny, P. G. (2000). Political agency in a globalizing world: Toward a structurational approach. *European Journal of International Relations*, *6*(4), 435–463.

DeLeon, R. E. (1992). *Left coast city: Progressive politics in San Francisco, 1975–1991*. Lawrence, Kan.: University Press of Kansas.

Downs, A. (1957). An economic theory of political action in a democracy. *Journal of Political Economy*, *65*(2), 135–150.

Feler, L., & Senses, M. Z. (2016). Trade shocks and the provision of local public goods, IZA Discussion Paper no. 10231. Bonn: Institute of Labor Economics, available at SSRN: https://ssrn.com/abstract=2846322.

Frug, G. E. (1980). The city as a legal concept. *Harvard Law Review*, *93*(6), 1057–1154.

Frug, G. E. (1999). *City making: Building communities without building walls*. Princeton, N.J.: Princeton University Press.

Frug, G. E., Ford, R. T., & Barron, D. J. (2006). *Local government law* (4th edn.). St. Paul, Minn.: Thomson/West.

Introduction 17

Harvey, D. (1990). *The condition of postmodernity: An enquiry into the origins of cultural change*. Malden, Mass.: Blackwell.

Leigh, N. G., & Blakely, E. J. (2013). *Planning local economic development: Theory and practice* (5th edn.). Thousand Oaks, Calif.: SAGE Publications.

Molotch, H. (1976). The city as a growth machine: Toward a political economy of place. *American Journal of Sociology, 82*(2), 309–332.

National Education Association (2017). Rankings and estimates: Rankings of the states 2016 and estimates of school statistics 2017. Washington, D.C.: National Education Association.

Nevarez, L. (2003). *New money, nice town: How capital works in the new urban economy*. New York: Routledge.

O'Brien, K. (2015). Political agency: The key to tackling climate change. *Science, 350*(6265), 1170–1171.

Paulsen, K. E. (2004). Making character concrete: Empirical strategies for studying place distinction. *City and Community, 3*(3), 243–262.

Peterson, P. E. (1981). *City limits*. Chicago: University of Chicago Press.

Peterson, P. E. (1995). *The price of federalism*. Washington, D.C.: Brookings Institution Press.

Ramsay, M. (1996). *Community, culture, and economic development: The social roots of local action*. Albany, N.Y.: State University of New York Press.

Sassen, S. (1991). *The global city: New York, London, Tokyo*. Princeton, N.J.: Princeton University Press.

Savitch, H. V. (1998). Global challenge and institutional capacity: Or, how we can refit local administration for the next century. *Administration and Society, 30*(3), 248–273.

Savitch, H. V., & Kantor, P. (2002). *Cities in the international marketplace: The political economy of urban development in North America and western Europe*. Princeton, N.J.: Princeton University Press.

Simon, H. A. (1997). *Administrative behavior: A study of decision-making processes in administrative organizations* (4th edn.). New York: Free Press.

Smith, M. P. (2001). *Transnational urbanism: Locating globalization*. Malden, Mass.: Blackwell.

Thorson, G. R., & Anderson, J. L. (2006). The Minnesota Miracle abandoned? Minnesota school funding 2001–2007. *Rural Minnesota Journal, 1*(2), 27–43.

Tiebout, C. M. (1956). A pure theory of local expenditures. *Journal of Political Economy, 64*(5), 416–424.

Weaver, T. P. R. (2016). *Blazing the neoliberal trail: Urban political development in the United States and the United Kingdom*. Philadelphia: University of Pennsylvania Press.

Wolf, M. A. (2008). *The zoning of America: Euclid v. Ambler*. Lawrence, Kan.: University Press of Kansas.

Wolman, H., & Goldsmith, M. (1990). Local autonomy as a meaningful analytic concept: Comparing local government in the United States and the United Kingdom. *Urban Affairs Review, 26*(1), 3–27.

1 A Theory of Institutional Capacity and Governance for Economic Development

This book is about analyzing and trying to answer, in a small town context, the question of whether and how local governance still matters. This includes studying the institutional organization, policies and leadership of government. It addresses both economic development – direct grant, loan, infrastructure or other assistance to private business – and community development, which here means building the infrastructure and public services necessary for a better quality of life and more opportunity for individuals, neighborhoods and businesses alike. Despite the obvious economic and financial constraints, there are powerful opportunities, at least on paper, for even a small community with effective leadership, political openness to change and shared policy goals to gain a great deal from better and more stable organization and processes.

The institutional governance of economic and community development plays a major role in defining the scope of this opportunity. Economic development boards, city administrators, planning and zoning commissions and other entities influence decision-making in these policy areas, and city councils may or may not choose to directly intervene in most actions. However, the capacity of such institutions to foster agreement and enact change varies greatly. Consider intergovernmental relations. The peer-to-peer relations among states range from administrative arrangements that can be made or broken without legislative approval, such as tuition remission and highway planning, to arrangements covered under the Compact Clause of the Constitution[1] and ratified by Congress, such as the Colorado River Compact (Hundley, 2009), that have the force of a treaty and are difficult to alter. Agreements among local governments are as diverse; they range from ad hoc contracts for specific services to long-term standing obligations mutually held with other governments (Feiock, Steinacker, & Park, 2009); in the absence of direction from regional or state institutions of governance they may be the only framework local government has to solve problems that overlap boundaries, as seen, for example, in the rapidly expanding Denver metropolitan region (Spensley, 2001).

Governance within the community also counts. For example, while council-manager systems do not assure an impact on government spending (Carr & Karuppusamy, 2009), the city manager has more delegated power and more direct authority (Ruhil, Schneider, Teske & Ji, 1999) than a city clerk or city administrator, who is merely one of several department heads reporting to the city council, and there is also evidence of a reduction in conflict in council-manager systems (Folz & French, 2005). Then again, council-manager systems do not automatically improve the odds for policy delivery, as large-sample research has demonstrated (Carr, 2015). Sidelining of political debate, for example, can introduce a bias toward less active policy output, austerity limits on public services and infrastructure and more dependence on deregulation and lowering costs (Davies & Blanco, 2017). Thus, we must consider more universal values in addition to bureaucratic "best practice." The institutional framework of government interacts with, influences and is sometimes deeply affected by the political culture of a community: trust in public officials, leadership, the level of voter resentment, precedent and practice. Concentration of the ability to define policy ("steering") and fund and deliver it ("driving") in a single venue can strongly empower a government. It can also prevent those seeking concessions from government from "venue-shopping" (Baumgartner & Jones, 1991; 2009; Pralle, 2003) for a board or commission to agree to a proposal that other bodies may reject or have rejected.

Accordingly, a central concept for this study is institutional capacity. I take this term beyond the "increasing ability of organizations to absorb responsibilities, operate more efficiently, and enhance accountability" (Savitch, 1998) to include the presence of standing, long-term, coherent and often binding arrangements for setting policy agendas, and developing, funding and delivering policy. The central theory of this book is that greater institutional capacity delivers a higher output of public support for public policy. We look here at public-sponsored economic and community development. Public-sponsored economic development means public support, through any combination of tax breaks, subsidies, incentives, worker training, discounted land or acceleration of the planning and zoning process, for private-sector jobs schemes. Community development implies a broader approach of building amenities in a municipality; the focus here is public infrastructure for local, but the term can also be taken to mean public services and quality-of-life improvements in general. Institutional capacity, influenced by elected and appointed leaders who can enhance or diminish it, interacts with the economic, institutional and intergovernmental context addressed in Chapters 2 and 3 to influence the policy-making process. These institutional arrangements do not necessarily need a council-manager system to function; they simply need to be established and generally accepted as part of the policy process, providing a degree of continuity and a forum in which both brainstorming and implementation can take place. The stronger these arrangements and leadership, the more coherent the policy process.

Measuring Governments' Institutional Capacity to Make Policy

Institutional capacity has the potential for a broad and deep influence on both local community and economic development outcomes, even in situations in which a community is short of financial resources or what would be conventionally viewed as bargaining power with private business. Communities with high institutional capacity in their governance deliver more policy than those with lower capacity; they may also be more responsive and accountable to their constituencies. Favorable signs include management stability, a defined and transparent process for delivering public policy, and handling of management functions that enables a city council to direct policy with a minimum of personal and minor disputes. For economic development, it may also include a city board or commission and/or a development corporation that answers to a city board or commission, specifically charged with the task of promoting economic development. Financial support for local government from the state is also an important element of institutional capacity, especially if it is redistributed to local governments on a need-based formula to ensure basic levels of public services and facilities are provided.

Examples of low institutional capacity in local governance may include internal dysfunction and conflict, such as in a commission government in which each council member is head of a city department and political rivalries may be imposed on interdepartmental bureaucratic functions; or weak arrangements for developing policy among municipal and township governments in an economic region that is politically fragmented. Low-capacity governance may also depend disproportionately on the intervention of outside public officials with lobbying and grant money when it comes to getting economic and community development projects done.

Institutional capacity is not the only determinant of economic and community development. The political, cultural and financial strength of a small town matters as well, particularly in broader-based community development projects – the efforts in downtown revitalization, worker training, parks and recreation, housing, streets and infrastructure, and other initiatives to boost a town's image, quality of life and, hopefully, its economy. Even within the United States there are major variations from one state to the next in terms of how local government is supported and empowered or constrained by state law. In the Dillon's Rule world of North American politics, the laws of the state or provincial level of government determine a local government's taxing powers, its ability to borrow for capital projects, and even managerial issues such as whether a local jurisdiction is allowed to require employees to reside within its municipal boundaries.

Additionally, the state level of government can choose how to finance local governments. For example, some US states simply share a proportion of state revenue based on population and/or on where the revenue was generated in the first place. Others use a redistributive approach, providing need-based assistance to local government or offsetting local property taxes in tax-poor areas. States can choose whether to allow localities to levy sales taxes, and where to cap those sales tax rates; they can and often do impose levy limits on property tax revenues, and some states grant income-tax-raising powers to certain municipalities. Taken together, state and local rules regarding how government and governance are organized influence whether an agenda for economic development gets implemented, whether action is taken and which policies get chosen.

How Institutions Frame Small Town Policy-Making: Plans of Governance, Territory and Internal Organization

The roots of this theory come from literature and experience regarding collective action problems, organizational process and fragmented governance. A successful process of local governance will likely minimize collective action problems, geographical fragmentation in terms of external relations among local government entities, and institutional fragmentation in terms of competing centers of power within local government entities. In other words, it is built to transcend situations that result in competing lines of authority or emphasize conflicting interests. The application of Mancur Olson's definition of collective action problems (Olson, 1965) is relevant, in that people without institutional responsibility toward the group (or, in this case, the community as a whole – not simply the municipality) are less likely to work toward group goals. Fragmentation among local governments (Feiock, 2005) or within them (Cook, 1993) can aggravate these problems in situations in which the economic community is divided among several governmental units (Dreier, Mollenkopf & Swanstrom, 2001; Swanstrom, 2006; Scholz, Berardo & Kile, 2008). On the other hand, when a local or regional government encompasses multiple communities it may inadequately serve and represent certain communities (Savitch & Vogel, 2004; Imbroscio, 2004; 2006). Collective action problems are particularly strong in small communities if institutions are weak, as peer pressure is a bigger factor in this context than in a larger city (Cook, 1993; Vidich & Bensman, 2000).

The nature of city–county consolidations and annexations in medium-sized to larger metropolitan areas is a case in point. A common theme has emerged in the United States on such consolidations that goes back 50 years. Louisville with Jefferson County, Kentucky; Indianapolis with Marion County, Indiana; and Nashville with Davidson County, Tennessee, all ostensibly sought governance that would bring about better and more efficient government and make the central cities – or, at least, the downtown areas – more financially secure and viable and more of an equal player in the economies of their metropolitan areas.

But, in every case, regional or metropolitan political elites drove the process rather than citizens of the central cities. For example, in Indianapolis

22 *A Theory of Institutional Capacity*

they bypassed the referendum altogether (Scott & Nathan, 1970), securing an act of the Indiana state legislature that made consolidation between city and county automatic in "first class cities", defined as places of more than 250,000 population – a definition that in 1970 comfortably excluded all Indiana cities but Indianapolis.[2] Such plans heavily diluted central city populations with large suburban populations, giving the latter the dominant political voice, and sometimes, even as plans were under way, exclusions were made (such as certain municipalities and all fire protection and schools from the Indianapolis Unigov project) that limited the liability of annexed suburban residents for central city problems (Savitch, Tsukamoto & Vogel, 2008).

All these state-driven institutional reorganizations succeeded to at least some extent in terms of their goals, which centered on stabilizing downtown business districts. The fact that they did little for the surrounding inner cities reflects the fact that the promoters of these consolidations were not particularly concerned with inner city problems but, rather, with downtowns losing their viability and threatening the economic security and jobs of often suburban residents. Longtime Indiana State Senator Tom Wyss (R–Fort Wayne) bluntly captured both the flaws and the benefits of the late 1960s merger of local governments in his state's capital city at a 2003 public forum regarding his home town's annexation proposals, saying that "the reason it's so ugly is because Unigov[3] was designed to make the Republican Party dominant in Indianapolis. That's why, though, at the same time, Indianapolis has been able to move forward with the things that they've done with the pro teams, with Circle Center Mall, all of these other things that they've done."[4]

Equally important to the exercises of designing processes and institutions for policy results are the locally devised or chosen arrangements *within* a unit of government. One obvious distinction within the chosen cases concerns the difference between mayor-council governments without a city administrator, mayor-council governments with a city administrator and council-manager governments. Consolidating the governance of a municipality through a city manager or city administrator does not automatically mean better government (Banfield & Wilson, 1963), but it often opens opportunities to deliver policy because such governments are less prone to internal political conflicts (Nelson & Nollenberger, 2011; Folz & French, 2005; Orfield, 2002; Fainstein, 2001; Savitch & Kantor, 2002). Concentrating most responsibility for economic development in the hands of a single entity, such as a board or commission with a budget or a loan fund, is also likely to insulate that process from conflict and controversy, whether by enabling grievances to be publicly aired and quickly acted upon, shielding the ugly or "sausage-making" aspects of policy from the debate of a full city council, or providing space for a private business partner that may not wish to engage in preliminary negotiations on a deal in a forum bound by open meeting law requirements. Relations between governments are also a key part of the definition, because they address institutions that are shared among governments as well as the role of citizen participation and oversight such as voting, membership of boards and commissions, and public hearings. They also represent an institution-based attempt to channel the strengths and neutralize the alleged weaknesses of the politics of "local culture" (Banfield & Wilson, 1963) and its connotations of biases and leaving results up to chance.

The question of where and how decisions on economic and community development are made is central to this study. The four cases presented here vary widely from centralizing both the definition and the funding of economic development policy on the city council to delegating substantial powers over both features to boards and commissions that meet separately from the council (Bliss, 2016) and may have only a minority of elected officials serving with a private citizen majority. Economic development in the form of direct subsidies to businesses can be unpopular and distrusted by experts and voters alike (Peters & Fisher, 2004).[5] Consequently, a strong possibility exists that, the more power over economic development is concentrated in the city council, the more policy tends to favor general-purpose infrastructure and public services over direct business assistance – a pattern that shows among these cases. Direct assistance to private business is more evident in the cases with more delegation of authority and funding of economic development away from the city council.

The Importance of Obligating Community Leaders

Having relatively few institutional players in an uncomplicated process is only half the battle in the war against free-rider problems (Olson, 1965). The process itself must be durable; it must last beyond a single policy or crisis, and to do that it must impose standing obligations upon participants. As such, this concept contradicts a key component of one of the most popular and powerful current metaphors in urban politics for explaining the development and delivery of public policy: civic capacity. The general idea of civic capacity, in the words of its leading advocate, Clarence Stone, namely "the ability to build and maintain a broad social and political coalition across all sectors of the urban community in pursuit of a common goal," grew from the studies of "regime politics" that began with Stone's landmark study of metropolitan Atlanta in the late 1980s (Stone, 1989), widely seen as a model for studying US cities. Few previous studies of urban power had so extensively examined the role played by informal but powerful players such as business groups and executives outside public and elected office; none have had such impact. Stone effectively propagated the idea with his own shift into researching the effects of regime on urban education reform (Stone, Henig, Jones & Pierannunzi, 2001). Overall, it represents a broad treatment of the question of the "power to" effect change – and who wields that power, and how.

24   *A Theory of Institutional Capacity*

But there is a major problem with civic capacity and regime studies in practice; while they measure the input of public mobilization for public policy reform, and the output of reform policies implemented, they pay relatively little attention to the processes and structures through which mobilization is translated into action. They also depend heavily on measuring episodes of activity more than the structures behind a community's standing, ongoing capacity to deliver policy. Regime has proven a highly effective concept for analyzing a particular type of local governance: devolved, market-oriented, making extensive use of informal actors and institutions. The insights on informal players alone have dramatically broadened analysis of urban politics in North America and beyond (Mossberger & Stoker, 2001). But, for comparing governance of different types, across multiple settings or in countries outside North America with more all-encompassing, formal and bureaucratic forms of general-purpose local government and for considering the impacts of local political choices and structures as opposed to only those settings working within a predominantly free-market and small government orientation (Davies, 2002), a broader framework is needed.

However, civic capacity provides more of a basis for studying and comparing municipalities and their governance the more one goes the extra step of analyzing how it might be reproducible in different organizational and cultural situations. In 2008 sociologist Xavier de Souza Briggs claimed that analyzing civic capacity is a means to "understand the process of building and using civic capacity in specific revelatory contexts that provide lessons for other contexts" (de Souza Briggs, 2008). Although the concept is still at times short on specifics, de Souza Briggs' statement about process implies obligations for delivering policy that are secured, long-standing and repeatable. Such attributes point to a process that becomes effective and is seen by the public as such because it can handle multiple problems over an extended period of time. It may also be adaptable to other contexts – for example, applying a governance structure that has successfully delivered public infrastructure to addressing other policy problems, such as economic development.

The interaction of obligation and process as a component of institutional capacity means that standing arrangements for the delivery of policy cannot readily be swept away through a single council vote, the death or retirement or sudden non-cooperation of a principal, or adversity, such as a cut in outside funding. This continuity is delivered through institutions such as city councils, economic development authorities, service boards or joint powers agreements with a defined mission to deliver, in this case, economic and community development. When configured appropriately, these institutions provide venues in which to overcome factional disputes; obligate major political players through the duties of membership; establish accountability with and support from the public; and connect steering and driving mechanisms for defining and delivering policy, as opposed to

A Theory of Institutional Capacity   25

having steering and driving separated between different individuals or entities. The choices of policy may depend on the membership of these institutions and on the type of institution involved, be it a city council, economic development corporation, public–private partnership or private development entity. Institutional mechanisms and reform efforts can take the form either of general-purpose governments that are functional, networked with each other and/or consolidated with one another, or government agencies assigned to a specific task (Horak, 2013).

The theoretical reasons for this approach draw on several strains of general political science that have been insufficiently applied to urban, state and local political science. Together, they demonstrate the importance to policy-making of political processes being made routine, through the "credible commitment" imposed on policy-makers by institutional obligations (Shepsle, 1991); through providing a standing venue for agenda-setting (Kingdon, 2003; Baumgartner & Jones, 2009); and through the generally greater effectiveness of well-"embedded" or stable and difficult-to-dislodge institutions (Ragsdale & Theis, 1997). For example, neighboring municipalities' policies on economic development are likely to converge – and therefore more likely to be implemented – when those municipalities are operating within a shared institutional and organizational arrangement for setting agendas and implementing policy (Savitch & Kantor, 2002; DiGaetano & Klemanski, 1999). Furthermore, such positive results are more likely to be repeated if that institutional arrangement is widely accepted and difficult to repeal. In contrast, even the strongest mayor cannot ensure policy continuity from higher office, retirement, the nursing home or the grave if the procedure for delivering policy can be easily removed or altered by a single council vote or administrative action (Hoyman, 1997).

The Dimensions of Institutional Capacity

How does this theoretical justification get put into operation? To begin with, this book uses a framework based in part on theories from comparative political science, identifying – among other things – why apparently similar cases produce different outcomes and apparently different ones can converge (Przeworski & Teune, 1982). Comparing these four communities requires evaluating their institutions, processes and both policy and political outcomes. Effectively, I am analyzing whether institutional capacity adds value to economic and community development. These dimensions include how agendas for economic development are set, how effectively geography and political processes match one another, whether the organizational process of policy adoption is coherent or fragmented, the nature of state involvement and – ultimately – the policy outcomes themselves. Within this broader context I also consider the role of leadership and the level of political consensus in the community.

26 *A Theory of Institutional Capacity*

The first question to ask is where the processes of agenda-setting, policy definition and deal-making take place. A diverse literature in American politics (Dahl, 1956; Schattschneider, 1960; Stone, 2002; Kingdon, 2003; Baumgartner & Jones, 2009; Edelman, 1988; DiGaetano & Lawless, 1999) has amply demonstrated the importance of how agenda-setting by policy-makers[6] frames political debate, and – through the study of "venue-shopping," or, in other words, political and business players searching around for a government body or jurisdiction most likely to support their plans – where that agenda-setting takes place. Local policy-makers are likely to have different preferences on economic development from state leaders, and local leaders may better reflect the preferences and the needs of the local community in situations in which their community is an "outlier" by the standards of regional or state politics and economics. Whether or not those preferences are acted upon – even in relatively centralized states – depends not only on state preferences but also on whether or not there is a political and governmental venue for local preferences to be defined and become part of a governing agenda.

Such agenda-setting takes place within whatever institutions in each community are responsible for economic and community development. There are many such institutions: statutory economic development authorities, which may or may not consist entirely of city council members; private associations formed with a remit for promoting economic and community development; joint powers boards that coordinate the policies of several different local government units and may jointly administer a program or department; community development corporations; public–private partnerships with funding from general taxation; and city staff, including city managers, administrators and economic development directors. All the above are represented in this sample, but the most notable variation is the extent to which these institutions are given standing, respected or deferred to by city government. From Hibbing, where policy development is handled by a statutory authority populated by various city officials and private-sector actors, to Ely, where the council itself sits as the statutory authority, there is a dramatic range in the level of devolution, institutionalization and politicization of economic development policy.

As for deal-making and implementation, I posit that communities with "stronger" institutions for economic development – which enjoy a broader combination of professionalism, autonomy, outside support, geographic coherence and organizational streamlining, along with less fragmentation of responsibility for making decisions – are more likely to see a pattern of high output of economic development projects. This is because these institutions provide a critical venue for building the kind of unity of purpose already documented in political science and public administration literature as leading to more active policy-making. A single economic development board with the "steering" responsibility to brainstorm policy and the "driving" power to at least make preliminary deals with business without a full vote by elected officials tends to produce more consistent results in line with its mission than a process in which policy definition, deal-making and implementation are all handled by separate entities or individuals. On the other hand, "weak" institutions or centralization of power on city councils leads to more intermittent output of economic development projects characterized by a "stop-go" pattern in which the "go" depends upon strong personalities and coalition builders in local government and dissipates upon their departure from office. These places are also more likely to have a pattern of economic and community development that reflects state preferences rather than their own preferences – or, if they succeed in blocking state policy, to have a pattern of very low output of economic development.

The alignment between economic geography and political geography matters for economic and community development because, when they converge, successful policies are more likely to get implemented. If a political unit is either substantially smaller or larger than the economic problem it aims to solve, the incentives for solving that problem become weak. In terms of political geography, this can take several forms. The Iron Range Resources and Rehabilitation Board, for example, is a state government agency with a long past (founded in 1941) and a large service area that covers the entire current and former iron ore mining region of Minnesota; additionally, it commands both substantial mine production tax revenues and the ability and political support to intervene throughout its service area in both supporting business and community infrastructure. This goes far beyond programs such as Illinois' enterprise zone boards or Minnesota's former Job Opportunity Building Zones (JOBZ) program that coordinate or at least mobilize local political leaders in targeting specific acreages for economic development through tax abatement.

But, with such broad geographical coverage, its agendas can conflict with local needs that differ from the "typical" IRRRB community. Although created with the goal of transitioning the region away from heavy dependence on iron ore mining, in practice it serves the mining industry itself more effectively than any other sector. This has triggered conflicts over how best to support local job growth, especially in areas without current mining that may depend on light manufacturing and services such as tourism and are characterized by businesses too small to be viewed by the IRRRB board as economically or politically significant. Additionally, local government boundaries themselves vary so sharply that they influence politics and policy-making. Hibbing covers what has been traditionally thought of as the city of Hibbing, its outskirts and the surrounding countryside, including the local airport southeast of the built-up area and vast iron ore pits to the northwest. By contrast, the Ely area is divided among several units of local government, with sharply varying levels of personal income, education, job skills and retired population, and consequently with meaningful differences in political agendas.

28 *A Theory of Institutional Capacity*

Fragmentation of policy-making manifests itself both geographically and through the institutions of governance. The process of setting agendas and making decisions varies, depending often on how many different boards and commissions must come to an agreement. An effectively designed process can help in reaching the consensus that outside funders or investors look for on economic development. Barriers to such a process are very different between a community in which only one government jurisdiction exists, and economic development is run as a department of that jurisdiction, and a community that is geographically fragmented into political units and/or has overlapping statutory bodies handling economic development policy.

The configuration of these institutions influences decision-making as much as their presence or absence. Local communities make strategic decisions about what kind of community leaders and residents want (Savitch & Kantor 2002: 19) and "who makes decisions over what" (Savitch & Kantor 2002: 21); the city of Hibbing's large-scale annexation in 1979, Ely's proactive approach to infrastructure and Sterling's managerialist governance are all cases in point in this study. Decisions on what kinds of projects are pursued are themselves often the functions of the institutional differences among the cases (Wassail & Hellman, 2005; Eisinger, 1988; Reese & Fasenfest, 2004; 1996). The influence of state government upon local government reveals itself in this study in the form of significant differences between a community's effectiveness in delivering public-sector community development (for example, new infrastructure or public buildings) and private-sector economic development (such as new or expanded employers in the community). But, in the end, weak and fragmented local processes impede policy-making on almost every level regardless of the state's role.

State finance plays a major role. Every US state has some form of general-purpose, non-designated assistance to local government in the form of shared revenue, grants or need-based equalization, with Illinois' revenue-sharing of income and sales tax revenues and Minnesota's need-based Local Government Aid program represented in this study. However, there are large variations domestically among US states and Canadian provinces (and internationally, for example among European Union members) in the amount of state-level funding for local government. Among the cases in this study, Minnesota provides both Ely and Hibbing with around 50 percent or more of their municipal operating budgets from LGA, a far higher proportion than communities of comparable size but superior tax base elsewhere in the state. Sterling and Rock Falls receive only approximately a third of their funding from the state of Illinois through revenue-sharing – with Sterling, the richer of the two communities, receiving a higher share due to its stronger retail sector generating more sales tax revenue, an approach sharply at odds with how LGA, Minnesota's main revenue support system, is determined. Thus, the Illinois avoidance of redistributive measures in revenue-sharing has implications for tax-poor communities in Illinois, such as Rock Falls, and other states with similar approaches to revenue-sharing, that merit comparison to other cases.

There are also variations in the freedom that states afford to municipalities. For example, Minnesota is more administratively centralized than Illinois, and the Taconite Assistance Area (TAA) is more centralized still on a regional basis under its IRRRB oversight. Thanks to its control over and distribution of taconite production taxes for economic and community development projects, the IRRRB is a critical funding partner for Ely and Hibbing and thus a major determinant of whether projects get done. Another example concerns local control over revenue: a home-rule municipality in Illinois can levy a sales tax through a vote of its council or board; a non-home-rule one can do the same with a vote of the elected council or board along with a referendum. Minnesota, on the other hand, stripped the ability of municipalities to initiate sales taxes without a vote of the state legislature in the 1970s, though existing cases, notably Duluth, were grandfathered.

Leadership emerges as a dimension of comparison because of how individual elected officials and business leaders influence local policy outcomes and institutional relationships among boards, commissions and even city councils (Judd & Parkinson, 1990; Stone, 1989; Nelles, 2012). Good leadership and effective institutions are mutually beneficial, and good leadership can sometimes paper over the inadequacies of poor institutions (Holli, 1999; Jones & Bachelor, 1993), especially in more informal structures of governance; this includes private-sector leaders (Stone, 1989) or "civic entrepreneurs" (Henton, Melville & Walesh, 1997). This is especially evident in small towns, which are more likely to lack the kinds of institutions that keep collective action problems and political conflict under control (Folz & French, 2005; Vidich & Bensman, 1958). This is due to the more voluntary, less funded and smaller-scale nature of governance in small towns than in major cities, even while such towns are more homogeneous and therefore presumably easier ground for a consensus than large cities. In such a situation, asking *how* things get done and *what* gets done may not be the most important questions; the simple question of *whether* things get done (Frieden & Sagalyn, 1989) needs to be discussed, whether in a big city or small town context. However, this phenomenon is subject to limitations; even strong leadership struggles in the face of institutional structures within a community that is configured in such a way that sows conflict or blocks implementation.

Finally, I also compare outcomes in these cases. These include economic development projects – boosting jobs and business activity in the private sector, whether by developing from within or recruiting from outside – and community development projects such as public infrastructure. The two are increasingly considered together because of the importance local governments have attached to multiple strategies, not

30 *A Theory of Institutional Capacity*

only "demand-side" economic development to subsidize businesses for job creation or "supply-side" strategies for boosting labor skills and availability, but also infrastructure and amenities to improve the general attractiveness of a community.

In some cases, municipalities set a strict priority on economic development defined as job creation – landing a major distribution center, expanding manufacturing, aid to small business. In others, stakeholders tend to favor the broader strategy of community development: developing amenities, infrastructure and public facilities such as improved schools, streets, utilities, parks and a higher grade of local services.[7] This broader strategy is politically popular and evident on policy agendas in communities with a high degree of political activity, but also hypothesized to depend more upon the support and involvement of the state or even federal government. Such amenities depend more on direct funding than subsidies for private development, which often entail giving up future revenues in the form of reduced taxes from the client business or in-kind support such as a land swap between the city and the client. An offer by the county, state and/or federal government to cover most or all of the cost of essential public facilities therefore makes a much bigger difference to a municipal budget than an offer of support for economic development funding. In other words, the conditions that encourage aggressive and proactive economic development are not necessarily the same as those that encourage a broader amenity-driven approach, even in cases in which amenities are viewed as central to supporting economic development.

Indeed, drawing a line between direct business assistance and the overall improvement of infrastructure and public services is often not helpful to economic development policy, or reflective of the way in which it is adopted. For example, a shared vision among leaders of a community's future (Pagano & Bowman, 1995) can be met in a far broader paradigm than growth-seeking subsidies to business, to include an ecological perspective, sustainability or business growth that fits grassroots political preferences or other models aside from those considered "typical" in the economic development field (Audirac, 1997; Shaffer, Deller & Marcouiller, 2006), Legal, policy-making and tax-raising powers are all likely to significantly affect a city's ability to pursue economic and community development on its own terms in this manner, no matter how poor that city actually is. Even in more resource-poor communities, a smoothly functioning network of political actors (Monge & Contractor, 2003) – often aided by appropriately configured institutions – reduces conflict-driven transaction costs such as delays, misconfigured policy and abrupt changes of direction (Lubell, Feiock & Ramirez, 2005). These organizational structures can also be fine-tuned to the point that they shape the predisposition of institutions to act in a particular way just as much as the preferences of institutional leaders (Ha, Lee & Feiock, 2016). The implication is that reform and alteration of institutions and organizational structures can deeply affect policy choices.

Economic Development Governance in the Study Cases: An Overview

The political and policy differences among these communities are highly visible in the governance and the assigning of responsibility for economic development policy within and around municipal government. At the core is an implication that the level of delegation of economic development away from the elected city council influences the type of policy chosen. More delegation, and the policies tend toward technical aspects of recruiting and/or retaining businesses. Less delegation and more city council control, and the policies blend with general-purpose strategies for building up infrastructure and public services (Bliss, 2016).

Hibbing runs economic development through a statutory authority, the Hibbing Economic Development Authority (HEDA), with support from city staff and a board of directors that includes both current and former council members and leading businesspeople; it has tended to work closely with businesses on technical and financial issues regardless of political currents on the council. In the Ely area, economic development policy, for over a decade, was developed through an independent agency run and funded through a joint powers agreement between Ely and three other local government units at which an additional Ely-area municipality (the city of Babbitt), a local school district and the Ely Chamber of Commerce each had observer status.[8] However, that leadership role is now back in the hands of the Ely City Council, which also serves as the statutory economic development authority and no longer funds the joint powers board; policy since this changeover, at the end of 2010, has seen less conflict over policy and an emphasis on "shovel-ready" or lease-ready property development and amenity-driven community development, such as general infrastructure and a new public library.

The Illinois cases provide their own distinction; in Sterling, a semi-private corporation, the Greater Sterling Development Corporation (GSDC), steers economic development, with some funding from City Hall. GSDC runs a business incubator and helps network private businesses with resources ranging from startup capital to government support. Across the river, the Rock Falls Community Development Corporation (RFCDC), for over a decade, administered a project to reclaim derelict areas along the city's riverfront following factory closures affecting some of the community's biggest employers. Once RFCDC and the city of Rock Falls had completed environmental remediation and installed the infrastructure to allow property to be resold for development, RFCDC was defunded in 2015 by the city council, with the newly elected mayor taking the lead role in leading economic development policy; RFCDC was subsequently dissolved. Prior to the CDC's creation, the Rock Falls City Council had not significantly engaged in economic development policy; yet it was carrying out community development policies ranging from

32   *A Theory of Institutional Capacity*

housing subsidies to managing and expanding the role of its municipal hydroelectric utility, with the recent launch of a community-owned gigabit Internet service.

A major state policy difference between Illinois and Minnesota provides the opportunity to examine a further question: the effect on local governance of empowered state institutions. The IRRRB, whose service area covers the TAA,[9] redistributes mine production tax revenues – which the mines pay in lieu of local property taxes – for economic development, streets and infrastructure, schools and even investment in facilities at the mines themselves and is the largest source of economic development aid for the region. All nine IRRRB board members are members of the Minnesota legislature, meaning that good legislative relations are at a premium for local governments in this region seeking economic development support.[10] This governance arrangement, while highly politically empowered at the state level, was called into question in 2016 by the Minnesota Legislative Auditor, who has suggested it may be vulnerable to a constitutional challenge due to the combining of executive- and legislative-branch functions.[11] In contrast, the leading economic development policy-makers for the Illinois cases are local institutions: the Sterling and Rock Falls city governments, private entities such as GSDC and RFCDC, and the Whiteside/Carroll Enterprise Zone Board. The Illinois enterprise zones[12] are governed entirely by local elected officials from the municipalities with land designated under the enterprise zone, placing responsibility for handling tax breaks in the hands of the board members while leaving property tax revenue in the hands of municipalities.

These differences in both local policy and state direction may cause major differences in how each community deploys economic development projects. One such example is attempting to apply large-scale solutions in a small-scale situation. Nowhere is this more evident at first glance than in Ely, where, in 2006, a $4 million state grant aimed speculatively at a hypothetical single employer in the Ely area went unclaimed after state legislators who also served on the IRRRB refused a request from leaders in Ely and the surrounding municipalities to divide the grant between multiple projects that reflect the smaller scale of the businesses that tend to operate there than in other TAA communities.

Nonetheless, these differences are not presumed to apply evenly across policy areas. They are expected to operate differently between economic development assistance to businesses and general-purpose community development aimed at improving amenities and services for residents and the attractiveness of a community to business. Consensus among policy-makers, particularly local officials, is expected to have a greater effect on private-sector economic development than the delivery of public facilities and infrastructure, simply because local economic development policy depends more heavily than local public works and infrastructure on local decisions. Powerful forces support general public spending among

A Theory of Institutional Capacity 33

municipalities, including broad public demand for at least a basic level of services from within (Einstein & Kogan, 2016) and the so-called "flypaper effect": the exogenous impact of increased general-purpose state aid driving increased public spending on projects and services (Deller, Maher & Lledo, 2007; Office of the State Auditor, State of Minnesota, 2003). Business-oriented economic development is driven by a different process: a steady trend of ever greater devolution toward local government (Eisinger, 1988), which places greater demands on local officials to reach agreement and direct and deliver results. Even in Minnesota's more centralized system, IRRRB grants for economic development depend on a strong local show of approval.

A further possibility, less well addressed by existing literature, is that direct public assistance to private business is subjected to tougher scrutiny by local government. At least some evidence indicates this trend is rising (Lingwen & Warner, 2010), with the cities that impose more accountability generally succeeding in passing a larger volume of economic development assistance (Sullivan, 2002). As local governments can influence this process because of the devolution that has taken place, it is not a stretch to suggest that local officials may be much more reluctant to take on political opponents in economic development policy than they are with, say, a major new piece of public infrastructure.

A Survey-Based Case Study

The analytical approach hinted at so far is necessarily complex in that it considers variations in local, regional and statewide governance driving choices involving policy and government institutions, all in the face of a more deregulated and competitive global economy and declining intergovernmental aid. Yet the concept is simple: reviewing a selection of economically comparable towns of diverse political backgrounds and in two states with dramatically different approaches to funding and empowering local government, and analyzing the way they develop and deliver economic and community development projects. This format, a two-level comparative case study, enables us to look more closely at how different institutional systems and different politics explain variances in policy outcomes among socially, demographically and economically similar communities (see Table 1.1 for a schematic of the cases demonstrating how they are organized). In other words, it is designed to answer the question of whether local politics still affects outcomes in a deregulated economy characterized by limited government.

The research gathers information through elite interviewing (George & Bennett, 2005), backed up by process tracing (Tansey, 2007) of governmental actions through archival research of newspaper coverage and public meeting minutes to track key decisions. A total of 105 local and regional political, business and community leaders were interviewed in 2006 and

34   *A Theory of Institutional Capacity*

Table 1.1 Schematic of the study

Variable	Internal delegation of economic development policy-making in local government		
	Policy outcome	*Policy-making authority, including management decisions concentrated on city council*	*Management and technical decisions delegated to staff, commission and/ or development corporation*
Centralization of state government	Higher state centralization; strong financial safety net for municipalities, less discretion over policy and revenue	Ely, Minnesota Population 3,390 2015 median household income $36,059	Hibbing, Minnesota Population 16,093 2015 median household income $43,831
	Less state centralization; weaker safety net but broad discretion policies and taxes	Rock Falls, Illinois Population 8,993 2015 median household income $35,361	Sterling, Illinois Population 14,908 2015 median household income $39,670

Source: US Census Bureau 2016 population and housing unit estimates; 2015 American Community Survey for median household income data.

2007, and many additional follow-up interviews were conducted from 2011 to 2015; four Minnesota respondents with stakes in both Ely and Hibbing answered questions for both communities. The survey interviews were designed to gauge elite opinion in each community, framing in general terms governmental performance in carrying out high-priority projects. Elite interviewing is also essential to process tracing (Tansey, 2007), and, in this book, it becomes a powerful qualitative tool for tracking success and failures in policy delivery. In lieu of probability sampling, the survey uses "purposive" sampling – in other words, maximizing the interviewing of key leaders and decision-makers in the community (Judd, Smith & Kidder, 1991); and expanding and enhancing the interview field, in part by asking respondents to name relevant and promising candidates for survey interviews (Biernacki & Waldorf, 1981; Seldon & Pappworth, 1983), in order to keep the focus on relevant actors.

Each case study has a largely separate field of interviewees. Ely, with 50 survey respondents mostly in the city itself and its surrounding townships, represents the largest subsample. Hibbing – with a unified local government within whose jurisdiction almost all local respondents live – featured 24 respondents. An additional four interviewees are common to both the Ely and Hibbing surveys due to their stake in both communities. The Illinois pool – 27 interviewees in neighboring Sterling and Rock Falls, which form the core of a single micropolitan area by a US Census Bureau definition that encompasses Whiteside County – is treated as a unit due to the immediate proximity and economic interdependence of the two cities. Nonetheless, the governments are separate, and the political culture and institutional configuration of the two cities are significantly different. Finally, the qualitative nature of the study makes for broad historical and contextual analysis and extensive use of meeting minutes and archives. Each interview – which ranged from around 40 minutes to as much as three hours – consisted largely of detailed questions on a city's general performance in handling economic development and on the delivery of specific development goals and projects.

A Two-Level Comparison: Local and State Government

This study takes place within the context of the structure of government and its influence on political choice, oriented toward the following question: why do apparently similar cities produce substantially different solutions to policy problems in economic and community development? Producing a set of cases that are broadly similar in terms of their social and economic situation but different in terms of the way in which they are governed helps us to do a better job of connecting variances in governance with policy outcomes. With cities such as these, which are short of resources to effect economic and community development, the added value gained in terms of institutional organization can provide a vital edge in producing better public policy and a better outcome for local taxpayers.

There is also the possibility of organizational convergence among municipalities in their forms of governance, resulting in them adopting a more common set of policies as well. Suppose conditions that on closer inspection proved to differ strongly – a strong tendency for consensus and economic intervention in one town; dissension and inaction in a neighboring town – might become much more similar over time as the "failing" community reorganizes its governance and both governments increasingly share tasks and even governing arrangements. This can be analyzed through the more recent "most-different systems" research design (Przeworski & Teune, 1982) – in other words, a common factor such as a shared local, regional or state political arrangement producing similar results even in significantly different situations, such as Hibbing, with its ongoing iron mining and reorganized governance, versus Ely, with its more traditional government structure and much greater dependence on service industry and commuting.

This study includes elements of both the most-similar and most-different systems approaches. In the terms of comparative political science, this is a

36   A Theory of Institutional Capacity

qualitative, small-sample study that uses for the most part a most-similar systems case study design. In other words, these communities share common circumstances particularly in economics, social makeup, local amenities and demographics. These are the similar systems. Essentially, these towns have much in common in terms of context. However, when it comes to their political and governmental organization and traditions, each town is distinct; in other words, structural differences are coming into play in terms of both state government and municipalities. Change in these structures may trigger change in policy; one vital question is whether it becomes a prerequisite to policy change.

The two-level approach arises because of the substantial organizational roles of both local and state government in making economic development policy. It is derived from methods used in political economy studies (Putnam, 1988) and occasionally in urban politics (Denters & Mossberger, 2006; DiGaetano & Klemanski, 1999; Goertz & Mahoney, 2005) in order to consider both factors. Thus, we can compare the impact upon local policy of states' delegation of powers to local government and their financing of local government; and evaluate local policy-making in the context of local expectations of state officials and their actions. We can address local government powers and actions in terms of raising revenue or making policy decisions on their own or in concert with others. We can consider how state aid is delivered, whether means-tested or through an allocation formula such as population or geographical source of revenue. We can consider how local governance is organized, through city councils, economic development authorities or private bodies.

This research design and the lessons drawn from it provide a methodological template with applications far beyond this study: they can serve as a guidepost for studying and comparing the effects of different types of city and community governance in different countries as well as different states. The considerable difference among US states in their handling of Dillon's Rule in particular (Sbragia, 1996; Frug, Ford & Barron, 2006; Frug & Barron, 2007) or local government finance in general is not unlike the differing approaches of different European countries. Consider municipal fragmentation, a popular theme for progressives who lament the inequality and disorganization of local communities in the United States (Dreier, Mollenkopf & Swanstrom, 2001; Orfield, 1999; 2002). A tremendous contrast exists within Europe between the inability of France's traditionally powerful national government to consolidate its notoriously fragmented local governments to the almost matter-of-fact merger of local governments undertaken in the United Kingdom and Denmark. France's tally of 36,000 local governments is not only orders of magnitude above the number in the United Kingdom, despite the two countries' similar populations,[13] but half the EU total and comparable on a per capita basis to Illinois, municipally the most fragmented state in the United States.

A Theory of Institutional Capacity   37

Similar contrasts exist within the United States, ranging from Illinois' 7,000 local government units to Hawaii's 19.[14] Thus, not only is state-level comparison an essential component of this primarily urban politics project, but it can inform researchers who compare cases between almost any number of countries, states and provinces. In the realm of local government, an effective comparison of multiple cases in two different US states can serve as a lesson for subnational or even international comparisons of local government in other countries. And, as much as local institutional capacity matters, the state-level framework has a major impact on the success or failure of even the most coherent applications of local power. In the face of the challenging economic context of today's local government, higher-level support is a key resource for local governments seeking to maximize their effectiveness in economic and community development.

Notes

1 "No State shall, without the Consent of Congress, lay any Duty of Tonnage, keep Troops, or Ships of War in time of Peace, enter into any Agreement or Compact with another State, or with a foreign Power, or engage in War, unless actually invaded, or in such imminent Danger as will not admit of delay.": Article 1, Clause 10, Section 3.
2 As Fort Wayne, Indiana's second city, passed 200,000 in population in the 2000s, the Indiana legislature narrowed the definition of first-class cities – to 600,000. The intent of the legislature that only Indianapolis should have this status is clear.
3 Indianapolis's 1969 merger of municipal (though not school) government between the central city and most Marion County, Indiana suburbs, conducted under mayor and later Republican US senator Richard Lugar.
4 *Fort Wayne News-Sentinel*, August 25, 2003: transcript of roundtable discussion on consolidation of Fort Wayne, Indiana, area government.
5 See the SurveyUSA/Kansas Policy Institute poll of Wichita residents in April 2014 on proposed new economic development spending compared with other spending lines, at www.surveyusa.com/client/PollReport. aspx?g=79f09fe6-f6cb-4c05-a391-3b2639a6ce1c.
6 Note that this field is distinct from, but involves processes sometimes connected to, the phenomenon of agenda-setting in the media, which has its own large body of academic research arising from work in the late 1960s on political communications (McCombs & Shaw, 1993; 1972).
7 These projects are frequently referred to here as community development, in view of their integral role in building a broader community. They are typically the beneficiaries of federal Community Development Block Grants, which are a critical component of development funding on the Iron Range.
8 For more information on the role of joint powers boards as implemented in the state of Minnesota, see the website of the League of Minnesota Cities at www. lmc.org/page/1/joint-powers.jsp.
9 The Taconite Assistance Area derives from the 1941 legislation that created the Iron Range Resources and Rehabilitation Board. The IRRRB was created

38   *A Theory of Institutional Capacity*

under Governor Harold Stassen with a remit to economically diversify local economies in view of what was seen at the time as rapidly declining high-grade "soft" iron ore resources. The achievement of an economically efficient process for low-grade "hard" taconite iron ore in the 1950s, and the arrival of seven new processing facilities for taconite between 1957 and 1972, changed the equation dramatically, and in 1977 the current TAA was created along with an elevated production tax to distribute to current and former mining communities.

10   During the 2000s and early 2010s the IRRRB also included three "citizen" members. As of 2010 the IRRRB's membership included the following three citizen members; Jack Ryan, nominated by Governor Tim Pawlenty, a prominent business leader in Hibbing widely identified in the survey research for this book as being a key player in economic development; Joe Begich, a former Democratic state legislator from Eveleth and uncle of Alaska US Senator Mark Begich, who was originally nominated by then Senate Majority Leader Roger Moe, of the Minnesota Democratic–Farmer–Labor Party (DFL–Erskine); and Chisholm resident Shelley Robinson, the executive director of a leading Iron Range provider of mental health services, nominated by House speaker Margaret Anderson Kelliher (DFL–Minneapolis).

11   Evaluation report: Iron Range Resources and Rehabilitation Board, March 2016, Office of the Legislative Auditor, State of Minnesota, Program Evaluation Division.

12   Illinois enterprise zones were created in 1982 by the Illinois Enterprise Zone Act, under Governor James R. Thompson. The act, which – unlike the IRRRB – applies statewide, enables local communities to form their own zones, in which eight different state tax deductions and breaks are granted and a variety of local tax and regulatory breaks are also typically offered. Enterprise zone boards determine which parcels of land are eligible for the tax breaks; sites are typically chosen with regard for attributes such as proximity to existing utilities and roads and renewal of brownfield sites. A smaller-scale counterpart in Minnesota, the JOBZ (Job Opportunity Building Zone) program, adopted in 2003 under Governor Tim Pawlenty, differed from the Illinois program both in that the tax abatements were less extensive and in that sites and projects were not chosen cooperatively on a regionwide basis by board local officials operating independently of the state but, rather, by each municipality subject to state approval.

13   Source: Council of European Municipalities and Regions (2009): 4–5, 38–57.

14   Source: US Census Bureau, Census of governments, 2012.

References

Audirac, I. (1997). *Rural sustainable development in America*. New York: John Wiley & Sons.

Banfield, E. C., & Wilson, J. Q. (1963). *City politics*. Cambridge, Mass.: Harvard University Press.

Baumgartner, F. R., & Jones, B. D. (1991). Agenda dynamics and policy subsystems. *Journal of Politics, 53*(4), 1044–1074.

Baumgartner, F. R., & Jones, B. D. (2009). *Agendas and instability in American politics* (2nd edn.). Chicago: University of Chicago Press.

Biernacki, P., & Waldorf, D. (1981). Snowball sampling: Sampling and techniques of chain referral sampling. *Social Methods Research, 10*(2), 141–163.

A Theory of Institutional Capacity 39

Bliss, D. (2016). Frameworks for growth: How local institutions and state governance influence economic development policy. *Illinois Municipal Policy Journal, 1*(1), 93–108.

Carr, J. B. (2015). What have we learned about the performance of council–manager government? A review and synthesis of the research. *Public Administration Review, 75*(5), 673–689.

Carr, J. B., & Karuppusamy, S. (2009). Reassessing the link between city structure and fiscal policy. *American Review of Public Administration, 40*(2), 209–228.

Cook, H. K. (1993). Small town talk: The undoing of collective action in two Missouri towns. PhD dissertation, Washington University, St. Louis, Mo.; available at http://artsci.wustl.edu/~anthro/blurb/b_cook.html.

Council of European Municipalities and Regions (ed.) (2009). *Balancing democracy, identity and efficiency: Changes in local and regional structures in Europe.* Brussels: Council of European Municipalities and Regions.

Dahl, R. A. (1956). *A preface to democratic theory.* Chicago: University of Chicago Press.

Davies, J. S. (2002). Urban regime theory: A normative-empirical critique. *Journal of Urban Affairs, 24*(1), 1–17.

Davies, J. S., & Blanco, I. (2017). Austerity urbanism: Patterns of neo-liberalisation and resistance in six cities of Spain and the UK. *Environment and Planning A, 49*(7), 1517–1536.

De Souza Briggs, X. (2008). *Democracy as problem solving: Civic capacity in communities across the globe.* Cambridge, Mass.: MIT Press.

Deller, S., Maher, C., & Lledo, V. (2007). Wisconsin local government, state shared revenues and the illusive flypaper effect. *Journal of Public Budgeting, Accounting and Financial Management, 19*(2), 200–220.

Denters, B., & Mossberger, K. (2006). Building blocks for a methodology for comparative urban political research. *Urban Affairs Review, 41*(4), 550–571.

DiGaetano, A., & Klemanski, J. S. (1999). *Power and city governance: Comparative perspectives on urban development.* Minneapolis: University of Minnesota Press.

DiGaetano, A., & Lawless, P. (1999). Urban governance and industrial decline: Governing structures and policy agendas in Birmingham and Sheffield, England, and Detroit, Michigan, 1980–1997. *Urban Affairs Review, 34*(4), 546–577.

Dreier, P., Mollenkopf, J. H., & Swanstrom, T. (2001). *Place matters: Metropolitics for the twenty-first century.* Lawrence, Kan.: University Press of Kansas.

Edelman, M. J. (1988). *Constructing the political spectacle.* Chicago: University of Chicago Press.

Einstein, K. L., & Kogan, V. (2016). Pushing the city limits: Policy responsiveness in municipal government. *Urban Affairs Review, 52*(1), 3–32.

Eisinger, P. K. (1988). *The rise of the entrepreneurial state: State and local economic development policy in the United States.* Madison, Wis.: University of Wisconsin Press.

Fainstein, S. S. (2001). *The city builders: Property development in New York and London, 1980–2000.* Lawrence, Kan.: University Press of Kansas.

Feiock, R. C. (2005). Institutional collective action and local governance. Paper presented at "Creating collaborative communities: Management networks, services cooperation, and metropolitan governance" symposium, Detroit, October 31.

40   *A Theory of Institutional Capacity*

Feiock, R. C., Steinacker, A., & Park, H. J. (2009). Institutional collective action and economic development joint ventures. *Public Administration Review*, *69*(2), 256–270.

Folz, D. H., & French, P. E. (2005). *Managing America's small communities: People, politics, and performance*. Lanham, Md.: Rowman & Littlefield.

Frieden, B. J., & Sagalyn, L. B. (1989). *Downtown, Inc.: How America rebuilds cities*. Cambridge, Mass.: MIT Press.

Frug, G. E., & Barron, D. J. (2007). *Boston bound: A comparison of Boston's legal powers with those of six other major American cities*. Boston: Boston Foundation.

Frug, G. E., Ford, R. T., & Barron, D. J. (2006). *Local government law* (4th edn.). St. Paul, Minn.: Thomson/West.

George, A. L., & Bennett, A. (2005). *Case studies and theory development in the social sciences*. Cambridge, Mass.: MIT Press.

Goertz, G., & Mahoney, J. (2005). Two-level theories and fuzzy-set analysis. *Sociological Methods and Research*, *33*(4), 497–538.

Ha, H., Lee, I. W., & Feiock, R. C. (2016). Organizational network activities for local economic development. *Economic Development Quarterly*, *30*(1), 15–31.

Henton, D. C., Melville, J., & Walesh, K. (1997). *Grassroots leaders for a new economy: How civic entrepreneurs are building prosperous communities*. San Francisco: Jossey-Bass.

Holli, M. G. (1999). *The American mayor: The best and the worst big-city leaders*. University Park, Pa.: Pennsylvania State University Press.

Horak, M. (2013). State rescaling in practice: Urban governance reform in Toronto. *Urban Research and Practice*, *6*(3), 311–328.

Hoyman, M. (1997). *Power steering: Global automakers and the transformation of rural communities*. Lawrence, Kan.: University Press of Kansas.

Hundley, N. (2009). *Water and the West: The Colorado River Compact and the politics of water in the American West*. Berkeley, Calif.: University of California Press.

Imbroscio, D. L. (2004). Can we grant a right to place? *Politics and Society*, *32*(4), 575–609.

Imbroscio, D. L. (2006). Shaming the inside game: A critique of the liberal expansionist approach to addressing urban problems. *Urban Affairs Review*, *42*(2), 224–248.

Jones, B. D., & Bachelor, L. W. (1993). *The sustaining hand: Community leadership and corporate power* (2nd edn.). Lawrence, Kan.: University Press of Kansas.

Judd, C. M., Smith, E. R., & Kidder, L. H. (1991). *Research methods in social relations*. New York: Holt, Rinehart and Winston.

Judd, D. R., & Parkinson, M. (eds.) (1990). *Leadership and urban regeneration: Cities in North America and Europe*. Newbury Park, Calif.: SAGE Publications.

Kingdon, J. W. (2003). *Agendas, alternatives, and public policies* (2nd edn.). New York: Longman.

Lingwen, Z., & Warner, M. (2010). Business incentive use among US local governments: A story of accountability and policy learning. *Economic Development Quarterly*, *24*(4), 325–336.

Lubell, M., Feiock, R. C., & Ramirez, E. (2005). Political institutions and conservation by local governments. *Urban Affairs Review*, *40*(6), 706–729.

McCombs, M. E., & Shaw, D. L. (1972). The agenda-setting function of mass media. *Public Opinion Quarterly*, *36*(2), 176–187.

A Theory of Institutional Capacity   41

McCombs, M. E., & Shaw, D. L. (1993). The evolution of agenda-setting research: Twenty-five years in the marketplace of ideas. *Journal of Communication*, *43*(2), 58–67.

Monge, P. R., & Contractor, N. S. (2003). *Theories of communication networks*. New York: Oxford University Press.

Mossberger, K., & Stoker, G. (2001). The evolution of urban regime theory. *Urban Affairs Review*, *36*(6), 810–835.

Nelles, J. (2012). *Comparative metropolitan policy: Governing beyond local boundaries in the imagined metropolis*. Abingdon, UK: Routledge.

Nelson, K. L., & Nollenberger, K. (2011). I – Conflict and cooperation in municipalities: Do variations in form of government have an effect? *Urban Affairs Review*, *47*(5), 696–720.

Office of the State Auditor, State of Minnesota (2003). *Special study: Local government aid and its effect on expenditures*. St. Paul, Minn.: Office of the State Auditor, State of Minnesota.

Olson, M. (1965). *The logic of collective action: Public goods and the theory of groups*. Cambridge, Mass.: Harvard University Press.

Orfield, M. (1999). *Metropolitics: A regional agenda for community and stability*. Washington, D.C.: Brookings Institution Press.

Orfield, M. (2002). *American metropolitics: The new suburban reality*. Washington, D.C.: Brookings Institution Press.

Pagano, M. A., & Bowman, A. O. (1995). *Cityscapes and capital: The politics of urban development*. Baltimore: Johns Hopkins University Press.

Peters, A., & Fisher, P. (2004). The failures of economic development incentives. *Journal of the American Planning Association*, *70*(1), 27–37.

Pralle, S. B. (2003). Venue shopping, political strategy, and policy change: The internationalization of Canadian forest advocacy. *Journal of Public Policy*, *23*(3), 233–260.

Przeworski, A., & Teune, H. (1982). *The logic of comparative social inquiry*. Malabar, Fla.: R. E. Krieger Publishing.

Putnam, R. (1988). The logic of two-level games. *International Organization*, *42*(3), 427–460.

Ragsdale, L., & Theis, J. J., III (1997). The institutionalization of the American presidency, 1924–92. *American Journal of Political Science*, *41*(4), 1280–1318.

Reese, L. A., & Fasenfest, D. (1996). Local economic development policy in Canada and the US: Similarities and differences. *Canadian Journal of Urban Research*, *10*(3), 100–121.

Reese, L. A., & Fasenfest, D. (2004). *Critical evaluations of economic development policies*. Detroit: Wayne State University Press.

Ruhil, A. V. S., Schneider, M., Teske, P., & Ji, B.-M. (1999). Institutions and reform: Reinventing local government. *Urban Affairs Review*, *34*(3), 433–455.

Savitch, H. V. (1998). Global challenge and institutional capacity: Or, how we can refit local administration for the next century. *Administration and Society*, *30*(3), 248–273.

Savitch, H. V., & Kantor, P. (2002). *Cities in the international marketplace: The political economy of urban development in North America and western Europe*. Princeton, N.J.: Princeton University Press.

Savitch, H. V., & Vogel, R. K. (2004). Suburbs without a city: Power and city–county consolidation. *Urban Affairs Review*, *39*(6), 758–790.

42   A Theory of Institutional Capacity

Savitch, H. V., Tsukamoto, T., & Vogel, R. K. (2008). Civic culture and corporate regime in Louisville. *Journal of Urban Affairs*, *30*(4), 437–460.

Sbragia, A. M. (1996). *Debt wish: Entrepreneurial cities, US federalism, and economic development*. Pittsburgh: University of Pittsburgh Press.

Schattschneider, E. E. (1960). *The semisovereign people: A realist's view of democracy in America*. New York: Holt, Rinehart and Winston.

Scholz, J. T., Berardo, R., & Kile, B. (2008). Do networks solve collective action problems? Credibility, search, and collaboration. *Journal of Politics*, *70*(2), 393–406.

Scott, S., & Nathan, H. (1970). Public referenda: A critical reappraisal. *Urban Affairs Review*, *5*(3), 313–328.

Seldon, A., & Pappworth, J. (1983). *By word of mouth: Élite oral history*. London: Taylor & Francis.

Shaffer, R., Deller, S., & Marcouiller, D. (2006). Rethinking community economic development. *Economic Development Quarterly*, *20*(1), 59–74.

Shepsle, K. A. (1991). *Models of multiparty electoral competition*. Chur, Switzerland: Harwood Academic Publishers.

Spensley, J. W. (2001). Using intergovernmental agreements to manage growth. *Natural Resources and Environment*, *15*(4), 240–278.

Stone, C. N. (1989). *Regime politics: Governing Atlanta, 1946–1988*. Lawrence, Kan.: University Press of Kansas.

Stone, C. N., Henig, J. R., Jones, B. D., & Pierannunzi, C. (2001). *Building civic capacity: The politics of reforming urban schools*. Lawrence, Kan.: University Press of Kansas.

Stone, D. A. (2002). *Policy paradox: The art of political decision making* (rev. edn.). New York: Norton.

Sullivan, D. M. (2002). Local governments as risk takers and risk reducers: An examination of business subsidies and subsidy controls. *Economic Development Quarterly*, *16*(2), 115–126.

Swanstrom, T. (2006). Regionalism, equality, and democracy. *Urban Affairs Review*, *42*(2), 249–257.

Tansey, O. (2007). Process tracing and elite interviewing: A case for non-probability sampling. *PS: Political Science and Politics*, *40*(4), 765–772.

Vidich, A. J., & Bensman, J. (1958). *Small town in mass society*. Princeton, N.J.: Princeton University Press.

Vidich, A. J., & Bensman, J. (2000). *Small town in mass society: Class, power, and religion in a rural community*. Urbana, Ill.: University of Illinois Press.

Wassail, G. H., & Hellman, D. A. (2005). Financial incentives to industry and urban economic development. *Review of Policy Research*, *4*(4), 626–639.

2 The Economic Context of Municipalities

Cities in the United States and beyond face globalization, open markets and federal and state policy changes that produce a triple threat to their finances and their stability. Three crises of declining manufacturing employment and tax base, intergovernmental aid cuts and the overhead from costs of current and former employees coincide with and in part result from a worldwide phenomenon: the intense competition for tax revenue from business spawned by what has become the second great age of globalization. Open markets and intergovernmental arrangements, such as delegation of power to local government, local government aid and revenue-sharing, have implications for the theoretical questions about economic and community development studied here, and are more highly politically contested than often acknowledged. I also address the question of how local governments might configure themselves institutionally or with regard to leadership to deliver results in terms of economic and community development policy or influence policy choices even when resources are short.

Powerful economic challenges face local governments and the constituents they serve alike. Just like its predecessor, the "Gilded Age" of the late nineteenth century, today's era of globalization and open markets has allowed footloose capital and businesses to relocate with ease. But, unlike in the 1880s and 1890s, the United States and its peers are now mature economies, with inherently low rates of economic growth and strong competition from emerging economies. Thus, whereas industrial employment in Western economies was growing strongly during the "Gilded Age," today it has dropped in the face of emerging economy competition, deregulation, freer trade and automation. As free trade expands economies overall, it carries a larger downside for a majority of people: as trade becomes freer, the ratio of redistribution to net gains rises,[1] which means that, absent nationwide attempts at managing the consequences of these trends, freer trade redistributes more and more wealth up and away from middle- and low-income households and from places dependent on shrinking industries (Bivens, 2015). Some national governments choose to intervene extensively to redistribute a large proportion of these gains in the form of social

44 *The Economic Context of Municipalities*

benefits or lower taxes for the poor and middle-income groups. Others, including the United States, have scaled back redistribution to the point that it is insufficient to overturn the negative side effects of free-trade-driven market forces (International Monetary Fund, 2007: chap. 4).

The adversity of this imbalance between strong free trade, growing and industrializing economies abroad and low levels of domestic wealth redistribution at home should not be underestimated. For example, as the overall population of the United States rose from 220 million in 1980 to more than 280 million in 2000, an increase of more than 25 percent,[2] manufacturing employment – for the better part of a century the bedrock of good-paying jobs for much of middle America – dropped from 19 million to 17 million, a decline of more than 10 percent. Even that drop was just the prelude to a far bigger collapse: manufacturing employment dropped by more than another third during the decade of the 2000s, even as the nation's population rose by another 30 million. Only after 2010 did a reversal emerge, with manufacturing employment in the United States rising from a low of 11,453,000 in March 2010 to over 12.3 million by mid-2015 and 12.4 million by mid-2017.[3]

Smaller towns such as those studied in this book face a large share of this challenge, which makes them ideal candidates for the study of economic development on both theoretical and empirical grounds. Theoretically, smaller communities should be more likely to engage in "race to the bottom" maneuvers than their big city counterparts. Their exposure to global market forces is as great – arguably greater – but their options for cutting overheads are fewer and their revenue streams fewer and less diverse. Empirically, they are relevant because, as larger US cities were losing manufacturing jobs in the 1960s, 1970s and 1980s, small towns were still gaining them and became much more dependent on manufacturing than major cities.

For example, manufacturing employment in the Chicago area peaked around 1970 and then started to fall rapidly. But manufacturing employment nationally in the United States did not peak until 1979, followed by a sharp but short recession, disproportionately concentrated in heavy industry in major cities, and then nearly two decades of near-stability, with continued industrial job growth in small towns masking the aftermath of the devastation of urban areas in the Rust Belt. The decline in manufacturing employment since 1999 has thus disproportionately hit smaller towns, which are now proportionally more exposed to the manufacturing sector in the United States than larger cities. And, while the major coastal cities that heavily lost manufacturing jobs in a previous era have more than made up for those losses with vast gains in service and technology sectors, small towns remote from the agglomeration effects that characterize global cities (Sassen, 2012; Friedmann, 1986) often appear to lack clear economic opportunities and political solutions to their troubles.

The Economic Context of Municipalities   45

This situation also raises political questions and questions about democratic choice, because local municipal governments find themselves on the front line of the political response to these changes, even as, theoretically speaking, they are the least empowered to cope with them. They have lost tax base. Their political and legal position appears weak. Retiree liabilities are often large, due to slow growth or decline, with unfunded pension liabilities alone ranging from $1 trillion to $3 trillion depending on how much the risk of stock market investments by public pension plans is taken into account.[4] And intergovernmental aid from state and federal governments has dropped sharply, especially federal support for economic and community development. States have themselves suffered a long-term decline in their own financial standing. The 2001–03 downturn[5] and the 2007–09 Great Recession brought unprecedented levels of deficit spending and resulted in a decline of state spending as a share of gross domestic product (GDP),[6] despite a strong trend in federal assistance away from aid to cities toward aid to states and a large overall increase in aid to states. They too face major financial burdens, including large employee benefit costs of their own, more responsibility for formerly federal government functions, and reduced federal grants. In several states, revenue-sharing with local government has been significantly reduced, though not eliminated.

Accordingly, municipalities face intense pressure to maintain the revenue needed to provide the services the voters expect. Federal aid to municipalities for community development in the United States dropped by more than half during the 1980s, from almost $24 billion a year to just over $10 billion a year in inflation-adjusted 2008-equivalent funds, as the Reagan administration withdrew from the then prevailing US federal practice of providing aid directly to cities[7] as well as via state government (Judd & Swanstrom, 2010).[8] Combined with the pressure on state spending, this has put local governments in perhaps the least favorable situation for intergovernmental aid since the Second World War.

Municipalities have thus had to respond with their own political and policy initiatives in economic and community development. The efforts of politically visible "builder mayors," such as Federico Pena in Denver, Richard M. Daley in Chicago (Spirou & Judd, 2016) or, more recently, Michael Bloomberg in New York, also have their counterparts in smaller communities, which are often playing a higher-stakes game due to inherently lower per capita revenues. The resulting evolution in local policy reflects not so much an economic and market imperative as change in state and federal fiscal policy toward lower intergovernmental support and a less regulated market. This fiscal devolution or offloading of costs to local government that has occurred from the 1980s "New Federalism" onward means political choice or agency matters greatly to the success and failure of economic and community development efforts. The choice at stake is whether those efforts will primarily take the form of a "race to the bottom" heavy on business subsidies and tax breaks, a

46 *The Economic Context of Municipalities*

community development approach of infrastructural, labor market and service improvement predicated on economic growth, centered on the idea of "If you build it, they will come," or a blended approach that includes elements of both strategies.

This is an important story to tell, because scholars, journalists and pundits alike have widely assumed that these economic factors mean a community's economic and tax base is highly vulnerable to capital flight. Put simply, businesses are theoretically free to exit a jurisdiction whenever they want, and will often do so when faced with even slightly onerous regulatory burdens or taxation (Tiebout, 1956; Schneider, 1985). In this narrative, local governments likely cannot provide the services and facilities that the public expects and votes for without such regulations and taxes, thus precluding a systemic political response that prioritizes citizen interests over business ones or treats them as being complementary to one another. Even the largest, most economically vibrant, new-economy-oriented global cities are seen as likely to compromise general infrastructure and service provision as they engage the specific task of encouraging businesses to make major capital investments in their communities. This viewpoint implies inherently worse conditions for the small town industrial belt of the American Midwest and South, where overall job losses in the past 15 years are proportionally greater and the presence of the new economy proportionally much smaller than that found in larger cities.[9]

The implication is that such places are even more driven than their big city counterparts to subvert local spending and tax policy in favor of making deals with businesses willing to relocate into their communities, because it is the only realistic means of expanding the tax base. These circumstances indeed impair spending on community development and essential services that might be popular with the public but take years to register in the minds of business owners and investors as a worthwhile asset. However, such policies are not a given. First, if they exist, they are often partly driven by a conscious choice for a more "market-led" or neoliberal approach that has been exercised by local elites, and not simply an economic necessity (Weaver, 2016). Second, higher levels of government remain involved, in some cases providing a support structure for local governments; and local government and communities sometimes choose activist governance in the form of higher taxes and spending, citywide and neighborhood amenities that are often seen as at least as useful as low taxes to business or to the workers they need to hire (Stone & Stoker, 2015; Vanderleeuw & Sides, 2016), or political choices that center on issues other than providing a "low-cost" business environment – despite the apparent risks of alienating capital or encouraging capital flight. My object is to tell the story, through the theoretically unfavorable situation of smaller towns, of how the local and state-driven organization of municipal governance influences such choices and drives outcomes.

Economic Pressure on Cities and City Governments in the "Heartland"

The intense economic pressure on most local governments (half of all new business startups in the first four years of the post-2007–09 recovery occurred in just a score of counties nationwide)[10] is driven above all else by competitive pressure on industries that have traditionally had large numbers of higher-paying jobs. Nowhere is this more visible than in manufacturing. The current era of globalization and deregulation has seen the number of "good-paying jobs" of manufacturing employment, which grew in the 1950s and 1960s and was approximately stable (though with sharp regional variations) through the 1970s, 1980s and 1990s, fall during the 2000s by more than a third below its 1979 peak of 19.5 million.[11] To start with, the decline was gentle, driven mostly by big productivity gains in domestic manufacturing in the 1980s and 1990s. But, as federal policy changed and outsourcing took hold, the pressure grew. Changes including the abolition of foreign exchange controls, reform of corporate governance, expansion of shareholder rights, expanded free trade and deregulation combined with broader trends such as declining labor unions and rising natural resource costs to put further pressure on the manufacturing sector, especially the line jobs overrepresented in small to medium-sized towns and cities in the Midwest and South. Manufacturing was the leading sector of the economy in 1990 in 36 US states; by 2015 that had dropped to seven states.[12]

As international trade barriers and tariffs have come down, developing economies for many years also increased their productivity far more rapidly than their wage rates. Overall, since the 1971 abandonment of fixed exchange rates, world trade in goods and services has risen by more than 1,000 percent in real terms.[13] The fastest-growing trade has been between developed economies and developing countries where wages are significantly lower, putting serious pressure on wages and salaries in the United States and other developed economies given the open trade environment.[14] The US trade deficit rose steadily from around $2.5 billion a month in the early 1990s, accompanied by an accelerating decline in manufacturing employment, until it reached a steady $60 billion or more a month during the three years prior to the 2008 economic crash.[15] It abruptly dropped during the ensuing recession; it then rose with the recovery through 2012, since when it has dropped significantly, only to flat-line at a still high $40 billion or so per month, equivalent to around two percent of GDP.[16]

In cities without a strong alternative base of high-paying employment – such as financial services, government administration, oil drilling, health care and technology – the decline of industrial employment is particularly problematic, because mining and manufacturing are among the highest-paying industries. For many small towns and even medium cities, especially away from the coasts, these jobs are the highest-paying form of mass

48   *The Economic Context of Municipalities*

employment, with the best benefits, while the plants are at the heart of commercial tax bases. The Economic Policy Institute's studies of manufacturing employment tell the story succinctly. Nationally, manufacturing's share of GDP strongly exceeds its share of employment: 12.2 percent as opposed to 10.4 percent.

The leading manufacturing states in the United States also tend to lack large concentrations of the types of service and financial jobs that have seen growth in numbers and pay, making them especially vulnerable to these trends. Of the four most manufacturing-dominated states in the United States as of 2016, three – Indiana, Iowa and Wisconsin[17] – are upper Midwestern states without a top 20 metropolitan area, and with hundreds of small towns that depend significantly on manufacturing for the best of their employment base. This is a particularly significant factor in the United States because of the way modern employment patterns are shifting toward services. The overall balance conceals a manufacturing trade deficit of around $60 billion a month during 2016, and a services trade surplus of around $20 billion a month during the same period.[18] The jobs under the highest pressure, therefore, are the manufacturing jobs likely to be the highest-paying jobs in smaller communities away from the coasts and with a smaller services sector.[19] What was once a churn in manufacturing – plant closings offset by openings – turned to sharp declines in 1999–2002 and steady further declines until 2011 in terms of employment, even as the overall contribution to GDP remains strong and manufacturing job growth has picked up slightly in the years since then.

These patterns are seen clearly in the areas and communities analyzed in this study. On Minnesota's Iron Range, the end of underground mining of iron ore and the exhaustion of open-cast deposits of high-grade "soft" iron ore was offset by the opening of a new generation of mines and plants handling low-grade "hard" ore, or taconite. In the manufacturing heartland of the Midwest, such as northern Illinois, as heavy industry became less important in the years after the Second World War, new jobs opened in sectors such as consumer goods and hardware manufacturing. Peak manufacturing employment in the United States did not arrive until the end of the 1970s – and employment levels remained close to the 1979 peak for another 20 years. Even as late as the 1980s, massive heavy industrial job losses in the steel and auto industries of the Ohio Valley and parts of the Midwest were offset by continuing gains elsewhere, in technology, aerospace and consumer goods; major cities that were losing manufacturing jobs were more than making up for these losses with service sector employment; smaller communities were still making net gains in manufacturing.

The Rust Belt, including the four case studies of this book, saw trouble earlier than most other parts of the country. Starting with the peak of manufacturing employment at the end of the 1970s, the situation not only for large, older cities but also for small towns heavily dependent on manufacturing became steadily more difficult, a trend that intensified with the sharp decline in manufacturing employment after 1999 and through the decade of the 2000s. This applies both to communities that depend on producing the raw materials for manufacturing and those that produce the finished goods. For example, from 1978 to 2005 more than 11,000 mining jobs were lost on Minnesota's Iron Range, with most of the decline between 1981 and 1986, modest rehiring in the late 1980s, and another substantial decline in the early 2000s (Power, 2007).

What was worse in small town regions of the United States was that these were the most numerous high-paying jobs in the community; there were few jobs of comparable pay on which to fall back. This first became evident during the recession of the early 1980s, when, particularly in the Minnesota communities in this study, the shortage of alternative employment with middle-class standards of pay became cruelly evident. Unemployment rates on the Iron Range stayed close to the 20 percent mark throughout the mid-1980s, with some house prices dropping below $10,000 – about the price of a decent pickup truck to move out with – and with average prices on the Range lagging even statewide depressed levels at the time.[20] Today the Range's mining industry produces approximately 1979 tonnage with only one-quarter of the previous employment.

In manufacturing-dependent areas that in many cases use the steel produced from what is mined in northern Minnesota, the story is similar. In Sterling, Illinois, the plant that was once Northwestern Steel and Wire

Figure 2.1 The Hull–Rust–Mahoning mine pit in Hibbing, now part of Hibbing Taconite, August 2017

Source: Daniel Bliss.

50   *The Economic Context of Municipalities*

employs just 400, versus almost 4,700[21] at its 1979 peak, and production has dropped as well, though by not nearly the same proportion. In the end, whether in raw materials or finished goods, industrial jobs that provide a middle-class standard of living[22] have declined in number, to be replaced, if at all, by jobs that all too often carry what in a major metropolitan area would be considered at best entry-level pay.[23] For small, blue-collar communities in particular, it means constant efforts to protect jobs and maintain the tax base. Economic and community development have become central to local policy agendas – yet at a time that the resources with which to conduct such policy are extremely short.

Deindustrialization and Its Characterization in Literature

How has this situation been characterized in the academic literature on urban politics and economic development? Technological change, globalization, deregulated trade and deindustrialization in the United States have combined to profoundly affect US urban economies over the past three decades. Technological change and international competition are seen as by far the two biggest contributors to declining manufacturing employment (Fisher & Rupert, 2005). This change is not confined to major metropolitan areas. A substantial portion of US manufacturing has traditionally taken place far away from the corporate headquarters of major cities (Sassen, 2012; 1991). For much of the industrial sector, including mining, steel, automobiles, hand tools, consumer goods and meatpacking, activity tends to take place in plants in small towns with poorly diversified economies where a single closure could knock out a community's major source of living-wage jobs and a city government's largest share of tax revenue.

These challenging circumstances explain why the narrative of local powerlessness can be so compelling. Even the most economically attractive and diversified global cities, such as New York and London, are seen as vulnerable to capital flight (Sassen, 1991). Indeed, they have lost a disproportionate share of middle-income blue-collar jobs and tax base, in part as skilled workers and plants alike leave these overheated property markets. In that context, one might not hold out much hope for activist governance in a mid-size city dominated by a single business sector, or a small town dominated by a single major employer and/or a handful of smaller businesses. Renowned geographer David Harvey goes farther, suggesting local governments are locked by capitalism into "economic imperatives" to confine public services to as limited a role as possible (Harvey, 1990).

The idea that economic conditions render local places' ability to set their direction beyond their control is a tempting one. Economic changes, driven in considerable part by the decisions of national governments, have been dramatic in scope and scale. Cities are seen to be facing "economic imperatives" to become active seekers of outside capital, building the value of

The Economic Context of Municipalities   51

the place they occupy, keeping tax rates to a minimum and eliminating or reducing programs that may interfere with that goal (Molotch, 1976). Policy is often driven by the perception that increases in the taxes needed to fund a municipality will inevitably drive holders of capital to look elsewhere to invest.

Accordingly, the recent histories of cities, both big and small, are dominated by narratives of continuing decline. Most large-scale manufacturing has disappeared from the metropolitan area of New York, its manufacturing workforce declining from two points above the national average in 1950, mostly in smaller businesses producing non-durable goods (Freeman, 2001), to less than two percent, one-fifth of the national average, by 2016.[24] Cities such as Detroit and Cleveland have also seen huge declines in manufacturing employment but without anything like New York's gain in service employment, dragging down the broader economy and leaving both central cities at less than half their historic population highs.

These huge declines in urban areas have left manufacturing jobs in the United States more concentrated in small communities in less urbanized states; the most manufacturing-centered states are Indiana (17.0 percent of workers in manufacturing), Wisconsin (15.9 percent), Michigan (13.9 percent) and Iowa (13.6 percent) as of 2016.[25] Cities that were dependent on a few large employers have been especially vulnerable to the trends in manufacturing industry. Examples of cities experiencing major plant closures include Waterloo, Iowa, which lost its meatpacking industry and much of its farm implement production in the 1980s (Portz, 1990); Wooster, Ohio, whose flagship Rubbermaid factory closed in 2004 following cost-cutting demands from retail customers such as Walmart, which forced the company to offshore production to China after 2004 (New York State School of Industrial and Labor Relations at Cornell University, 2005) in order to absorb raw materials costs;[26] and Galesburg, Illinois, whose biggest employer, Maytag, relocated production to Mexico that same year.[27]

The Untold Story of Small Communities and the Policy Response

What cities – indeed, citizens – everywhere are searching for in the face of these pressures is a prospect of greater self-determination and self-direction. But much of the public and academic discussion of these economic and policy trends leaves three major questions largely untouched. First, it focuses on larger cities, using an argument centered on economic resources whose logic implies that smaller cities – with their smaller per capita tax base,[28] failure to recover from recessions,[29] and relative weakness in location, education and economic diversification – should be inherently even more vulnerable to economic "imperatives" than their big city counterparts. This discussion has barely entered the small town space to determine whether this logic holds or whether policy choices in small communities might suggest broader horizons for both them and bigger cities.

52   *The Economic Context of Municipalities*

Second, it pays insufficient attention to the role of institutional and governmental organization in producing a policy response to these economic changes. Parameters affecting policy decisions include intergovernmental connections among municipalities or between local and state government, the process of policy development and adoption and how functions are delegated within a municipality. The confinement of much of the discussion on economic and community development to market forces and private economic resources means the neglect of a large area of policy and politics. This is a problem because of how highly politically structured the role of municipal government is; in the United States, it depends on state law and constitutional provision, as the tools and/or money that states provide or fail to provide local government can make or break municipalities. In Massachusetts, for example, communities are forbidden from levying a local sales tax, making for little incentive to recruit retailers. In Alaska, on the other hand, they depend on them, and no sales taxes go to the state. Similar differences are evident among the cases analyzed here. In Illinois, revenue is shared by the state with local government, based on population (for a cut of 10 percent of the state's income tax revenue) and where revenue was generated (based on sales and motor vehicle excise tax). These arrangements place a clear premium on recruiting retailers. Another approach is attempting to ensure the broad provision of basic local services without resorting to aggressive policies aimed at importing capital. In Minnesota, the state supports municipalities with Local Government Aid, a program means-tested through a property-valuation-based formula that, even after several rounds of cuts, still distributed more than $519 million for 2016, around $100 per citizen on average.[30] Additionally, school funding, once heavily based on property taxes and through the 1970s, 1980s and 1990s based on the 1971 "Minnesota Miracle" reform of means-tested state funds to offset property taxes, now takes place largely with the support of state income and sales taxes. The general idea since the early 1970s has been to ensure that even the poorest community has sufficient funds for basic services without heavy pressure to increase property tax revenue (Berg, 2012).

Third, the private-sector, large-city-centered discussion on economic and community development glosses over real evidence in scholarly literature and elsewhere of different policy choices being made, often successfully, by local government. When the argument of structural economic imperatives and inevitable policy choices is modified to take account of individual success stories, the anecdotes are usually about economics and luck rather than political choice or agency. Many cities that have been analyzed in the economic and community development literature – to take a few examples: Santa Barbara, California (Nevarez, 2003); Huntsville, Alabama (Pagano & Bowman, 1995); or even, in the more distant past, Muncie, Indiana (Lynd & Lynd, 1929) – are those that still have significant material resources at their disposal, such as land or a well-educated workforce, that give them enhanced bargaining power with private business (Savitch & Kantor, 2002). Other such structural assets include institutions of higher education, a well-trained workforce or market proximity to one or more major metropolitan areas. Less commonly, analysis may identify a broader context of leadership or institutional structure to the process of trying to make economic development work better and more efficiently. This occurs through structured regulation of business subsidy and support among governments across a region or country or even internationally (Thomas, 2011), or establishing sufficient unity of purpose among community leaders to deliver major community development projects despite a weak local economy (Pagano & Bowman, 1995).[31]

Examples of small towns with at least some success in these respects in economic development are scattered across the United States, particularly in the Midwest, where rural economies are proportionally less weak than in the South and West. The last two decades have seen – in most US central cities, at least – an end to the hemorrhaging of population of the 1950s to the 1980s, as downtowns have recovered, inner city neighborhoods have gentrified and social problems have increasingly become shared with the suburbs. As for smaller towns, many – particularly in the Farm Belt – have continued to slowly decline in population and economic base; some have reinvented themselves as hubs of commerce and industry. Some of these strategies, such as in Hutchinson, Minnesota, a city of 14,000 located 60 miles west of Minneapolis, are vulnerable due to lack of economic diversification, meaning that outsourcing or offshoring by a single major employer, such as hard drive component manufacturer Hutchinson Technology, can deeply harm an entire community.[32] When small towns, such as Grinnell, Iowa, have a higher-paying and more diversified job base (in this case, insurance, higher education, manufacturing, health care and biotechnology), they become regional long-distance commuting magnets; local competition for jobs remains intense.

How Do Small Towns Stand Out on Economic Development and Organization?

Local governments, large and small alike, must deal with the consequences both of economics and of higher-level political decisions – and satisfy their own citizen and business constituencies. Many medium- to large-sized city governments have increasingly pursued economic development and entrepreneurial activity since the 1970s (Eisinger, 1988; Frieden & Sagalyn, 1989; DiGaetano & Klemanski, 1999; Fainstein, 2001; Savitch & Kantor, 2002). These efforts have typically involved revitalizing business districts, particularly downtowns, and retooling cities for service industries and tourism, often through land use and zoning changes (Rast, 2002). This is because land use is a tangible way to measure a community's bargaining capability; it is a resource with extensively reported data on

54 *The Economic Context of Municipalities*

measurements such as tax capacity, environmental remediation grants and the value added by building improvements. It is also, thanks to its inherent immovability, a useful resource for political leaders (Bowman & Pagano, 2004; Rast, 1997; Pagano, 2003). Especially in smaller and/or economically marginalized cities, retention and development of manufacturing jobs is also at the forefront of local government policy (Jones & Bachelor, 1993; Hoyman, 1997; Portz, 1990; Eisinger, 1988). But, detailed though this subset of the literature is, it also misses crucial parts of the basic process by which policy responses to economic change are formed, and often neglects smaller communities.

This book explores two underexamined aspects of organizational influence on politics and policy. The first is the question of how the process of politics affects power over outcomes in general. These political processes can include decisions over the role of city councils, and various organizational choices such as weak versus strong bureaucracies, shared services versus for each his own, and policy choices such as beggar-thy-neighbor economic development versus regional boards and joint powers arrangements for developing policy. We know more about the value of material resources, such as tax base, grants from federal and state government or a business community heavily invested in the city, than we do about institutional effects on economic development politics. There is a robust literature on the political fragmentation of urban areas in the United States, motivated in part by concerns over inequality between central cities and first-ring suburbs, on the one hand, and affluent suburban enclaves, on the other (Orfield, 1999; 2002; Savitch & Vogel, 2004; Dreier, Mollenkopf & Swanstrom, 2001; Oliver, 2001). Yet cities' institutional and organizational power within themselves, or among themselves, to deliver policy is little addressed. Public administration literature has addressed the impact of forms of government (for example, mayor-council versus council-manager) on politics and policy (Folz & French, 2005; Nelson & Nollenberger, 2011). Political science has studied the culture of city institutions and politics and the effect of that context on economic development in the form of civic capacity (Reese & Rosenfeld, 2001; de Souza Briggs, 2008; Nelles, 2013). Additionally, a study in the Chicago metropolitan region has indicated that fragmentation among local governments significantly weakens their bargaining power with private business (Chicago Metropolitan Agency for Planning, 2013).

The second is how such processes and the institutions that manage them might affect a city's ability to perform economic and community development (Imbroscio, 1997) – potentially enhancing it even when it is otherwise short of resources. Given the increasing levels of financial pressure upon local government, this question is becoming more and more pertinent, encompassing cities of all types and sizes. The small towns studied here represent an inherently good situation for testing this question. They are particularly dependent on the types of industry in which employment is particularly under pressure from global competition and technological advance. Their governments are also inherently vulnerable; they have per capita spending and tax bases that are well behind their statewide averages and that of major cities such as Minneapolis and Chicago. Added to that, the small size of these city staffs – approximately 200 in Hibbing, 30 in Ely – makes it difficult or impossible for them to achieve economies of scale in the provision of essential public services. For example, key city functions such as planning and zoning or coordination of economic development can form simply a part-time portion of a broad job description for a particular employee. Given these constraints, spending cuts may well mean not eliminating a certain percentage of positions in a department but, rather, a choice between sharing services with neighboring municipalities and elimination of the services altogether. At once, we see both the particularly deep vulnerability of small towns and a possible solution to a problem based on the organization and institutions of governance rather than new spending.

The overwhelming large city focus of literature on urban economic renewal and revitalization (Frieden & Sagalyn, 1989; Fainstein, 2001; Fainstein, Fainstein, Hill, Judd & Smith, 1983; DiGaetano & Klemanski, 1999; Ferman, 1996; DeLeon, 1992; Stone, 1989; Molotch, 1976) has left little space for discussion in small towns; This is especially problematic in view of the distinction between the white-collar "global cities" economy of the United States from the manufacturing, light industrial and back-office base of most of the rest of the country. In analyzing this part of the question, the historical economic functions and business presence of various communities stand out as an important predictor of future patterns of success in economic development (Abu-Lughod, 2000; Doussard & Schrock, 2015). The major metropolitan areas, such as New York, enjoy vast surpluses of trade with the rest of the world, even as their manufacturing has largely disappeared and other blue-collar trades have downsized, and, accordingly, they have been far more concerned with maintaining their financial service sectors. But smaller towns rarely have such diversification; the "company town" model remains widespread, and in many cases towns must reinvent themselves and find a new function, a far greater challenge in many respects than for New York to maintain Wall Street. In this respect, there are a handful of studies, not unrelated to regime studies, that analyze the way power is wielded in community decisions in general (Lynd & Lynd, 1929; Vidich & Bensman, 1958; Cook, 1993) or economic development in particular (Ramsay, 1996; Hoyman, 1997).

This functional challenge implies an even greater "imperative" for smaller towns: to pursue economic development as a core strategy of maintaining themselves as viable communities. But what do these communities do? Do they engage in a "race to the bottom," pursuing tax incentives and other direct aid to often outside-owned business, frequently at the expense of public facilities and services? Do they build community assets, in the

56   *The Economic Context of Municipalities*

hope that they will prove attractive to those looking to expand, relocate or open a business? Or do they blend strategies? What does the governance of these communities produce in terms of public and private assets? And to what extent do institutional geography and organization influence the outcome? In the rest of this chapter, I review evidence of local choices being made on economic development; in the next, I tackle the question of institutions and organizations, both local and intergovernmental, including the steering and driving of economic development and the role of state governments.

Local policy-making: Imperatives, Public Choice or Guided by Institutionalized Power?

When considering why a small town government might try to intervene forcefully to shape its community, one might ask whether it does so because it should, or because the citizens want it to or simply because it can. In a political choice between doing nothing and taking major action, local governments will often choose to do the latter even if a new development appears highly speculative or the intervention constitutes a desperate measure to retain what economic base the community already has (Hoyman, 1997; Portz, 1990).

A case in point within one of the regions addressed here, the Iron Range of Minnesota, exists in the city of Cohasset, population 3,000, which lost an amount of money greater than its annual operating budget on a failed project. In 1996 the city guaranteed $2.4 million of a $12 million revenue bond to support Technimar, the then US licensee for Stonite,[33] an Italian granite product used in manufacturing kitchen counter tops, as part of a financing package that saw the Iron Range Resources and Rehabilitation Board contribute $2 million in incentives and the Minneapolis police and firefighters pension plans invest $5 million each. The venture collapsed without any production, with Cohasset levying for its entire loss in calendar year 2000 (more than 80 percent of the burden fell on Minnesota Power, by far the town's dominant taxpayer).[34] The city of Cohasset subsequently adopted an ordinance limiting business subsidies to a maximum of $200,000 and establishing other safeguards. Litigation in the case continued for many years. In 2000 David Welliver, the Grand Rapids, Minn.-based investment adviser who brokered the deal, lost a $14.6 million judgment to both pension funds for mismanaging fund assets,[35] and in 2007 the Minnesota appeals court panel rejected a lawsuit by Technimar's bankruptcy trustee against its auditors.[36]

What is striking in the Technimar case is how loose the definition of "economic imperative" (Harvey, 1990) is in the eyes of local political leaders. After all, they may choose a variety of ways of handling business and capital, ranging from corporate welfare to minor regulatory changes or community amenities and infrastructure. The Technimar aid package was

The Economic Context of Municipalities 57

not a response to an emergency but, rather, a reflection of long-term economic stress that created political pressure. The Iron Range of the mid-1990s had recovered considerably from the mass unemployment of the 1980s, but still faced a situation of chronically subpar wages typical of support and service industry in mining regions (Power, 2007). This decision from Cohasset and the IRRRB and the pension fund backing was a calculated strategic move that went disastrously wrong due to inadequate vetting of the business. Cohasset took a risk because of the immense outside backing and seal of approval from major public bodies.

In short, the Technimar project was not an economic imperative but, rather, the function of a political choice driven both by an economically anxious local community and by bigger institutions with an agenda. Indeed, politics and governance explain a great deal of the variation between local governments to these kinds of economic development problems (Savitch & Kantor, 2002; Clarke & Gaile, 1998; Pagano & Bowman, 1995; Stone, 1989). Local governments make decisions, often politically driven, on whether to recruit prospective businesses from within or outside the community, how much trust to place in a potential business partner, how much to give them, how much to lend them, and – if resources are available – how much to engage other levels of government. These decisions, though they are influenced profoundly by economic circumstances, do not take place in a vacuum. Substantial institutional and organizational influences also exist. Local governments are configured differently from one another. States (or national governments, when applicable) provide both limitations on and opportunities to local governments seeking to enhance policy outcomes for their citizens. Accordingly, a close look at these broader institutional frameworks is in order.

Notes

1 Source: D. Rodrik, What is wrong (and right) in economics? May 7, 2013, blog post, available at http://rodrik.typepad.com/dani_rodriks_weblog/2013/05/what-is-wrong-and-right-in-economics.html.
2 Based on US Census data.
3 Source: US Bureau of Labor Statistics, Employment, hours and earnings from the current employment statistics survey, August 2017.
4 Source: W. G. Gale and A. Krupkin, Financing state and local pension obligations: Issues and options. Brookings Institution, 2016.
5 Source: research brief, National League of Cities, May 2003.
6 Source: Center for Budget and Policy Priorities, A brief update on state fiscal conditions and the effects of federal policies on state budgets. September 13, 2004; available at www.cbpp.org/archives/9-13-04sfp.htm.
7 US Office of Management and Budget, Budget of the United States government, fiscal year 2009, Historical tables, pp. 62–71, Table 3.2, Community and regional development: federal spending on regional and community development, 1962–2002.

58 *The Economic Context of Municipalities*

8 See Judd & Swanstrom (2010), p. 193, Federal spending on regional and community development, 1962–2008 (Figure 8.1), which documents the approximately 60 percent inflation-adjusted decline in the 1980s in federal spending supporting municipally based economic and community development efforts.

9 See County business patterns, US Census Bureau, 2000 and 2014. East North Central, East South Central and New England census divisions lost total employment during that time; the country as a whole lost almost 35 percent of previous manufacturing employment, with total employment rising just over 6 percent. In the regions representative of the communities in this study, non-manufacturing employment declined as well as manufacturing employment.

10 See Economic Innovation Group (2016). This report, which uses US Census Bureau County business patterns data and was widely covered in US media, documented the growing geographic concentration of economic recovery and growth following recent recessions. The 1992–6 recovery from the 1990–1 recession saw the top 125 counties of 3,142 in the United States account for half of all new business startups; the 2002–6 period after the 2001 recession saw 64 counties account for half of new business startups; and the 2010–14 period after the 2007–9 recession saw a mere 20 counties account for half of all new startups. This concentration has occurred even though all three recoveries have ended up attaining similar annual levels of new business startups nationally.

11 Source: US Bureau of Labor Statistics, US Department of Labor. A complete data series on manufacturing employment is available at http://research.stlouisfed.org/fred2/data/MANEMP.txt.

12 Source: US Bureau of Labor Statistics, US Department of Labor, The economics daily, Major industries with highest employment, by state, 1990–2015, August 5, 2016; available at www.bls.gov/opub/ted/2016/major-industries-with-highest-employment-by-state.htm (visited August 12, 2017).

13 Organisation for Economic Co-operation and Development (OECD) data, International trade (main economic indicators) dataset, available at http://stats.oecd.org/index.aspx?queryid=167. Total world exports in goods and services were $343.24 billion (2005 dollars) in 1971, $3,473.71 billion (2005 dollars) in 2009.

14 Ibid. Exports from non-OECD countries grew the most rapidly from 1971 to 2009, rising from $76.86 billion to $1,259.69 billion, or around 1,700 percent.

15 Source: US Census Bureau, US trade in goods and services – balance of payments basis, 1960 through 2015. Annualized chart available at www.census.gov/foreign-trade/statistics/historical/gands.pdf.

16 Source: US Bureau of Economic Analysis, US Department of Commerce, April 2016 trade gap is $37.4 billion, June 3, 2016, beablog, blog.bea.gov/category/trade-deficit.

17 Scott (2008), based on figures from the US Bureau of Economic Analysis of the US Department of Commerce and the Economic Policy Institute. In 2006 Indiana depended on manufacturing for 28 percent of gross state product (GSP), Iowa and Louisiana 21 percent, and Wisconsin 20 percent. By 2013, according to the National Association of Manufacturers' State manufacturing data table, Indiana had risen to 30 percent of GSP derived from manufacturing, with Oregon at 29.8 percent and Louisiana at 23.4, but Indiana, Wisconsin and Iowa remained the top three by employment.

The Economic Context of Municipalities 59

18 Source: US Census Bureau, US international trade in goods and services, October 2016 report. Monthly reports are accessed at www.census.gov/foreign-trade/statistics/highlights/Congressional.pdf.

19 See US trade in goods and services – balance of payments (BOP) basis, value in millions of dollars 1960 through 2009; US Census Bureau, Foreign Trade Division, available at www.census.gov/foreign-trade/statistics/historical/gands.pdf. The US trade balances in 1960 were a goods surplus of $4.892 billion and a services deficit of $1.384 billion; in 2009 they included a goods deficit of $517 billion (following three consecutive years of goods deficits of more than $800 billion) and a services surplus of $138 billion, just slightly below 2008's all-time record of $144 billion. Since the recession the services surplus has continued to soar, reaching a peak of $262.2 billion, while the goods deficit, though it has not set any new records during this time, reached $762.6 billion in 2015 before starting to drop again in 2016.

20 See Population notes – Minnesota state demographer, State Planning Agency OSD 87-43, March 1987.

21 Interview 94. Northwestern Steel and Wire, Inc. (NWSW), had dropped from 4,000 under the Dillon family's ownership to 1,500 under its new ownership by its 2001 bankruptcy, and successor Sterling Steel, Inc., employs approximately 300.

22 In 2000 the president of the Iron Mining Association of Minnesota, Anne Glumac, in a presentation for an Ely Area Development Association quarterly meeting, estimated average assembly line salary and benefits in the Minnesota taconite industry at $65,000 annually.

23 Jobs at Sterling's newly opened Walmart distribution center averaged $12 to $14 an hour in 2006–7 – a rate considered good by service industry standards in the area and well ahead of rates of pay in Walmart stores.

24 Source: US Bureau of Labor Statistics, New York City economic summary, updated May 2, 2016.

25 Source: US Bureau of Labor Statistics, State area employment 2016 annual average tables.

26 See G. Burns, Closure of Rubbermaid factory tears at fabric of hometown Wooster, Ohio, *Chicago Tribune*, June 1, 2004.

27 See C. Broughton, The last refrigerator, *The Atlantic Magazine*, September 16, 2014; available at www.theatlantic.com/business/archive/2014/09/the-last-refrigerator/380154.

28 Median house prices are far lower for rural areas than for urban ones; in 2013 median house prices in central cities were $170,000, in major metro suburbs $180,000, in micropolitan areas $110,000 and in rural areas $95,000. Source: US Census Bureau, American housing survey table creator.

29 As of the second quarter of 2014 urban America had surpassed its pre-Great-Recession employment peak, while rural America remained around four percent below its pre-recession peak; 779 of 1,985 rural counties had continued to see job losses in just the previous year. Source: US Department of Agriculture (2014).

30 Minnesota LGA statistics are available in both total amount and per capita from 2002 onward, at www.house.leg.state.mn.us/hrd/lgahist.aspx, and summary statistics are available at www.revenue.state.mn.us/local_gov/prop_tax_admin/aclb/lga_16_summary.pdf.

60   *The Economic Context of Municipalities*

31 Pagano & Bowman compared ten mid-size US cities, including Duluth, Minn. – near to the Iron Range cases in this book, and with often similar politics – for how they mobilize economic and community development projects.

32 See C. Serres, With ax poised to fall, Hutchinson is on edge, *Star Tribune* (Minneapolis), March 24, 2011. This article marked the announcement of major layoffs by Hutchinson Technology, the town's home-grown producer and developer of disk drive components, whose employment in Hutchinson has since dropped from 2,300 to only a few dozen as production has been outsourced and the company has been bought out by a rival. See also S. Alexander, More layoffs for Hutchinson Technology workers, *Star Tribune*, May 21, 2014; and J. Hammerand, Hutchinson Technology plans more Minnesota layoffs, *Minneapolis/St. Paul Business Journal*, April 12, 2016.

33 David Welliver, the investment adviser who brokered the project, subsequently alleged Technimar had never paid the fee called for in the exclusivity agreement. See S. Sedgewick, Welliver says he was singled out in failed Technimar deal, *Grand Rapids Herald Review*, May 31, 2003.

34 See *Bemidji Northern Herald*, The Technimar story, February 28, 2001.

35 See D. Browning, Former investment adviser pleads guilty to securities fraud, *Star Tribune*, July 14, 2016.

36 See Julia A. Christians *v.* Grant Thornton, LLP, State of Minnesota in Court of Appeals no. A06-1309, July 3, 2007.

References

Abu-Lughod, J. L. (2000). *New York, Chicago, Los Angeles: America's global cities.* Minneapolis: University of Minnesota Press.

Berg, T. (2012). *Minnesota's miracle: Learning from the government that worked.* Minneapolis: University of Minnesota Press.

Bivens, J. (2015). The trans-Pacific partnership is unlikely to be a good deal for American workers, Briefing Paper no. 397. Washington, D.C.: Economic Policy Institute.

Bowman, A. O., & Pagano, M. A. (2004). *Terra incognita: Vacant land and urban strategies.* Washington, D.C.: Georgetown University Press.

Chicago Metropolitan Agency for Planning (2013). *Examination of local economic development incentives in northeastern Illinois.* Chicago: Chicago Metropolitan Agency for Planning.

Clarke, S. E., & Gaile, G. L. (1998). *The work of cities.* Minneapolis: University of Minnesota Press.

Cook, H. K. (1993). Small town talk: The undoing of collective action in two Missouri towns. PhD dissertation, Washington University, St. Louis, Mo.; available at http://artsci.wustl.edu/~anthro/blurb/b_cook.html.

De Souza Briggs, X. (2008). *Democracy as problem solving: Civic capacity in communities across the globe.* Cambridge, Mass.: MIT Press.

DeLeon, R. E. (1992). *Left coast city: Progressive politics in San Francisco, 1975–1991.* Lawrence, Kan.: University Press of Kansas.

DiGaetano, A., & Klemanski, J. S. (1999). *Power and city governance: Comparative perspectives on urban development.* Minneapolis: University of Minnesota Press.

The Economic Context of Municipalities 61

Doussard, M., & Schrock, G. (2015). Uneven decline: Linking historical patterns and processes of industrial restructuring to future growth trajectories. *Cambridge Journal of Regions, Economy and Society*, 8(2), 149–165.

Dreier, P., Mollenkopf, J. H., & Swanstrom, T. (2001). *Place matters: Metropolitics for the twenty-first century*. Lawrence, Kan.: University Press of Kansas.

Economic Innovation Group (2016). *The new map of economic growth and recovery*. Washington D.C.: Economic Innovation Group.

Eisinger, P. K. (1988). *The rise of the entrepreneurial state: State and local economic development policy in the United States*. Madison, Wis.: University of Wisconsin Press.

Fainstein, S. S. (2001). *The city builders: Property development in New York and London, 1980–2000*. Lawrence, Kan.: University Press of Kansas.

Fainstein, S. S., Fainstein, N., Hill, R. C., Judd, D., & Smith, M. P. (1983). *Restructuring the city: The political economy of urban redevelopment*. New York: Longman.

Ferman, B. (1996). *Challenging the growth machine: Neighborhood politics in Chicago and Pittsburgh*. Lawrence, Kan.: University Press of Kansas.

Fisher, E. O. N., & Rupert, P. C. (2005). The decline of manufacturing employment in the United States, policy brief. Cleveland: Federal Reserve Bank of Cleveland.

Folz, D. H., & French, P. E. (2005). *Managing America's small communities: People, politics, and performance*. Lanham, Md.: Rowman & Littlefield.

Freeman, J. B. (2001). *Working-class New York: Life and labor since World War II*. New York: New Press.

Frieden, B. J., & Sagalyn, L. B. (1989). *Downtown, Inc.: How America rebuilds cities*. Cambridge, Mass.: MIT Press.

Friedmann, J. (1986). The world city hypothesis. *Development and Change*, 17(1), 69–83.

Harvey, D. (1990). *The condition of postmodernity: An enquiry into the origins of cultural change*. Malden, Mass.: Blackwell.

Hoyman, M. (1997). *Power steering: Global automakers and the transformation of rural communities*. Lawrence, Kan.: University Press of Kansas.

Imbroscio, D. L. (1997). *Reconstructing city politics: Alternative economic development and urban regimes*. Thousand Oaks, Calif.: SAGE Publications.

International Monetary Fund (2007). *World economic outlook October 2007: Globalization and inequality*. Washington, D.C.: International Monetary Fund.

Jones, B. D., & Bachelor, L. W. (1993). *The sustaining hand: Community leadership and corporate power* (2nd edn.). Lawrence, Kan.: University Press of Kansas.

Judd, D. R., & Swanstrom, T. (2010). *City politics: The political economy of urban America* (7th edn.). New York: Longman.

Lynd, R. S., & Lynd, H. M. (1929). *Middletown: A study in contemporary American culture*. San Diego: Harcourt, Brace.

Molotch, H. (1976). The city as a growth machine: Toward a political economy of place. *American Journal of Sociology*, 82(2), 309–332.

Nelles, J. (2013). Cooperation and capacity? Exploring the sources and limits of city–region governance partnerships. *International Journal of Urban and Regional Research*, 37(4), 1349–1367.

Nelson, K. L., & Nollenberger, K. (2011). I – Conflict and cooperation in municipalities: Do variations in form of government have an effect? *Urban Affairs Review*, 47(5), 696–720.

62 *The Economic Context of Municipalities*

Nevarez, L. (2003). *New money, nice town: How capital works in the new urban economy*. New York: Routledge.

New York State School of Industrial and Labor Relations at Cornell University (2005). Wal-Mart imports from China, exports Ohio jobs. Ithaca, N.Y.: New York State School of Industrial and Labor Relations at Cornell University; available at http://digitalcommons.ilr.cornell.edu/cgi/viewcontent.cgi?article=1025&conte xt=laborunions.

Oliver, J. E. (2001). *Democracy in suburbia*. Princeton, N.J.: Princeton University Press.

Orfield, M. (1999). *Metropolitics: A regional agenda for community and stability*. Washington, D.C.: Brookings Institution Press.

Orfield, M. (2002). *American metropolitics: The new suburban reality*. Washington, D.C.: Brookings Institution Press.

Pagano, M. A. (2003). City fiscal structures and land development, discussion paper. Washington, D.C.: Brookings Institution Center on Urban and Metropolitan Policy.

Pagano, M. A., & Bowman, A. O. (1995). *Cityscapes and capital: The politics of urban development*. Baltimore: Johns Hopkins University Press.

Portz, J. (1990). *The politics of plant closings*. Lawrence, Kan.: University Press of Kansas.

Power, T. M. (2007). *The economic role of metal mining in Minnesota: Past, present, and future*. Missoula, Mont.: University of Montana.

Ramsay, M. (1996). *Community, culture, and economic development: The social roots of local action*. Albany, N.Y.: State University of New York Press.

Rast, J. S. (1997). Contested terrain: Downtown redevelopment, industrial displacement, and regime change in Chicago, 1955–1996. PhD dissertation, University of Wisconsin, Milwaukee.

Rast, J. S. (2002). *Remaking Chicago: The political origins of urban industrial change*. DeKalb, Ill.: Northern Illinois University Press.

Reese, L. A., & Rosenfeld, R. A. (2001). *The civic culture of local economic development*. Thousand Oaks, Calif.: SAGE Publications.

Sassen, S. (1991). *The global city: New York, London, Tokyo*. Princeton, N.J.: Princeton University Press.

Sassen, S. (2012). *Cities in a world economy* (4th edn.). Thousand Oaks, Calif.: SAGE Publications.

Savitch, H. V., & Kantor, P. (2002). *Cities in the international marketplace: The political economy of urban development in North America and western Europe*. Princeton, N.J.: Princeton University Press.

Savitch, H. V., & Vogel, R. K. (2004). Suburbs without a city: Power and city–county consolidation. *Urban Affairs Review, 39*(6), 758–790.

Schneider, M. (1985). Suburban fiscal disparities and the location decisions of firms. *American Journal of Political Science, 29*(3), 587–605.

Scott, R. E. (2008). The importance of manufacturing: Key to recovery in the states and the nation, Briefing Paper no. 211. Washington, D.C.: Economic Policy Institute.

Spirou, C., & Judd, D. R. (2016). *Building the city of spectacle: Mayor Richard M. Daley and the remaking of Chicago*. Ithaca, N.Y.: Cornell University Press.

Stone, C. N. (1989). *Regime politics: Governing Atlanta, 1946–1988*. Lawrence, Kan.: University Press of Kansas.

Stone, C. N., & Stoker, R. P. (eds.) (2015). *Urban neighborhoods in a new era: Revitalization politics in the postindustrial city.* Chicago: University of Chicago Press.

Thomas, K. P. (2011). *Investment incentives and the global competition for capital.* Basingstoke, UK: Palgrave Macmillan.

Tiebout, C. M. (1956). A pure theory of local expenditures. *Journal of Political Economy, 64*(5), 416–424.

US Department of Agriculture (2014). Rural America at a glance: 2014 edition, Economic Brief no. 26. Washington, D.C.: US Department of Agriculture; available at www.ers.usda.gov/media/1697681/eb26.pdf.

Vanderleeuw, J. M., & Sides, J. C. (2016). Quality of life amenities as contributors to local economies: Views of city managers. *Journal of Urban Affairs, 38*(5), 661–675.

Vidich, A. J., & Bensman, J. (1958). *Small town in mass society.* Princeton, N.J.: Princeton University Press.

Weaver, T. P. R. (2016). *Blazing the neoliberal trail: Urban political development in the United States and the United Kingdom.* Philadelphia: University of Pennsylvania Press.

3 Institutional Frameworks
Intergovernmental Support and Bureaucratic Organization

What are the non-economic structural factors that drive small town policy-making in economic and community development, and how do they interact with economics? Even in the limited scholarly literature in this field, there are tantalizing glimpses. Tradition, social class structures and ingrained habit emerge as explanatory factors for public policy and government actions in places as diverse as industrial Muncie, Indiana (Lynd & Lynd, 1929); agricultural Candor, New York (Vidich & Bensman, 1958); and Crisfield and Somerset on the Eastern Shore of Maryland (Ramsay, 1996; 2013). Problems or successes in community leadership tend to be magnified as factors influencing policy in these smaller towns (Hoyman, 1997), and tend to be addressed as personality conflicts (Vidich & Bensman, 1958; Cook, 1993),[1] or at least as rebellions against a dominant personality (Hoyman, 1997) more than functions of a municipality's institutional organization. Demographic change also emerges as a factor affecting policy changes (Hoyman, 1997; Vidich & Bensman, 1958); old establishments die off or are overwhelmed by new arrivals in the community.

When economic development is addressed, the findings, interestingly, tend to directly contradict the idea that municipalities are driven by an "economic imperative" (Harvey, 1990) to grow and seek private capital. The Maryland study is noteworthy for the way in which it documents small, poor towns on the state's Eastern Shore deliberately choosing to avoid economic development for fear of changing their culture, scenery and built environment, a phenomenon more often noted in communities with overheated economies that are highly attractive to outsiders (Nevarez, 2003; DeLeon, 1992). Michele Hoyman's 1997 analysis of small town recruitment of new car assembly emphasizes large variations in how towns treat the "imperative"; Smyrna, Tenn., Mayor Sam Ridley's successful hardball approach on tax concessions for Nissan did not survive once Ridley himself had left office and the council, now with members who had connections to the new plant, determined that the firm's costs needed to be lowered.

The academic research on the organizational ways in which local governments have responded to these economic challenges points toward

Institutional Frameworks 65

attempts to reconfigure institutions to promote agreement among political leaders. Literature in the public administration field (Frederickson, Johnson & Wood, 2004a) identifies the type and demonstrates the value of governmental structures that reduce conflict among leaders. Such reforms, by keeping city councils away from day-to-day micromanagement, allow them to better attend to general goals and policies (Folz & French, 2005; Nollenberger, 2009).

Prior to the 1960s the trend was for governments to reform themselves on the council-manager plan; for political reasons, many reforms in more recent years have involved the less drastic step of hiring a city administrator (chief administrative officer) while allowing councils to retain some managerial control (Protasel, 1988). In either case, the reform involves inserting a senior manager between city department heads and the city council, with at least the promise of preventing interdepartmental turf wars from spilling over onto the council. But – and this is an important consideration, especially in view of politicians' reluctance to cede authority to administrators – council-manager governance does not necessarily mean radical limitations on elected officials' influence. There is a considerable amount of convergence in American government toward what is known as an "adapted city", including both mayor-council governments that have hired strong administrators and council-manager governments that have elevated the administrative role of elected officials (Frederickson, Johnson & Wood, 2004b).

When multiple jurisdictions are involved, additional complications arise. Setting an agenda and setting policy goals, a part of policy-making just as important as finding funding and rounding up votes (Baumgartner & Jones, 2009; Kingdon, 2003), can be equally fraught if several different political jurisdictions must be reconciled. Yet the research on collective action problems (Olson, 1965) has not been widely used to guide research on economic development, though one noteworthy example studies how these problems have hindered small town development (Cook, 1993).

Nonetheless, local governments themselves have a wide variety of approaches to economic development policy. The differences in policy have been studied in detail (Hoyman, 1997; Portz, 1990; Eisinger, 1988), and reveal many ways in which local governments can succeed or fail in their goals, with solutions that range from "giving away the farm" to driving a hard bargain that effectively locks in jobs and tax base for the longer term. Even the general methods by which local government handles economic policy vary. Local government can choose to take a "bystander" role, largely avoiding intervention in economic policy; it can choose to attempt to "offset" economic circumstances, whether through trying to prevent a business from failing or trying to lure one to relocate; or it can become an active player in devising broader solutions to economic problems (Portz, 1990). Research demonstrates that resource-rich communities are generally in a stronger bargaining position and can more effectively assume

66 *Institutional Frameworks*

an activist role (Savitch & Kantor, 2002). Additionally, communities that enjoy broad agreement among elites and other stakeholders about defining a future vision tend to be successful in achieving their goals even when resources are short (Pagano & Bowman, 1995).

However, a major outside factor remains: the state. For local governments, especially the small, often non-home-rule ones we see here, state financial support, state grants of authority and the interaction of state and local institutions have a powerful impact on the sorts of decisions that emerge from local government. Therefore, studying the state and even federal frameworks within which local governments operate is also vital in order to determine the resources they can work with. A beneficial framework from the state can go a long way to enhance local government's effectiveness in dealing with the challenges of powerlessness, scarcity and economic stagnation. In the end, the interaction between state and local institutions has a profound influence on the economic development policies that are enacted, and accordingly merits close attention.

A Shifting Burden: Federal Abdication, State and Local Leadership

Institutional and bureaucratic influences on local government take several forms when it comes to economic and community development. There is the role of the state regarding statutory power over economic development and intergovernmental assistance to communities. Locally, bureaucratic and political organizations are a factor; many policy responses to problems are divided by geography, with often arbitrary city limits cutting across zones of common economic interest or vice versa, while others may be enhanced or compromised depending on how "steering" functions such as brainstorming and policy development are, or are not, aligned with "driving" functions such as funding and policy implementation. Within this context sits the role of leadership, which may or may not have talent and may or may not share a common vision of a community's direction. All of these combine to produce profound differences in policy outcomes even without dramatic changes in overall public spending. Done right, institutional enhancement can be a very affordable way of achieving positive policy outcomes; hence the interest in it demonstrated here.

The challenge posed by intergovernmental effects on municipalities' finances and power should not be underestimated. The current era of economic deregulation and deindustrialization in developed countries and small town and urban challenges has also been accompanied by a sharp withdrawal of the federal government from intergovernmental aid and pressure on state governments as well in the areas of both economic development and community development. Federal aid for urban renewal, such as Urban Development Action Grant (UDAG) schemes, has largely disappeared, while federal infrastructure spending has sharply declined

Institutional Frameworks 67

to the point where it assumes a secondary role relative to state and local government.

The result is that state government – and local government whenever it has sufficient autonomy, state aid and/or revenue-raising power – must increasingly take both the lead and the funding responsibility on economic and community development. This situation applies whether the project involves landing a plant with hundreds of new jobs or building a major new piece of community infrastructure. For example, the massive push by the federal government to fund wastewater treatment infrastructure in the 1970s has never since been replicated. The federal government has sharply cut spending on public housing, a change that not only impacts urban areas, with their high degree of inequality and racial segregation, but is also harmful to rural areas, with their elderly populations and demand for affordable and purpose-built senior housing. Overall, federal intergovernmental aid declined from 26 percent of municipal revenues in 1979 to around four percent by 2004 (Judd & Swanstrom, 2009: 292–294).[2] In inflation-adjusted dollars, funding for community and rural development dropped from $16.235 billion in 1980 to $6.371 billion by 1990, recovering slightly to $7.433 billion in 2005, a level at which it has generally stayed except for temporarily higher funding during the 2008 and 2009 economic stimulus. The Community Development Block Grant (CDBG) alone has dropped, as of 2016, by 49 percent in inflation-adjusted dollars since 2000 and 63 percent since its 1982 inception, when it replaced other larger government assistance programs; it currently stands at around $3 billion.[3] Federal spending on wastewater treatment facilities dropped by more than three-quarters in the two decades after 1980 in real terms. This has triggered major expenses, especially for smaller municipalities. Highway spending, though it eventually again surpassed its interstate-era peak, did not come close to keeping up with population growth (Congressional Budget Office, 1999: 12).

Furthermore, the burden of these shifts in federal policy on economic and community development has not gone away; instead, it has fallen upon state and local government. State and local spending on matters such as infrastructure and economic development has soared. In the decade after 1982, state and local spending on infrastructure increased by more than 50 percent, and by 1998 it exceeded federal spending on infrastructure by a three-to-one margin, reaching $130 billion in then current-year dollars (Congressional Budget Office, 1998: 4–6). The ideology of Ronald Reagan's famous 1981 inaugural address, containing the admonition that, "in this present crisis, government is not the solution to our problem, government *is* the problem,"[4] had some of its greatest impact on funding for economic and community development. While federal aid to some state-level programs, mostly highways and transportation, saw increases,[5] block grants for services such as education, policing and above all community and economic development were slashed (Feldstein, 1994). General

68   *Institutional Frameworks*

revenue-sharing from the federal government to municipalities, introduced only under the Nixon administration, was phased out by 1986 (Nathan & Lago, 1988). Even during the turn to the Democrats in national politics between 2006 and 2010, this trend against an intergovernmental safety net remained apparent; the largest portion of funds stripped from the 2009 stimulus bill in amendments in the Senate as Democrats attempted to break a Republican filibuster were non-transportation grants to state and local government. And other structural trends – retirement obligations, weak support from the states and increasing demands on local government – add up to what has been called a "permanent fiscal crisis" (Osborne & Hutchinson, 2004).

In this situation, the "permanent fiscal crisis" characterization is apt, given shrinking tax bases and locked-in employee benefit expenses. The losses in federal aid must be made up in state and local taxes, which fall proportionately more heavily than federal taxes on middle- and low-income people. Income taxes, the most progressive, tend to be weakly progressive or flat at the state level, and localities rely on property taxes and sales taxes that fall even more heavily on people of modest means. The problem is worst for local government, which has no lower level of government on which to offload expenses. States download their financial troubles to local government through cuts in aid to or revenue-sharing with local government, while voter tax revolts – often motivated by high local property taxes – have led either to reluctance on the part of government to push for more revenue or strong statutory limitations on revenue-raising.

The most important point about this trend is that it disproportionately affects resource-poor communities. Consider intergovernmental aid. When Minnesota reformed its school spending formula in 2001, a system that formerly provided state aid to school districts on the basis of need (defined by property tax capacity) was replaced with one that funded all schools at approximately the same level as the poorest school districts had been funded before – a change that shifted more than $1.6 billion a year in costs from local property taxes to the state income and sales taxes,[6] largely to the benefit of property-rich districts that had previously had much lower state aid. The resulting state budget deficit was then paid for in the following biennium with sharp cutbacks in Local Government Aid (LGA) to municipalities as well as need-based health and welfare programs. Overall general-purpose, need-based and categorical state aid to local government alone dropped by over $540 million between 2002 and 2004.[7] These changes were of minimal importance to the wealthy suburbs of Minneapolis and St. Paul that never had been eligible for LGA. But, to cities on the Iron Range, drawing LGA for 50 or even 60 percent of their budget or more as well as making use of other state programs, the results were obvious; an across-the-board percentage cut in LGA, for example, meant trouble for those communities that already depended heavily on it. Only when upper-bracket income taxes were increased in the early 2010s and the proceeds spent on programs including restoring some of the lost LGA was the previous structural budget balance partly restored.

Local Government's State-Provided Tools in Economic Development: A Brief History

The first part of the municipal response to this challenging situation very often concerns legal powers: the power to borrow for public infrastructure, the power to zone land, the power to work with private partners to achieve development. States in the United States, along with provinces in Canada, play a critical role in determining what these powers are. They began in England as a royal function, but in the United States for the past 150 years, and for the most part in Canada as well, they have been a function of state or provincial government. This has problematic implications for economic and community development because of city governments' long-standing preeminent role in these fields and the resulting perennial difficulty of funding them.

We begin with the history of the United States' local government framework and how it developed into its current state, with substantial but varied limits upon local government taxation and borrowing power and even the activities in which it may engage. The United States stands out because, as a relatively decentralized country with a variety of means for local governments to raise money, cities have had considerable freedom to shape their destiny and responsibility for their citizens' welfare. Indeed, prior to the post-Civil-War Dillon's-Rule-era crackdowns on local autonomy and local government ability to raise money, US cities moved well ahead of their European counterparts in providing public infrastructure. City governments' role was trying to ensure that they got a piece of the infrastructure and the money, for example subsidizing rail links to ensure they were not left off new transportation arteries. Local politicians also followed the legal path of least resistance. For example, in Wisconsin, where the state constitution banned the subsidy of railroads by the state but not by local government after 1848, the city of Milwaukee began massive construction subsidies (Sbragia, 1996: 45) – among other things, resulting in three competing routes to nearby Chicago alone, all of them still in operation.

As the nineteenth century progressed, city governments turned their attention to local infrastructure, building up water and sewage systems far beyond what was found even in European capital cities at the time. As long ago as the 1890s a daily water supply of more than 100 gallons per person was the norm in major northeastern US cities, yet it had not been attained in a single major European city (Teaford, 1984). Importantly, local governments underwrote these achievements. The most interventionist cities, in New England, accounted for by far the largest proportion of the investment and borrowing (Sbragia, 1996). But even cities in the South, historically tax-averse, eventually saw the benefits to economic growth of better

70   *Institutional Frameworks*

infrastructure, with Atlanta engaging in a crash program after a successful 1910 bond issue to tackle the third of the city without sewer lines or running water (Sbragia, 1996: 87).

Not surprisingly, growth in local public debt mirrored the growth in local infrastructure and public services. Cities and states could, and did, borrow heavily, availing themselves of capital from investors in London and New York who were skittish of lending to private business on the frontier but comfortable with lending to government. Massive borrowing – $231 million by states alone in 1843 – went into supporting the provision of canals, railroads and banks (Sbragia, 1996: 32–33). Between 1840 and 1880 local government debt in the United States rose twenty-fold, to over $800 million. However, of greater consequence for the entrepreneurial local governments of today, this increase in debt brought about a political reaction whose consequences remain entrenched, but vary sharply from one state to another.

Dillon's Rule, which in practice increased state power over municipalities, unleashed a raft of limits upon this kind of local government activity, especially in finance, and, drawing as it did on old precedent, it has endured strongly. Today the ability of local governments and local places to shape their destiny is in considerable part a function of the uneven but widespread "institutionalization of limits" on local government, mostly by the states (Sbragia, 1996; Robertson & Judd, 1989; Frug, 1980; Frug & Barron, 2008). This includes limits upon borrowing, limits upon taxation power, even limits upon the types of activities in which city governments may engage. Added to this are systems of local government finance in which many states do not equalize the revenue of poverty-stricken jurisdictions on the basis of need.

The end result is a strong historical pattern of cities serving as economic growth engines for the broader economy in interventionist ways, leveraging their historical economic roles for maximum effect (Abu-Lughod, 2000; Jacobs, 1984), but at the same time having to work around serious legal and constitutional limitations on their activity. At their best, cities are seen to effectively anchor national economies (Savitch, Collins, Sanders & Markham, 1993; Shachar, Kresl & Gappert, 1995), in much the same way that a major store or core attraction anchors a regional shopping mall. Political arrangements are viewed strongly through a pluralist prism within local governance. Competing interests within the city indeed formed a key basis of pluralist thought in political science (Dahl, 1961), with the continuity of business involvement in local government held to be evidence both of the existence of governing "regimes" and of a more limiting phenomenon – relations with the private sector being the most important constraint on local politics (Elkin, 1987; Stone, 1989; Logan & Molotch, 1987).

The stakes are especially high today because of the level of interregional and international economic competition. Local governments are fixed in place geographically; people and especially businesses can move. Yet both local governments and the state-level or national-level governments that provide the framework in which they operate make decisions based on far more than economics. So why has globalization not led to a standardization of approaches in local government? Very simply, the state-level rules remain different. The United Kingdom's national government, for example, gives less tax-varying power to English and Welsh local government than even the most centralized US states (Cox, 2004). Within the United States, the proportion of general-purpose local government operating expenses paid for by the state ranges from less than 10 percent (Hawaii) to more than 60 (Vermont).[8] Meanwhile, the state-provided economic development policy tools discussed here, such as the Illinois Enterprise Zone Act of 1982, which enables local or regional boards made up of local government officials to designate sites for tax-preferred development, or Minnesota's Iron Range Resources and Rehabilitation Board, which provides state agency direction over economic development for an entire region, are designed around sharply differing processes for making decisions. Local government organization operates within this context; both must be considered.

How Do Today's Institutions and Rules Affect Community-Level Economic Policy?

Central to the idea of institutional influence on economic and community development is the idea that institutional arrangements – strong versus weak intergovernmental support, matching regional political boundaries to regional economic problems, and so on – is the idea that it affects cities' bargaining power. Cities have been seen as standing in an inherently weak bargaining position (see Savitch & Kantor 2002: 32–34) with private business, due to being fragmented bodies that lack autonomy and political sovereignty. Here is the long-standing belief in the free market, a tendency to infer that local politics cannot meaningfully trump economics, or else perhaps should not attempt to do so. This is part of why so much literature has been devoted to fundamentally pessimistic notions such as economic imperatives (Harvey, 1990), or the idea that redistributive policies are self-destructive in a federal system (Peterson, 1995) or simply exhaustive analyses of economic facts on the ground that downplay political and social influences (Sassen, 2006). Nonetheless, there remain opportunities for institutionally derived political action. Cities opportunistically make use of political as well as economic resources to build bargaining power with the private sector as they attempt to outcompete one another (Savitch & Kantor, 2002); they move aggressively to regenerate themselves, especially when effectively "freed" by the declining authority of state and federal government (Parkinson, Foley & Judd, 1989); they follow the tone set by state-level and national-level government rather than the laws of

72   *Institutional Frameworks*

the market when choosing a course of action on regeneration (Fainstein, 2001); they even have the balance of power somewhat tilted in their favor by globalization, and are aggressively exploiting it (Clarke & Gaile, 1998).

Local government in the United States suffers from deficits of both self-help and state support, even though in many respects it is relatively independent by international standards. These have consequences for the kinds of economic and community development that are delivered (Peterson, 1981; 1995). Without a strong, redistributive safety net, local politicians are skittish about imposing taxation and regulatory regimes that would cause business to flee; hence, local government in the United States tends not to engage in social policy to the extent of its European and Canadian counterparts (Savitch, 2002; Fainstein, 2001), yet it has long taken the lead on economic development (Sbragia, 1996; Eisinger, 1988). Even when powerful state agencies exist, such as the Iron Range Resources and Rehabilitation Board for the Minnesota cases in this study, the overall framework for economic development policy is seen as limiting options (Manuel, 2015). For, ever since the 1870s, there has been a paradox regarding the power of local government in the United States: considerable power over money, yet significant political constraints. Dillon's Rule politically renders local governments as "creatures of the state," yet successive Supreme Court rulings in the twentieth century created not only local authority over land use but also a uniquely stable municipal bond market whose fundamental safety – due to the near-impossibility of default – resulted in local government access to large quantities of cheap capital (Sbragia, 1996).

There is plenty of evidence that state policy, not just the market, affects economic development outcomes even when the level of political intervention by local government is high. For example, there are fundamental differences in the types of development undertaken by cities with different state-mandated tax systems: sales-tax-dependent cities favoring edge-city developments to lure shoppers and sales tax dollars from neighboring jurisdictions; property tax cities favoring building up their downtowns to build property values; income tax cities doing whatever they can to lure a strong job base and residential neighborhoods within the city (Pagano, 2003; Bowman & Pagano, 2004).

But, within these constraints, cities attempt to do what they can to shape outcomes, even if they lack funding. For example, Chicago, with its revenue system centered on some of the highest sales taxes in the United States, opted at a critical point in its history for regulations to promote economic development in a way that city leaders saw as both providing social value and exploiting economic trends. The city government undertook massive rezoning in the 1960s, 1970s and 1980s, protecting factories and therefore manufacturing jobs when they could realistically be sustained and, closer to downtown, removing building height limits and enabling the construction of dozens of high-rise apartment buildings. At the same time, Chicago aggressively promoted the intensification of retail activity on Michigan Avenue's "Magnificent Mile" (Rast, 1997) in a visitor- and convention-centered strategy for boosting sales tax revenue that has seen the city become a premier tourist destination.

Institutional Tools for Government in Economic and Community Development

What organizational and institutional tools can municipalities use independently as they attempt to lead urban renewal and economic revitalization? The general theme here seems to be of cities enjoying varying degrees of success in filling the vacuum left by the financial retreat of higher levels of government. Among the most ambitious arguments from the standpoint of local government is that of Clarke and Gaile, who in surveying several dozen US cities point to the effect of contemporary economic change driven by globalization and deregulation as enhancing the role of city government (Clarke & Gaile, 1998: 6–11).

As a direct result of a less controlled economy and the shrinking of higher levels of government (i.e. lower federal and state spending in support of municipalities), cities effectively accrue political power even though they are, on paper, losing financial resources. Human capital (for example, a trained workforce) emerges as a critical measure of whether a particular city is at an advantage or a disadvantage compared to its peers. The decreasing support from higher levels of government means less funding and more volatility and makes the generation of local revenue more important. Municipalities and counties increasingly and by default fill a power vacuum, especially in economic development, left by federal and state government.

But what strategy will, and should, cities pursue? Clarke and Gaile outline the ideas of building upon a city's existing context; investing in human capital; and building citizenship and other forms of social capital. In a similarly broad study, this time of smaller to medium-sized cities, Pagano and Bowman (1995) study how agenda-setting and political consensus contribute to development policy. The finding here is that, regardless of the strategy pursued, a critical element in eventually successful policy is a "shared vision" of a city's future among its leaders. This finding is indicated across a wide range of local economies. Indeed, this fundamentally political variable often proves more important than economics in explaining both policy strategy and policy outcomes. Variations in political culture also profoundly influence this process (Reese & Rosenfeld, 2001).

The other studies discussed here are mostly comparative projects involving qualitative analysis of smaller groups of cities that show the palpable effect of higher levels of government – albeit mostly national government – upon how cities handle economic change. DiGaetano and Klemanski (1999) contrast British cities – operating in the 1970s

74 *Institutional Frameworks*

under a national government policy that emphasized community development, and then since the 1980s under a sharply changed regime with an emphasis on economic development and renewal – with American cities under a regime of declining federal influence. They study a growing and declining city in each country, and suggest that influences and constraints from above and community and social factors from below interact to produce a variety of distinctive types of governance ranging from coalitions or regimes that push a pro-growth set of policies to those that merely operate as caretakers. Critical to these outcomes, in their view, are which local groups participate in governance.

Savitch and Kantor (2002) develop both the argument and the method further, developing a hypothesis that political and social factors considerably affect cities' bargaining positions with private business. In analyzing ten cities in North America and Europe they reach the conclusion that a variety of resources, ranging from a strong local economy to intergovernmental aid to powerful political and social forces within the community, can trigger considerable levels of intervention in the marketplace – including intervention that, under the circumstances of globalization, might be considered risky in terms of encouraging capital and businesses to flee. We see the effect of higher-level governance (i.e. national and even international) upon economic development more clearly with Thomas's (2000; 2011) comparisons of business subsidies and state- or national-level supervision of local economic policy in the European Union and North America. The European Union's larger quantities of assistance to local government and the tight restrictions on competition among cities for jobs-related projects result in a situation in which beggar-thy-neighbor competition is less prevalent and taxpayer value for money greater on economic development.

Lastly, fragmentation of local government, especially in the United States, is a constant theme, particularly among progressives who favor varying forms of regionalism, building coalitions between inner city areas and their suburbs and providing more equitable funding and provision of public services. Orfield (1999; 2002) diagnoses the problem and the consequences of an inequitable tax base in fragmented urban regions; Dreier, Mollenkopf and Swanstrom (2001) go farther, suggesting that inequality is intractable due to its rootedness in geographical place, and arguing that change will require, among other things, a significant diminution of Republican Party influence in the federal government, given the GOP's strong skepticism about wealth redistribution.

However, the striking thing about all these studies is the relatively limited attention paid to institutional and organizational arrangements of governance. The single-case or small-sample studies of community power in the tradition of Dahl (1961) or Rae (2005) and their studies of New Haven, Connecticut, or the studies in small town Indiana (Lynd & Lynd, 1929) and upstate New York (Vidich & Bensman,

2000) stand out as studies of pluralism. In other words, they analyze the effect of different aggregations of interest groups as they compete with one another in gaining influence over their hometown's economic and political interaction with the outside world. They also study the changing patterns of these governing coalitions through major upheavals triggering economic and social change, be it urban renewal (Dahl), in-migration and population growth (Vidich & Bensman) or deindustrialization and globalization (Rae).

There is a parallel between these studies and the field of regime studies and its offshoot, civic capacity. The paradigm of urban regimes, pioneered by Clarence Stone's study of Atlanta from the 1940s to the 1980s (Stone, 1989), has been described as the dominant theoretical approach for studying local politics in major cities (Imbroscio, 1997). Stone's benchmark study of Atlanta politics was quickly followed by similar treatments of other cities. Single-case studies have been done, for example, in San Francisco (DeLeon, 1992); Detroit (Orr & Stoker, 1994); Philadelphia (Beauregard, 1997); Bristol, England (Bassett, 1996); and, narrowed to the single question of the delivery of sports stadiums, Denver (Marichal, 2000).

Multi-city comparisons have been done at least in larger cities on economic development (DiGaetano & Klemanski, 1993; 1999; DiGaetano & Lawless, 1999) and school reform. School reform has been a particular area of interest (Henig, 1999; Stone et al., 2001; Stone, 1999), with the development of a new metaphor – civic capacity – to describe the level of functionality of a community in delivering policy, solving problems and in general functioning as a model of what Stone has described as "social production." In the area of economic and community development, this has been expressed in de Souza Briggs' comparisons of non-profit and community organizations' role in promoting development in impoverished neighborhoods of cities in developed and developing countries alike (Christensen & Levinson, 2003; de Souza Briggs, 2004; 2008).

A defining feature of the civic capacity field is its "softness" (Mossberger & Stoker, 2001). While the role of government institutions and political economy is considered to varying degrees, research in this field has at times underplayed or even ignored the corrosive effect on policy of, say, a policymaking process in which the institutions charged with implementing policy are weak or overpoliticized, or especially remote from citizen preferences. More process-focused research has shown that institutional weakness, such as the weak representation of citizens in the organizations of city government or weakness in authority to deliver on government decisions, has a limiting effect on economic and community development policy well beyond prevailing economic factors (Fainstein et al., 1983; Elkin, 1987). Likewise, when economic motives of different levels of government are considered, the obligations of government can start to look much more complicated than the maximizing of a local economy's access to capital investment. However, scholars have struggled with theoretical limitations

76   Institutional Frameworks

(Feldman, 1997; Lauria, 1997), comparative analysis and attempting to apply the regime model in other countries (Davies, 2002).

Furthermore, single-city studies of political power and comparative analyses of urban economic renewal alike tend to neglect how city government decisions are affected by state policy structures. For the most part, the key intergovernmental relationship these studies visualize is that of the declining national or federal aid to cities, and cities' response to that situation. With certain exceptions (for example, municipal reorganizations such as the widespread province-driven amalgamations of city governments in Canada: Keil, 2000; Sancton, 2006), they do not sufficiently consider the relationship of cities with state-level governments. Thus, the independent power of cities to raise revenue, perform functions or associate in binding or non-binding arrangements with one another is neglected. Even research that specifically studies economic development policy (Eisinger, 1988) and comparative analyses of attempts at retaining or luring economic development (Lauria & Fisher, 1983; Portz, 1990; Hoyman, 1997) tends to downplay the structures in which these governments operate.

Particularly in a federal system, this is a serious omission. In the United States and Canada, states and provinces can effectively not only consolidate government but sharply alter its powers, amending charters, taxation power, borrowing limits and even peer-to-peer arrangements among governments. And in states that delegate considerable power to local governments, peer-to-peer arrangements such as regional government (Orfield, 1999), city–county consolidation (Savitch & Vogel, 2004) and locally directed enterprise zones can help to pool scarce resources, enhance bargaining power and limit beggar-thy-neighbor competition – not to mention being more responsive to local needs than a state-level agency.

The question is how to approach these omissions and at the same time tackle the question of whether local places can alter their destiny even if they are small and short of resources. This takes analyzing communities comparatively, and for both their local governing arrangements and for the state laws and finances under which they operate. This demands a potential theoretical solution that holds that, for communities to shape their destiny, a particular set of structural circumstances is needed. It also means a case for reviewing possibilities for local governance from outside the conventional urban studies literature, evaluating policy and institutional dimensions on which to select and compare different cases, leading finally to a set of hypotheses about how even the poorest and smallest communities might better shape their economic future.

Multi-level analyses that consider the effects of various forms of governmental organization are a potential resolution to this theoretical problem. Consider relations among governments. A great example is the difference between the city of Chicago's historical avoidance of debt-related crises and New York's immersion in them: Chicago was able, under Illinois law and with its historic influence on state politics, to "upload" costly and politically unrewarding functions such as jails and social services to higher levels of government, while New York, assuming the obligations of both a city and a county contiguously and facing an alliance of hostile suburban and upstate interests, was stuck with an array of obligations unparalleled in American local government (Fuchs, 1992). Consider also relations *within* governments. Pittsburgh derived great benefit, under mayor David Lawrence's groundbreaking regime in the 1940s and 1950s, from devolving control over economic development to a city commission with many connections to neighborhood organizations (Ferman, 1996). Here was an opportunity to see how the study of urban regimes and their influence on economic and community development might interact with governmental institutions and policy processes.

These methods are applicable here. The differences between Illinois and Minnesota, and between each of the two pairs of cases, have already been described. By considering these cases together, beginning with the smallest and most institutionally fragmented, and therefore the theoretically most vulnerable of them – Ely, Minnesota – and then drawing appropriate comparisons, we better understand how resources, local institutions, state law, fiscal support and leadership interact. Through methods ranging from extensive elite interviewing in each of the communities to the content analysis of newspaper coverage, official meeting minutes and documents and to observing public meetings, we gain a broad and rich view of each community. In each case, the study covers select policy initiatives, projects and institutional reforms and how they have worked in practice over the past ten years and more. This provides not just a snapshot but a timeline and tracking of the processes at work and of how governance in each community is performing.

Notes

1 See Cook (1993). Kathleen Cook's work, which focuses on the personality-based dysfunctionality of local government in two small Missouri towns, is important because of the way in which it maps the effect of such dysfunctionality on community and economic development.
2 See also US Census Bureau, Census of governments, 2002, 2007.
3 I. Shapiro, B. DaSilva, D. Reich & R. Kogan, Funding for housing, health and social services block grants has fallen markedly over time, Center on Budget and Policy Priorities, March 24, 2016.
4 President Ronald Reagan's first inaugural address, January 20, 1981, quoted from www.reaganlibrary.com/reagan/speeches/first.asp (accessed October 13, 2008).
5 See Historical tables: Budget of the United States government, fiscal year 2009, at www.whitehouse.gov/omb/budget/fy2009/pdf/hist.pdf (table accessed October 13, 2008).

78   *Institutional Frameworks*

6 Source: Minnesota Management and Budget: February 2009 forecast, Price of government, p. 4.

7 *Ibid.*, p. 3.

8 Source: US Census Bureau, 2014 State and local government, State and local summary tables, www.census.gov/govs/local (accessed August 17, 2017).

References

Abu-Lughod, J. L. (2000). *New York, Chicago, Los Angeles: America's global cities.* Minneapolis: University of Minnesota Press.

Bassett, K. (1996). Partnerships, business elites and urban politics: New forms of governance in an English city? *Urban Studies, 33*(3), 539–555.

Baumgartner, F. R., & Jones, B. D. (2009). *Agendas and instability in American politics* (2nd edn.). Chicago: University of Chicago Press.

Beauregard, R. (1997). City planning and the postwar regime in Philadelphia. In Lauria, M. (ed.), *Reconstructing urban regime theory: Regulating urban politics in a global economy*, 171–188. Thousand Oaks, Calif.: SAGE Publications.

Bowman, A. O., & Pagano, M. A. (2004). *Terra incognita: Vacant land and urban strategies.* Washington, D.C.: Georgetown University Press.

Christensen, K., & Levinson, D. (eds.) (2003). *Encyclopedia of community: From the village to the virtual world.* Thousand Oaks, Calif.: SAGE Publications.

Clarke, S. E., & Gaile, G. L. (1998). *The work of cities.* Minneapolis: University of Minnesota Press.

Congressional Budget Office (1998). The economic effects of federal spending on infrastructure and other investments, CBO Paper. Washington, D.C.: Congressional Budget Office.

Congressional Budget Office (1999). Trends in public infrastructure spending, CBO Paper. Washington, D.C.: Congressional Budget Office.

Cook, H. K. (1993). Small town talk: The undoing of collective action in two Missouri towns. PhD dissertation, Washington University, St. Louis, Mo.; available at http://artsci.wustl.edu/~anthro/blurb/b_cook.html.

Cox, K. R. (2004). Globalization and the politics of local and regional development: The question of convergence. *Transactions of the Institute of British Geographers, 29*(2), 179–194.

Dahl, R. A. (1961). *Who governs? Democracy and power in an American city.* New Haven, Conn.: Yale University Press.

Davies, J. S. (2002). Urban regime theory: A normative-empirical critique. *Journal of Urban Affairs, 24*(1), 1–17.

De Souza Briggs, X. (2004). Social capital: Easy beauty or meaningful resource? *Journal of the American Planning Association, 70*(2), 151–158.

De Souza Briggs, X. (2008). *Democracy as problem solving: Civic capacity in communities across the globe.* Cambridge, Mass.: MIT Press.

DeLeon, R. E. (1992). *Left coast city: Progressive politics in San Francisco, 1975–1991.* Lawrence, Kan.: University Press of Kansas.

DiGaetano, A., & Klemanski, J. S. (1993). Urban regime capacity: A comparison of Birmingham, England, and Detroit, Michigan. *Journal of Urban Affairs, 15*(4), 367–384.

DiGaetano, A., & Klemanski, J. S. (1999). *Power and city governance: Comparative perspectives on urban development.* Minneapolis: University of Minnesota Press.

DiGaetano, A., & Lawless, P. (1999). Urban governance and industrial decline: Governing structures and policy agendas in Birmingham and Sheffield, England, and Detroit, Michigan, 1980–1997. *Urban Affairs Review*, *34*(4), 546–577.

Dreier, P., Mollenkopf, J. H., & Swanstrom, T. (2001). *Place matters: Metropolitics for the twenty-first century*. Lawrence, Kan.: University Press of Kansas.

Eisinger, P. K. (1988). *The rise of the entrepreneurial state: State and local economic development policy in the United States*. Madison, Wis.: University of Wisconsin Press.

Elkin, S. L. (1987). *City and regime in the American republic*. Chicago: University of Chicago Press.

Fainstein, S. S. (2001). *The city builders: Property development in New York and London, 1980–2000*. Lawrence, Kan.: University Press of Kansas.

Fainstein, S. S., Fainstein, N., Hill, R. C., Judd, D., & Smith, M. P. (1983). *Restructuring the city: The political economy of urban redevelopment*. New York: Longman.

Feldman, M. M. A. (1997). A neo-Gramscian approach to the regulation of urban regimes: Accumulation strategies, hegemonic projects, and governance. In Lauria, M. (ed.), *Reconstructing urban regime theory: Regulating urban politics in a global economy*, 51–73. Thousand Oaks, Calif.: SAGE Publications.

Feldstein, M. S. (ed.) (1994). *American economic policy in the 1980s*. Chicago: University of Chicago Press.

Ferman, B. (1996). *Challenging the growth machine: Neighborhood politics in Chicago and Pittsburgh*. Lawrence, Kan.: University Press of Kansas.

Folz, D. H., & French, P. E. (2005). *Managing America's small communities: People, politics, and performance*. Lanham, Md.: Rowman & Littlefield.

Frederickson, H. G., Johnson, G. A., & Wood, C. H. (2004a). The changing structure of American cities: A study of the diffusion of innovation. *Public Administration Review*, *64*(3), 320–330.

Frederickson, H. G., Johnson, G. A., & Wood, C. H. (2004b). *The adapted city: Institutional dynamics and structural change*. Armonk, N.Y.: M. E. Sharpe.

Frug, G. E. (1980). The city as a legal concept. *Harvard Law Review*, *93*(6), 1057–1154.

Frug, G. E., & Barron, D. J. (2008). *City bound: How states stifle urban innovation*. Ithaca, N.Y.: Cornell University Press.

Fuchs, E. R. (1992). *Mayors and money: Fiscal policy in New York and Chicago*. Chicago: University of Chicago Press.

Harvey, D. (1990). *The condition of postmodernity: An enquiry into the origins of cultural change*. Malden, Mass.: Blackwell.

Henig, J. R. (1999). Building conditions for sustainable school reform in the District of Columbia, Occasional Paper no. 11. Washington, D.C.: Woodrow Wilson International Center for Scholars.

Hoyman, M. (1997). *Power steering: Global automakers and the transformation of rural communities*. Lawrence, Kan.: University Press of Kansas.

Imbroscio, D. L. (1997). *Reconstructing city politics: Alternative economic development and urban regimes*. Thousand Oaks, Calif.: SAGE Publications.

Jacobs, J. (1984). *Cities and the wealth of nations: Principles of economic life*. New York: Random House.

80 *Institutional Frameworks*

Judd, D. R., & Swanstrom, T. (2009). *City politics: The political economy of urban America* (7th edn.). New York: Longman.

Keil, R. (2000). Governance restructuring in Los Angeles and Toronto: Amalgamation or secession? *International Journal of Urban and Regional Research*, *24*(4), 758–781.

Kingdon, J. W. (2003). *Agendas, alternatives, and public policies* (2nd edn.). New York: Longman.

Lauria, M. (ed.) (1997). *Reconstructing urban regime theory: Regulating urban politics in a global economy*. Thousand Oaks, Calif.: SAGE Publications.

Lauria, M., & Fisher, P. S. (1983). *Plant closings in Iowa: Causes, consequences, and legislative options*. Iowa City, Iowa: Institute of Urban and Regional Research, University of Iowa.

Logan, J. R., & Molotch, H. L. (1987). *Urban fortunes: The political economy of place*. Berkeley, Calif.: University of California Press.

Lynd, R. S., & Lynd, H. M. (1929). *Middletown: A study in contemporary American culture*. San Diego: Harcourt, Brace.

Manuel, J. T. (2015). *Taconite dreams: The struggle to sustain mining on Minnesota's Iron Range, 1915–2000*. Minneapolis: University of Minnesota Press.

Marichal, J. (2000). We all win: Regimes and the symbolic politics of stadium development. Paper presented at 30th annual meeting of Urban Affairs Association, Los Angeles, May 5.

Mossberger, K., & Stoker, G. (2001). The evolution of urban regime theory. *Urban Affairs Review*, *36*(6), 810–835.

Nathan, R. P., & Lago, J. R. (1988). Intergovernmental relations in the Reagan era. *Public Budgeting and Finance*, *8*(3), 15–29.

Nevarez, L. (2003). *New money, nice town: How capital works in the new urban economy*. New York: Routledge.

Nollenberger, K. (2009). *Cooperation and conflict in the decision-making process: Governmental decision-making in middle size cities in the USA*. Saarbrücken: VDM Publishing.

Olson, M. (1965). *The logic of collective action: Public goods and the theory of groups*. Cambridge, Mass.: Harvard University Press.

Orfield, M. (1999). *Metropolitics: A regional agenda for community and stability*. Washington, D.C.: Brookings Institution Press.

Orfield, M. (2002). *American metropolitics: The new suburban reality*. Washington, D.C.: Brookings Institution Press.

Orr, M. E., & Stoker, G. (1994). Urban regimes and leadership in Detroit. *Urban Affairs Review*, *30*(1), 48–73.

Osborne, D., & Hutchinson, P. (2004). *The price of government: Getting the results we need in an age of permanent fiscal crisis*. New York: Basic Books.

Pagano, M. A. (2003). City fiscal structures and land development, discussion paper. Washington, D.C.: Brookings Institution Center on Urban and Metropolitan Policy.

Pagano, M. A., & Bowman, A. O. (1995). *Cityscapes and capital: The politics of urban development*. Baltimore: Johns Hopkins University Press.

Parkinson, M., Foley, B., & Judd, D. R. (1989). *Regenerating the cities: The UK crisis and the US experience*. Glenview, Ill.: Scott, Foresman.

Peterson, P. E. (1981). *City limits*. Chicago: University of Chicago Press.

Institutional Frameworks 81

Peterson, P. E. (1995). *The price of federalism.* Washington, D.C.: Brookings Institution Press.

Portz, J. (1990). *The politics of plant closings.* Lawrence, Kan.: University Press of Kansas.

Protasel, G. J. (1988). Abandonments of the council–manager plan: A new institutionalist perspective. *Public Administration Review, 48*(4), 807–812.

Rae, D. W. (2005). *City: Urbanism and its end.* New Haven, Conn.: Yale University Press.

Ramsay, M. (1996). *Community, culture, and economic development: The social roots of local action.* Albany, N.Y. State University of New York Press.

Ramsay, M. (2013). *Community, culture, and economic development: Continuity and change in two small southern towns* (2nd edn.). Albany, N.Y.: State University of New York Press.

Rast, J. S. (1997). Contested terrain: Downtown redevelopment, industrial displacement, and regime change in Chicago, 1955–1996. PhD dissertation, University of Wisconsin, Milwaukee.

Reese, L. A., & Rosenfeld, R. A. (2001). *The civic culture of local economic development.* Thousand Oaks, Calif.: SAGE Publications.

Robertson, D. B., & Judd, D. R. (1989). *The development of American public policy: The structure of policy restraint.* Glenview, Ill.: Scott, Foresman.

Sancton, A. (2006). Why municipal amalgamations? Halifax, Toronto, Montreal. In Young, R., & Leuprecht, C. (eds.), *Municipal–federal–provincial relations in Canada,* 119–137. Montreal: McGill-Queen's University Press.

Sassen, S. (2006). *Cities in a world economy* (3rd edn.). Thousand Oaks, Calif.: Pine Forge Press.

Savitch, H. V. (2002). What is new about globalisation and what does it portend for cities? *International Social Science Journal, 54*(172), 179–189.

Savitch, H. V., Collins, D., Sanders, D., & Markham, J. P. (1993). Ties that bind: Central cities, suburbs, and the new metropolitan region. *Economic Development Quarterly, 7*(4), 341–357.

Savitch, H. V., & Kantor, P. (2002). *Cities in the international marketplace: The political economy of urban development in North America and western Europe.* Princeton, N.J.: Princeton University Press.

Savitch, H. V., & Vogel, R. K. (2004). Suburbs without a city: Power and city–county consolidation. *Urban Affairs Review, 39*(6), 758–790.

Sbragia, A. M. (1996). *Debt wish: Entrepreneurial cities, US federalism, and economic development.* Pittsburgh: University of Pittsburgh Press.

Shachar, A., Kresl, P. K., & Gappert, G. (1995). *North American cities and the global economy.* Thousand Oaks, Calif.: SAGE Publications.

Stone, C. N. (1989). *Regime politics: Governing Atlanta, 1946–1988.* Lawrence, Kan.: University Press of Kansas.

Stone, C. N. (1999). Poverty and the continuing campaign for urban social reform. *Urban Affairs Review, 34*(6), 843–856.

Stone, C. N., Henig, J. R., Jones, B. D., & Pierannunzi, C. (2001). *Building civic capacity: The politics of reforming urban schools.* Lawrence, Kan.: University Press of Kansas.

Teaford, J. (1984). *The unheralded triumph: City government in the United States 1870–1900.* Baltimore: Johns Hopkins University Press.

82   Institutional Frameworks

Thomas, K. P. (2000). *Competing for capital: Europe and North America in a global era.* Washington, D.C.: Georgetown University Press.

Thomas, K. P. (2011). *Investment incentives and the global competition for capital.* Basingstoke, UK: Palgrave Macmillan.

Vidich, A. J., & Bensman, J. (1958). *Small town in mass society.* Princeton, N.J.: Princeton University Press.

Vidich, A. J., & Bensman, J. (2000). *Small town in mass society: Class, power, and religion in a rural community.* Urbana, Ill.: University of Illinois Press.

4 Ely
Infrastructure Delivered, Governance Contested

In August 1980, in the heat of a fiercely contested presidential election, the sitting Democratic vice president of the United States came to the then Democratic Party stronghold of Ely, Minnesota, an odd place to deploy a person who was doubtless in demand in the true "swing" states. But, for Walter Mondale, this was not purely about campaigning (see Figure 4.1). He was answering to higher authorities: baseball, and the long-time mayor of Ely, Dr. J. P. "Doc" Grahek. In throwing out the first pitch at the American Legion World Series at Ely's newly opened Veterans Memorial Field, Mondale was paying tribute to the role of Mayor Grahek in Ely and state politics. Grahek had dominated Ely politics since his first mayoral election in 1956, he was influential in the state's Democratic–Farmer–Labor Party and (more importantly in terms of this study) he had cemented his local power and authority through leading opposition to restrictions on the use of the many public lands in the area, and through the successful delivery of a series of major infrastructure projects.[1]

Grahek succeeded in part because, as a well-connected mayor of more than two decades' seniority,[2] he had the influence and the clout to drive projects. Additionally, he had the good fortune to be running Ely during relative economic boom times for the Iron Range, and the question of government policy to promote economic development rarely arose. He was also a political force of nature with no clear successor.[3] His retirement reduced, though did not eliminate, Ely's influence with higher-level politicians. Moreover, economic challenges loomed. The 1981–2 crash in the US steel industry drove major layoffs in nearby mines, soaring unemployment and a crash in the local real estate market. A major transition in local tourism driven by stricter federal regulation of US Forest Service lands, in particular the nearby Boundary Waters Canoe Area (BWCA) Wilderness, created further big challenges, but also opportunities. In the 1980s Ely was in a new era of scarcity it had not anticipated and felt ill prepared to face. However, in the 1990s things changed dramatically. Tourism and retail sales boomed, on the back of strong growth in ecotourism, and a steady influx of newcomers throughout the 1980s and 1990s significantly changed the town's culture. The 2000s brought further challenges: a sharp drop

Figure 4.1 Vice President Walter Mondale, President Jimmy Carter and Ely Mayor J. P. Grahek, image undated. Mondale and Grahek were long-time allies in the Minnesota DFL (Democratic–Farmer–Labor Party); Grahek clashed with national Democrats over environmentalism and economic development

Source: Ely-Winton Historical Society.

during the first half of the decade, and then a post-recession revival – so far more modest than the 1990s – that has seen the town named "Coolest Small Town in America" by a leading travel magazine.[4]

From a theoretical standpoint, the most instructive aspects of Ely's experience with governance and economic development arose after Grahek's 1980 retirement (he returned for one final three-year term in 1987–9). The challenge has been generating continuity and the capacity to make policy. With functions ranging from city administration to economic deal-making centralized on the council, even technical and managerial details can become mired in conflict, and periods of better-functioning government have generally coincided with strong personalities in city administration. Stop-go leadership has been a fact of life, with a reduction in the mayoral term to two years after 1998 and no mayor from 1980 to the time of writing serving more than four consecutive years. Former city councilman Eugene "Butch" Pecha, who declined to run for re-election after just one term in 2006, decried the cost to the city and taxpayers of this tendency toward conflict and memorably described it to a local newspaper as

Ely: Infrastructure Delivered   85

a matter of local leaders suffering from "Iron Range Alzheimer's – they've forgotten everything except the grudges."[5]

Today the structure of Ely government has changed only modestly from the Grahek days, which is a problem from the point of view of building consensus, in view of the absence of dominant leadership and the nature of Ely's plan of governance. Indeed, conflicts have been frequent. Only at the end of the decade of the 2000s did the city council finally resolve a long-standing dispute over chains of authority by consolidating administration of both city government and public utilities in a single director of operations. Intergovernmental relations, a heavy responsibility in the Ely area's fragmented local governance, have proved especially challenging. A joint powers board designed to develop an economic and community development agenda for the area became largely inactive following Ely's departure from the agreement in 2011, although the city has since rejoined board meetings. The problem is compounded because of the difficulty in getting many community leaders, notably businesspeople, to run for public office. As one small business respondent put it, "If you want to be a successful businessman in Ely, stay out of politics. People don't like politicians, and if they don't like you they'll boycott your store."[6] Another factor limiting the emergence of leaders is Ely's tightly drawn city limits; as more people treat former summer cabins as year-round residences, many who might take a strong interest in running for office are ineligible due to non-residency.[7]

Despite this, the city has delivered major achievements in the public sector, especially in projects with state and federal support, with large improvements in infrastructure since the 1980s. Financial management has been consistently sound, with the city currently running a bond rating of AA – that far bigger cities would envy. Municipal projects of the past three decades include a new water supply plant, a rebuilt sewage plant, several major street reconstruction projects, a far more reliable electrical supply system and the reconstruction and expansion of water supply and sewer capacity. The state has expanded the local community college and located a major tax collection facility in the city, and, through the IRRRB, assisted many projects ranging from streets to senior housing; the federal government has built a new district ranger headquarters for the US Forest Service; and the local community hospital has partnered with a regional provider to build a new clinic and renovate the existing hospital, taking advantage of the city's credit rating. Small business owners and real estate developers have steadily improved and restored old downtown buildings, helped by improvements to business district infrastructure, and in recent years easing a shortage of usable commercial space and reviving long-vacant properties.

In contrast, the city's performance on economic development projects is spotty. Aside from the defunding of the joint powers board, several other projects have either failed or been significantly delayed. A municipal business park on former railroad land that now counts as a major success took more than a quarter-century to fill its original footprint, while disputes occurred

86   *Ely: Infrastructure Delivered*

along the way over poor provision of city infrastructure to an adjacent privately run business park.[8] New housing development is sluggish, with many newcomers and long-time locals alike choosing to live in the surrounding townships, where larger homes and lakefront property are widely available. The year-round (as opposed to seasonal) population continues to decline. One of the most significant economic development coups of the past 20 years, the early and widespread arrival of rural broadband Internet in 2000–2001, had more to do with state intervention from above and grassroots organizing from below than with city leadership. And the city's aspirations to expand its land area[9] – dating from a 1973 agreement for "orderly annexation" inked when Grahek was at the height of his power – remain mostly unfulfilled, even though some small parcels in useful locations for business have recently been added.

So, the principal question that needs to be answered is why a tax-poor small town that performs as effectively as it does in renewing public infrastructure has been so inconsistent on high-profile economic development projects. This chapter establishes the challenges of Ely's recent economic history: the economic crash of the 1980s, which followed an era of many years of growth; a modest recovery in the 1990s, driven by tourism and government services; and stagnation from 2000 to the early 2010s, from the general state of the national economy and a transition from large-volume resort and ecotourism to a lower-volume industry increasingly driven by high-income people or retirees summering in the area. We then look in detail at how the city's institutional governance has shaped the policy response to these challenges, especially in economic development. Ely has been marked by periods of instability within city government, especially during the decade of the 2000s, and by often rocky relationships with neighboring local governments. Finally, we consider both the successes and failures of economic development implementation. This includes the impact of governance on the city's major successes at maintaining, improving and modernizing infrastructure, and its inconsistent record on major economic development projects.

The Economic Context

Ask a local politician, bureaucrat or business leader what the economy needs most in Ely, Hibbing, or elsewhere in northeastern Minnesota, and the phrase "good-paying jobs" will soon emerge. On the Iron Range, the large-volume private-sector source of employment that best fits that definition is iron ore mining (see Figure 4.2).[10] The fortunes of cities of the Iron Range, whether they still host local mining or merely workers who commute to mining jobs, remain strongly influenced by the area's iron mining industry. The challenge of "good-paying jobs" arises because,

Figure 4.2 Pioneer Mine "A" shaft, Ely, Minnesota, image undated. This was the point at which iron ore from the underground mine was brought to the surface and shipped out by rail

Source: Ely-Winton Historical Society.

since 1982, employment in the iron mining industry has declined from around 17,000 to fewer than 4,000, through industry-wide mechanization and the 2001 closure of LTV Steel Mining, one of the region's seven original taconite iron ore plants.[11] Although overall production of iron ore in northeastern Minnesota remains near its 1970s average and ore reserves are substantial, the automation has permanently lowered blue-collar wage scales across the region.[12]

Ely itself saw the closure of its last local mine in 1967 (see Figure 4.3). Ever since then it has played the role of a commuter town as far as the mining industry is concerned, seeing more than 50 job losses out of the 1,100 from the 2001 closure of LTV Steel Mining.[13] So it shares in the impact from the dramatic shrinkage of the area's preeminent industry, with a concomitant loss of high-benefit, middle-income jobs. This context makes for a political environment in which interest in lobbying for large-scale state support for a large-scale industrial project is never

Figure 4.3 Iron ore miners Frank Godec, Bif Niemela and Fred Kaplan at Ely, Minnesota's, Pioneer Mine, shortly before the mine's closure in 1967
Source: Ely-Winton Historical Society.

very far from the surface, even at times such as the 1990s and early 2000s when Ely took more incremental approaches to developing business-oriented infrastructure.

The broader impact on the community of these job losses has been most visible among families with school-age children. More of them left the area, while fewer young families moved in than before. Ely schools' total kindergarten through grade 12 enrollment dropped from 1,750 in 1977 to 821 by 2000[14] and 542 by 2010 before stabilizing, rising slightly to 594 by 2017.[15] This decline has taken away both state funding – the state of Minnesota covers almost all instructional costs – and support for administrative overhead. Another legacy of the mining industry's arc has been relatively poor housing stock, with housing within the city limits dominated by older, smaller and more outdated homes than most young families or retirees want to buy. More than half the city's housing was built before 1941 according to Census Bureau statistics; relatively few homes within the city limits are large enough for a medium to large family, many have just two bedrooms and very few are handicapped-accessible for the large senior population. The town's population has dropped from close to 6,000 to under 3,400 during this time, with the city general fund operating budget

Ely: Infrastructure Delivered   89

of just over $3.8 million in 2015 dependent on Local Government Aid from the state for more than 54 percent of funding.[16]

What alternatives does Ely have? Uniquely among these four cases, Ely has long had a thriving tourism industry, especially in the summer. But this too has profoundly changed, thanks to stricter regulation and changing consumer tastes.[17] The federal environmental protection legislation from the late 1940s to the late 1970s that culminated in the 1978 BWCA Wilderness Act sharply reduced the portion of this region along the Canadian border that was open to resorts and motorized recreation such as snowmobiling and outboard-equipped boats (Proescholdt, Rapson & Heinselman, 1995), as well as reducing the scope of a traditional off-season source of employment: logging. At the same time, substantial support for the arts in Ely from city government and private citizens alike has produced another facet of the community appealing to tourists and new residents alike.

At first the industry shifted to ecotourism, cultivating customers who were drawn by a non-motorized "wilderness experience" and an often counter-culture atmosphere. During the 1990s the long-term decline in population slowed;[18] retail sales almost tripled; and summer festivals became major draws for visitors throughout Minnesota and beyond. But, more recently, the stronger tourism emphasis has drawn people from the Twin Cities and Chicago at or close to retirement age and able to buy lakefront property; the ensuing increase in property values in the 1990s made affordable housing for Ely natives a significant policy challenge by the end of the decade. Additionally, the new trend saw many of the area's resorts converted to condominiums, a process enabled by a laissez-faire St. Louis County Board of Adjustment, whose zoning decisions regularly caused controversy among local residents.[19] Whereas cabins had once been occupied more or less continuously – albeit by a different guest every week – through the summer, now their new owner-occupiers spent only a few weeks a year.[20] Furthermore, stagnating national incomes for middle- and working-class Americans put downward pressure on the market for short-distance tourism and travel, with declining rates of travel in the 2000s for all income groups except those making more than $100,000 a year.[21]

The eventual result for Ely was a sharp drop in visitor numbers and retail sales in the early 2000s that took a decade to come close to full recovery. Even the annual Blueberry/Art Festival, the area's biggest tourist event, saw three-day attendance level off at around 40,000 visitors before resuming modest growth (see Figure 4.4);[22] a blues festival, begun only in 2000, relocated 120 miles west to Grand Rapids, Minn. in 2009 due partly to disagreements over the site of the event.[23] And Ely saw a reduction in retail sales in current-year dollars during the 2000s[24] before finally setting a new mark of $109 million in 2015, still well below its inflation-adjusted 1998 peak. Many vacant storefronts emerged downtown, even as the market for

Figure 4.4 Ely's annual Blueberry/Art Festival, July 2012. Around 45,000 visit this three-day event each year, with around 250 exhibitors in attendance
Source: Daniel Bliss.

lakefront property including second homes remains strong, and more commercial buildings are being renovated.

The community's support for the arts, even though the city does not classify it as an economic development policy, is also worth mentioning in this introduction. Much of this support centers on two developments in the 1980s: the creation of a local endowment for the arts and the emergence of a strong local nonprofit to support the arts. The endowment, the Gardiner Trust, dates from 1989, when a city-owned Post-Impressionist painting fetched more than $550,000 at auction, which the city council then turned over to create the endowment. Income from this and other donations has supported a wide range of local artists and craftspeople. The nonprofit Northern Lakes Arts Association has consistently maintained a dues-paying membership of more than 1,000, and has supported a wide variety of local community theater, musicals and other arts events and exhibitions as well as visiting professional acts from around the Midwest. This has made Ely a more attractive place to live and has been widely recognized around the region as an asset for the community. In economic development terms, it has helped to bring in new residents, and therefore bolstered the local workforce, but has not directly driven extensive job growth.

The overall shortage of higher-paying jobs in the area has helped to intensify the politics surrounding mining and the possibility that the needs of mining, tourism and local amenities will clash. The presence of large but low-grade deposits of copper, nickel, gold, platinum and palladium in the "Duluth Complex" of gneissic rocks such as gabbro and greenstone to the north of the Mesabi Iron Range has long been known, but only with commodities inflation in the 1960s and again in the 2000s has there been serious commercial interest. This time the interest has proceeded to a multi-million dollar effort by two consortia to establish the viability of proposed mines and obtain necessary permits. One, Twin Metals, a subsidiary of Chilean copper mining giant Antofagasta plc, which became sole proprietor when it bought out Canadian partner Duluth Metals in early 2015 after a run on the partner's stock,[25] is prospecting land just southeast of Ely on the edge of the Boundary Waters Canoe Area Wilderness, for which it proposes to develop a deep underground mine. The consortium's profile in the community is a high one, after an encounter at a Minnesota Twins baseball game between Twin Metals executives and then Ely mayor Roger Skraba in 2012, in which Skraba urged Twin Metals to ease its political troubles in the community by demonstrating commitment with a building; a local head office and logistics support facility was subsequently placed in the Ely Business Park. The other is a new Canadian-based company, PolyMet Mining, publicly traded but backed by Swiss mining firm Glencore, which is prospecting land at the former site of LTV Steel Mining, 40 miles southwest of Ely.

Both projects, especially Twin Metals, with its highly sensitive location, have run into serious opposition over the environmental impacts on water quality and the tourist industry, especially in the surrounding townships, but draw substantial support from within Ely and in general among multigenerational residents, many of whose parents fought tooth and nail against a previous prospecting attempt for precious metals mining in 1990 and 1991. Mining has proved to be a dominant and divisive issue in the area in both local and national elections, helping to drive an increase in Republican vote share, with, for the first time since 1928, a Republican nominee for president – Donald Trump – carrying the town even as some rural townships tilted Democratic. Nowhere has this divide been more visible than in the 2015 special election to fill the seat left vacant in the state's House of Representatives by David Dill, who died of cancer following more than 12 years as the area's legislator; the real contest was, once again, in the Democratic primary between eventual victor and United Steelworkers Local 159 president Rob Ecklund, a mining advocate, and Bill Hansen, a resort owner with a long record of involvement in environmental causes. Ecklund prevailed on the strength of his support in his hometown of International Falls, newly added to the district as its largest town, but Hansen dominated the eastern part of the district, except in the city of Ely itself, where he failed to reach even a third of the vote.

Economically, Ely therefore presents as an ideal test case for this study. Faced with structural declines in industrial employment and tourist

92   *Ely: Infrastructure Delivered*

revenue, the city provides an excellent example of economic scarcity. Faced with fragmentation among governments and within the city of Ely government, the community's means of mobilizing resources and delivering public policy are often disjointed. And, even though leaders have long recognized this to be a problem, successes have been limited and movement backwards has been evident in some policy areas. The key question is what effect these organizational issues have had on economic and community development policy.

The Governmental Context

Ely's governance is characterized by a major asset and two major problems. The asset is the high level of citizen involvement in governance. Voter turnout rates for city elections benefit from the scheduling of city elections on the same date as state general elections, and drop off only slightly from lines at the top of the ballot; rates of voluntarism in the community are high (and complimented by leaders elsewhere on the Iron Range); council seats rarely go unopposed; a large, rambling committee structure in city government is mostly fully "staffed"; and the impressive array of local nonprofits enjoy strong support. This environment also creates a situation in which the public tends to police questions of accountability. This involvement, even though it can lead to some combustible political fights, is reciprocated by the city council and government – a factor in how the city chose to support the arts so strongly and continues to provide extensive in-kind assistance for nonprofits and special events. Ely is a "hands-on" polity for its elected officials and voters.

The first of the problems is intergovernmental. This conflict has roots both within Ely city government and in Ely's relations with neighboring townships and cities and with the state of Minnesota. First, the Ely area is small in population but big in the number of local governments. Combined with neighboring townships, Morse, Fall Lake, Eagles Nest, Stony River, nearby unorganized territory and the tiny city of Winton, the population losses have taken the community's overall population below 6,000[26] and with no further consolidation in government and little annexation. Babbitt, 17 miles to the south, adds a further 1,500, a consideration in view of its role as an industrial employment center (through Cleveland-Cliffs subsidiary Northshore Mining, once the main facility of Reserve Mining Company and among the first of Minnesota's taconite iron ore plants to be developed) and Ely's role as the area's main service center. Nowhere has this fragmented governance been more visible than in intergovernmental arrangements, notably Ely's withdrawal of funding from the Community Economic Development Joint Powers Board in 2010 and the failure to establish a single regional fire department.

The second issue is internal. The city struggled for a generation to fill the power vacuum left by Mayor Grahek. With today's voters skeptical of the top-down governance that characterized Grahek's long rule, this means building process and continuity more than finding a particular leader. But, in practice, leadership has counted, in administration more than elected office, through the more successful and longer-lasting public officials, such as city clerk Lee Tessier (1986–2000) and director of operations Harold Langowski (since 2008 at the time of writing). The city council has seen serious disputes over Ely's form of government – council-manager versus weak mayor-council – and with how economic development policy should be formulated and managed. The general perception of weakness in city government helps to explain a level of distrust that might otherwise be surprising in view of the high level of citizen involvement. Nonetheless, consensus on the city council over the city's management has improved since Langowski's hiring heralded a structure that in practice makes for a strong city administrator with responsibilities close to that of a city manager.

Economic development policy has been central to the conflicts. Tessier, a hands-on city clerk who, among other things, managed the city's bond auctions directly (and successfully) rather than the normal practice of hiring consultants, had played a substantial but informal role in economic development policy. But, with a poorly defined and institutionalized process for setting the policy agenda, Tessier's retirement in 2000 created another political vacuum and a round of political conflict, forcing Ely to confront the high degree of fragmentation of agenda-setting and policy-making over economic development. From 2010 on, the city council has taken direct charge of economic development policy, with city staff under Langowski's management handling infrastructure and public services.

Economic Development in Ely: Who Governs?

Institutionally, there are several key players in the handling of economic development: the city council itself; the statutory economic development authority (EDA), whose membership consists of the city council and mayor and whose post-2010 revival makes it the leading player; senior city officials; and, prior to the Community Economic Development Joint Powers Board's defunding, its executive director and the economic development director for the joint powers board all have had substantial influence on policy within the city of Ely. The joint powers board was additionally used in an attempt to forge an area-wide consensus on policy.

Under legislation dating from 1986, Minnesota municipalities have the power to set up economic development authorities.[27] EDAs may exercise their own powers, the powers of housing and redevelopment authorities (which Ely also has), municipal powers in conjunction with development districts, and the powers of municipalities or redevelopment authorities in conjunction with industrial development. In other words, one agency can perform functions formerly performed by several. The default membership for an EDA is the city council; this is the case in Ely. Ely's EDA was created

94 *Ely: Infrastructure Delivered*

in 1993[28] and authorized by the council to handle housing development, economic development and redevelopment under the act. But it soon fell dormant, and only with Ely's end-2010 withdrawal from joint powers was it revived.

The relative inactivity of the Ely EDA resulted for many years in power over economic development being wielded in other areas. For example, the Ely Business Park was managed by a subcommittee of the city council, an apparently minor distinction but one that created an extra degree of separation in business meetings and management. Nor did it manage activity at Ely's airport, despite its importance for economic development and direct attempts by the city to use it as a business recruiting tool.[29] Instead, the airport remains under the sole control of the Ely Airport Commission, a body that has typically consisted of council members with an interest in aviation and members of the aviation community (for example, current and former bush pilots, and staff at the US Forest Service's logistics facilities in the area).

But, in practice, the most important authority above the city of Ely is the Iron Range Resources and Rehabilitation Board, the state agency that for almost 70 years has coordinated economic development policy on Minnesota's Iron Range. The IRRRB controls by far the greatest share of resources for economic development, not just in Ely but across the Iron Range. Spending of own-source revenue on economic development is usually less than two percent of the city budget. Even with IRRRB grants, a consistent pattern of $250,000 to $350,000 a year in economic and community development funding for Ely[30] left total spending in these categories at around or a little under 10 percent of the city's entire current general fund budget during the late 2000s and early 2010s. A challenge for Ely is the domination of the IRRRB by the state legislators within its jurisdiction. In the 2000s they were all labor-union-backed Democrats,[31] and they held a supermajority of the board's seats. Now the board consists entirely of legislators, one of whom is a Republican former IRRRB commissioner. In practice, the board has been far more familiar with and supportive of big business than of small, a stance that clashes with Ely's small population and small business orientation. This means the city's economic development spending often adheres more to IRRRB priorities than its own challenges. As one council member put it in 2006, "Everyone is continuing to ignore the problem – it is as simple as the city needs to increase its revenues. [It] has been a constant for more than a decade."[32]

Thus, the first instinct of many local leaders in terms of building the capacity to deliver on economic development was to attempt to put Ely more in charge of its policy agenda by making it more financially self-sufficient, through a local option sales tax. These are difficult indeed to obtain in Minnesota. Minnesota municipalities must petition for an act of the state legislature simply to hold a local referendum for a sales tax, whose use, if the referendum passes, must be designated and whose duration is time-limited. Thus, Ely's referendum in 1994 authorized by the legislature was a rare opportunity – and it failed by a margin of three to two, with opponents including a local car dealership running heavy radio advertising. The lack of a local option sales tax is cited by a clear majority of survey respondents in Ely as a limitation. Purely local approval of a sales tax is an option that home-rule cities in Minnesota are denied, but even non-home-rule municipalities in Illinois can gain if voters approve it in a referendum. Ely-area leaders are broadly in favor of some kind of sales tax, but since the failed referendum in 1994 they have differed on the details. Township officials have suggested an exemption for residents would be needed in the event of a new tax due to the thin margins local businesses already operate on during the off-season.[33] As the managing editor of the *Ely Echo* newspaper, Tom Coombe, has put the challenge of convincing the public to support a local sales tax, "I see an extra cent sales tax [going] into some sort of infrastructure. To sell it to people, they'd have to 'see' something, and economic development is hard to 'see.'"[34]

On the other hand, Ely's general revenue is relatively secure, thanks in part to Minnesota's system of local government finance. With general property tax revenue equalized by the state and substantial influence over finance and policy from above, the incentive to spend substantial city funds on economic development is relatively weak, especially in a political environment highly sensitive to property taxes. Thus, IRRRB funds remain the dominant factor in economic development spending. This has had major consequences for Ely's funding of assistance to business.

Ely's Joint Powers Board and the Attempt to Build Local Institutional Capacity

The failure of the 1994 sales tax referendum triggered a push in the Ely area to reform the governance of economic development. Elected authorities including the townships and the city council, as well as the Ely Area Development Association (EADA), a business group advocating economic development policies, believed building regional consensus would both bring better policy results and trigger another opportunity at a sales tax, legislative approval of which would likely require an area-wide endorsement.[35] Furthermore, the long-running disputes over matters such as annexation and fire coverage provided a ready motive for better cooperation among area governments.

Accordingly, from 1995 through 1997 Ely-area leaders participated in a regional project to boost public policy cooperation among neighboring towns and cities. The IRRRB and the Blandin Foundation[36] of Grand Rapids, Minn., funded the Inter-Community Cooperation Leadership Program (ICCLP), which paired six groups of Iron Range communities: the "quad cities" of Mountain Iron, Virginia, Eveleth and Gilbert; the central Iron Range cities of Hibbing and Chisholm; the East Range communities

96   Ely: Infrastructure Delivered

of Ely, Tower, Soudan, Babbitt and Embarrass; the eastern Mesabi Range communities of Aurora, Hoyt Lakes, White Township and Biwabik; the western Mesabi Range cities of Keewatin, Nashwauk, Pengilly, Calumet, Marble, Bovey and Coleraine; and the Cuyuna Range cities of Deerwood, Crosby, Ironton and Emily.[37] Hibbing and Chisholm's project under this program was notably modest and successful; a business park, the Hibbing Airpark, at the municipal airport jointly operated by both cities, and with the direct involvement of the Hibbing Economic Development Authority.[38] The East Range's leading project, creating a regional authority to supervise economic development policy, was much more ambitious. However, participating communities failed to achieve consensus, paid less heed to institutional organization and power and did not meet all the Blandin process's goals. When, in 1998, the authority finally emerged, it did so with few members. Babbitt eventually gained observer status, but the voting members were limited to Ely – which withdrew financial support from the agreement in December 2010[39] – the tiny neighboring city of Winton, Morse Township and the Ely School District (Independent School District 696); even nearby Fall Lake Township, with the largest property tax base in the area,[40] declined to join, having initially promoted the project.

The authority, called the Community Economic Development Joint Powers Board (hereafter referred to as the Joint Powers Board), paid the salary of a half-time executive director and three-quarter-time assistant director for EADA who would provide business recruitment and technical assistance for local government, as well as office expenses from a budget split among members on a formula based primarily on population, and to a lesser extent property value and board voting rights. Accordingly, during the 2000s the city of Ely and Morse Township shouldered more than 90 percent of the operating cost of the authority, with Ely accounting for the largest share. So at least one goal was met. Ely could bring in support from surrounding communities, primarily Morse Township, to cover management costs, a more professionalized approach to economic development and more active business recruitment. However, the Joint Powers Board never had the authority to pair policy brainstorming with the resources needed to deliver projects.

Central to the Joint Powers Board's early credibility was the official who became its principal staff member. When Ely's previous economic developer retired in 1995, the hiring of his replacement as EADA executive director, Bill Henning, a retired US Air Force lieutenant colonel, was something of an event. The typical Iron Range government official is a locally born and bred native, likely part of the area's Democratic–Farmer–Labor political alignment, and probably a career public employee. Henning, who, before his military career, had earned an MBA and worked in the private sector, was anything but the typical Range official. A New Jersey native who had never lived in Minnesota (having been through a series of military postings in the South, where he met his wife), politically conservative (he was later appointed to one of the Iron Range Resources and Rehabilitation Board's citizen representative positions in the 2000s by Republican governor Tim Pawlenty), temperamentally entrepreneurial and free-market-oriented, he dramatically raised the profile of the office. Indeed, Henning was instrumental in the creation of the Joint Powers Board.[41]

This created a dynamic in which the city council, despite its statutory power through the Ely EDA, was content for several years to allow Henning to take the lead on economic development, intervening only when necessary to provide funding, lobbying support and legal services. However, in a critical respect Henning was an excellent political fit for the region's leaders. His strategies were centered upon traditional supply-side economic development (see Eisinger, 1988), thus matching a long-standing approach of both IRRRB and local governments including the city of Ely. And they filled a vacuum in a city whose otherwise detailed Comprehensive Plan (75 single-spaced pages as of 2016) continues to feature just a single sentence on implementing economic development policy.[42]

By far Henning's biggest success during his nine years as economic developer was securing a call center from Sato Travel (later Navigant, and now CWTSatoTravel, a subsidiary of Carlson Wagonlit) in the Ely Business Park. This was an unexpected turn of events for city leaders, who had been increasingly concerned with what to do about a heavily indebted city-owned office building in the business park once its main tenant, the Minnesota Department of Revenue, moved next door into its own, state-owned facility. Ely officials had intended, with IRRRB support, to redevelop the office building as a "technology center" – in other words, an "incubator" for small, new, information-technology-related businesses.

The arrival of Sato, a privatized, formerly federal government airline ticketing office that provides travel management services to defense contractors, transformed the debate over the building. Sato was large enough to lease most of the space and was prepared to meet IRRRB rules on prevailing wages, a move that provided the politically advantageous situation of delivering many jobs quickly. The firm hired 60 people immediately at pay rates of $8 to $16 an hour,[43] rising to 120 over three years,[44] and, despite periodic episodes of layoffs and rehiring, has maintained a large presence ever since and continually extended its lease. The IRRRB, which had earmarked funds for the technology center project, entirely funded the city's $400,000 share of renovation costs. It is the largest private-sector for-profit workplace in Ely, and the only other comparable or larger local employers in Ely include the school district, community college, state Department of Revenue, US Forest Service and hospital.

Aside from Sato, Henning's successes were limited, despite his high profile. He helped to secure Ely's place in an IRRRB-backed project by Minnesota Power subsidiary MP Telecom to build a fiber optics backbone in the area in 1998 and 1999, ensuring the early arrival of broadband Internet[45] and paving the way for Sato; he also strongly supported

98   Ely: Infrastructure Delivered

expansion of the Minnesota Department of Revenue operation in Ely. But, in some respects, his view of limited government resulted in him not intervening in projects. For example, he declined to actively support an effort by rural residents to lobby state regulators to require that local phone companies provide them with service, suggesting the problem was best left to the private sector.[46] Undaunted, these residents went directly to the Minnesota Public Utilities Commission on their own, and won a resounding victory, forcing Citizens Communications (now Frontier Communications) to provide fiber-optic-standard service to often remote forest locations at the state's standard installation charge and monthly service fees.

But Henning, like every other economic developer in the area, was facing an uphill battle during this time. The high point of Sato's arrival quickly dissipated, with illegal dumping of steel on the US market combining with the 2001–2 recession to trigger the region's worst economic downtown in 20 years. LTV Steel went bankrupt in 2001 with the loss of 1,100 Iron Range jobs alone; several other firms were on layoff. Only profitable Cleveland-Cliffs, the parent of Northshore Mining, whose Peter Mitchell Mine near Babbitt is 20 miles south of Ely, avoided major layoffs, and even it cancelled a major expansion.

Henning's sudden decision to retire in May 2004 brought instability, with periodic conflict between the council, EADA and townships over the organization's recruitment efforts and even governance, and an overall shift in strategy at EADA that seemed to take hold regardless of the Ely City Council's periodic shifts and swings on economic development policy. The effort of then Ely city clerk John Tourville to take on economic development duties was merely the first step in the battle. After Tourville's departure – and the electoral defeat of his city council opponents – EADA took a new direction. With the failure of efforts to recruit further high-profile businesses, the organization hired a Minneapolis community organizer as executive director, Pat Henderson. She shifted EADA's focus from Henning's outside recruitment strategies to emphasizing the development of Ely-based businesses and encouraging local business startups.

At the core of Henderson's strategy was microlending, originating small business development loans, often little larger than typical consumer loans, to provide operating capital in situations in which banks were reluctant to get involved. Ely, like many other Minnesota communities, has operated its own microlending program for Main Street retail businesses to renovate their storefronts, with clear benefits both for downtown infrastructure and retaining businesses. Henderson proposed to establish a larger-scale microlending program that would be available to any local business, especially in manufacturing. Dubbed Project Firefly, the program received $50,000 in startup funding from the Blandin Foundation in early 2006 to survey local metal manufacturing capacity and establish a panel of local citizens with mechanical design and engineering experience, known as the 'Innovators

Circle," that was intended to identify products for development, financing and marketing.

Project Firefly quickly won support among local area governments, and in 2007 it secured $100,000 in grant funding from the IRRRB and the Blandin Foundation[47] as well as other smaller foundation grants.[48] As one former elected official put it, "It may not bring in a 250-person project or anything as big as Navigant or the Revenue Building, but these are the kind of things that create an entrepreneurial spirit and keep people coming here."[49] But, by this point, Firefly had already hit a serious snag. The area's highest political authority in the field of economic development remains the state legislators, who form a supermajority of the Iron Range Resources and Rehabilitation Board. The agenda of these officials – with their political base in large-unit industries dominated by organized labor – strongly favors "supply-side" economic development strategies and recruiting large, headline employers. And so it proved during 2006 and 2007. Two of the area's most senior legislators, state senator Tom Bakk (who became State Senate Taxes Committee chairman in December 2006) and state representative Tom Rukavina, earmarked $4 million in surplus taconite tax revenue for the recruitment of a single major business for the East Range. In announcing the project, Bakk told the EADA quarterly meeting: "We designed this program to attract a business that can put 200-plus jobs in one of the four towns or a business that has the potential to grow to that level of employment. We need to enhance local economies and school districts by working together."[50]

To the dismay of many Ely officials and business leaders, state politicians rejected Henderson's idea of distributing $300,000 of these funds for microlending.[51,52] Communities participating under Henderson's supervision in the Highway 1 Corridor Task Force, an ad hoc organization originally convened in 2000 to promote improvements to state highways in the area, would be expected to agree among themselves on a strategy and a location for this single project and then secure IRRRB support, a tough task in view of the 60-mile spread from one end of the area to the other. No concrete developments resulted from the initiative. The EADA board later rejected an additional proposal from Henderson to use interest to launch a marketing effort for a major business, whereupon she suggested business recruitment in general would have to be handled directly by elected officials rather than economic development staff.[53] The $4 million earmark remains unspent. And, while Project Firefly subsequently attracted limited foundation support, it came nowhere close to corralling the resources envisioned by Henderson. As one Ely City Council member put it, "[Local] government positions aren't full-time jobs; people are trying to do the best they can. They're not in the game politically 24/7. People in higher state offices are doing it all the time, and they just run you over."[54] Yet, from the state's standpoint, a major opportunity for regional cooperation was being missed.

100 *Ely: Infrastructure Delivered*

At this point, the standing of EADA and the Joint Powers Board agreement started to deteriorate. The 2006 council elections in Ely brought an increase in skepticism about EADA's increasingly incremental, demand-side strategy and a shift toward city demands to see more tangible results from economic development efforts. The election brought allies for the newly installed mayor, Chuck Novak: former council member Warren Nikkola, in a political comeback, and John Lindroos, who was appointed to fill the remainder of Novak's council term in a move that would later trigger a voter backlash in the form of Novak's re-election defeat and a charter amendment requiring special elections for vacancies.

Political fireworks took barely a month to arise. December's EADA quarterly meeting and holiday party degenerated into extended argument between Novak and Henderson.[55] Novak said he was sure that "everybody would be pleasantly surprised" if EADA efforts led to the creation of new jobs; Henderson shot back by asking if the city received a "volume discount" for plaques presented to retired and former employees. Henderson walked out of the meeting after the argument, which took place the day after a council meeting in which one member, Gordon Sheddy, had called for a 50 percent cut in funding to the Joint Powers Board to show the city's concerns over EADA's performance. Although no council action was taken, only one council member expressed support for the organization. A calmer meeting of the EADA board two weeks later involving Novak and Henderson simply clarified the difference in both approach and strategy between the two.[56]

Henderson eventually resigned in June 2008, to become executive director of Arrowhead Regional Development Commission. This put her in charge of a leading regional community development and planning body, in a position with more influence with the IRRRB. After an extended vacancy and a blown search for a replacement, the EADA board hired Nancy Larson, the community education director in Tower,[57] 20 miles west of Ely, as Henderson's replacement. Larson's background further shifted EADA away from economic development toward promoting more consensus and support for grant-writing among local governments[58] on infrastructure,[59] such as improved road links, and on tourism.[60] Project Firefly became inactive, despite its considerable startup grant, and saw no further developments.

In the end, the Ely City Council lost patience. The vote in late 2010 to end support for the Joint Powers Board left the Ely Area Development Association without the funds to maintain paid staff. In view of the clear differences between the city of Ely and surrounding townships on economic development – demographically younger Ely being in favor of it, the retiree-heavy townships being more skeptical of it – the policy direction moved more strongly in a development direction even as direct spending was cut and the townships' approximately $1 billion property tax base appeared more off-limits than ever.

Since 2011, with the city council in direct control of economic development policy, the city's strategy has concentrated on providing more general improvements of benefit to individual residents as well as business; the question of direct business assistance has proved more of a challenge, with much hope being pinned by pro-mining leaders in the community on state permission for copper-nickel mining and critics expressing concerns that this will damage other business sectors by threatening the environment. Ely has redoubled efforts to boost general infrastructure, with a string of projects dealing with long-unfinished business involving city buildings, including a new public library (leaving the future of the listed Ely Community Center very much in doubt) and a long-awaited renovation of City Hall that finally added building-wide wheelchair access. Another major recent priority has been building up the city's tourist infrastructure, with the city as of 2016 moving to identify a project to better support trailhead access for both non-motorized and snowmobile routes. And the city's biggest economic development initiative for the past two decades, the Ely Business Park, continues to see infrastructure expansion opening new properties for immediate development.

Measuring the Joint Powers Board's success as an economic development institution is difficult. The downgrading of Joint Powers was ignominious; a reflection of the failure to ameliorate conflicts on this and other issues, such as the collapse of an area-wide fire contract that led to Morse and Fall Lake Townships forming their own department and then being denied mutual aid by Ely for several years. On the other hand, it influenced policy. It surveyed area residents on their preferences and vision for the community, and in many respects local governments ended up reflecting those desires. It drummed up at least some support from surrounding townships for city-based services, both for the cost of administering economic development policy and the cost of regional library and recycling services. EADA by 2009 accounted for 12 percent of Morse Township's property tax levy, or about $29,000 a year,[61] before largely suspending its activities when township funding dried up following Ely's withdrawal of support. It helped to clarify an area-wide consensus on community development, including better roads and securing the future of amenities such as the school district. Perhaps in the end it was not fair to expect it to reconcile a more structural conflict: the demographic difference between retiree-led and tourism-heavy rural townships interested in sustainability and preservation, and the younger and poorer city of Ely pushing hard for more commercial and industrial economic growth.

Governance Disputed: The Question of City Management

The way in which the city handles this problem is best illustrated by the conflict over city administration during the decade of the 2000s, which saw six changes in the position of city clerk/administrator. Compared to the

102 *Ely: Infrastructure Delivered*

new business park projects and water and sewer infrastructure upgrades of the 1990s, and the uptick in city facilities and property development of the 2010s, this was a "lost" decade, mired in local conflict, in the context of a weak regional economy. The disputes over institutions and governance further distracted local government from economic and community development; indeed, they often centered on the governance of these policies.

This sequence of administrative instability began innocuously and with little warning of what was to come. First, a former municipal official from Colorado, Terry Lowell, was appointed as city clerk, holding the position for three years. September 2003 saw the entry of an experienced official with local roots, John Tourville. An Ely native who pursued a promising career in the private sector in the Twin Cities,[62] he had returned to the Iron Range and emerged in municipal politics there as city administrator and economic developer in Hibbing, at the start of that city's shift to a more activist approach to economic development that included recruiting business from outside the community. Within Ely he began with the respect and political influence that accrues to natives of the city in positions of bureaucratic authority.

On the surface, the first several months of Tourville's appointment passed relatively uneventfully. But the city's purported desire for a strong administrator or city manager was belied by a council whose composition had recently turned toward people against such a move. The council was now without administrator proponent Roger Skraba, a two-term councilman[63] who had given up his seat in 2002 in an unsuccessful run against local real estate broker and former League of Minnesota Cities vice president Frank Salerno for the open mayor's seat. In contrast, Mayor Salerno, in his third, non-contiguous term, was in little hurry to delegate authority, a situation that appears to have chafed at Tourville from the start. Salerno, a Chicago native who moved to Ely in the 1970s and was arguably the highest-profile local politician to date of the post-Grahek era, took a traditional view of city governance that upheld the mayor-council system and involved close supervision by the council.

The May 2004 retirement of the city's economic developer, Ely Area Development Association executive director Bill Henning, on just two weeks' notice, brought the issue to the fore. The motive for this abrupt decision after nine years on the job was not clear and has never been publicly elucidated since – for example, Henning retained his appointment on the Iron Range Resources and Rehabilitation Board as Governor Pawlenty's "citizen" representative. But Tourville quickly moved to stake a claim to absorbing Henning's position into his office. With his prior experience in Hibbing and his corporate contacts in the Twin Cities, Tourville was adamant that he could do a more effective job at lowering cost to the city than a separate economic developer working a half-time position. Some on the council, on the other hand, took the public stance of questioning whether one person could effectively combine both jobs.

Ely: Infrastructure Delivered   103

It soon became clear that the objections were far more serious. Salerno and long-standing council member Paul Kess appear to have sharply split from the other five members of the council on the question of Tourville's job performance. Local newspaper articles and columns in September 2004 raised the alarm, with *Ely Timberjay* editor Steve Foss openly suggesting based on an interview with the mayor that Salerno would be happy for Tourville to leave.[64] Official documents eventually suggested, though did not explicitly state, a similar story. In performance reviews conducted in August and October 2004, but not published until after Tourville had left office, he commanded good grades from a majority of the council, in part because of what was cited by one council member as him having "brought city employees closer to the core of city operations."[65] But two council members (all members were unidentified in the review documents) gave Tourville at least some below-average grades, with one of those officials marking him below-average across the board. In January 2005, after Tourville's departure from the job, it emerged that, while Tourville had been hired on the basis of directly supervising two long-established city department heads who had previously reported directly to the city council, public works superintendent Ken Hegman and Ely Utilities Commission general manager Terry Jackson, no one on the council had negotiated or discussed the change with Hegman and Jackson, leading to considerable friction at the top level of city management.[66]

Three weeks before election day the story broke that Tourville had made the shortlist for the Iron Range city of Virginia's director of operations and economic development. The election turned into what even some council members described as a strike by the voters on Tourville's critics.[67] Both Salerno and Kess were among council members up for re-election, and both were decisively beaten. Although Salerno had lost as an incumbent before, Kess's loss was particularly notable, a landslide defeat, leaving him in fifth place in a best-three-of-six race, following two comfortable re-elections (years later, both Kess and Salerno would make a comeback to the council, though in Salerno's case a comeback that was cut short by family matters and ill health).

The inevitable denouement came just days after the election. Tourville, ranked far ahead of the other Virginia candidates by a human relations consultant, was the unanimous choice of Virginia City Council,[68] and ruefully noted in comments to reporters that he had never had that degree of support from the Hibbing or Ely City Councils.[69] Shortly after that his Ely performance review was published (the report was written by a committee consisting of three Tourville allies: councilmen Butch Pecha, Jerome Debeltz and Mark Zupec).[70] The city took eight months to replace Tourville, during which time they appointed the eventual winner of their job search, Ely Butler, on an interim basis in order to handle a growing backlog at City Hall.

104 *Ely: Infrastructure Delivered*

Ely's difficulty in resolving the long-term direction of city administration did not end with Tourville's departure. Replacing Salerno and Kess were two people wanting reform of the weak mayor-council system, both Ely natives who would later run against each other. One, Skraba, who won the mayoral election that had eluded him two years earlier, had worked for most of his life in his home town. He had returned to Ely after college, a congressional internship and service in the military to start a fishing guide business, and had served almost a decade on the city council before his first attempt at the mayor's office in 2002. The other, Chuck Novak, who gained Kess's seat on the city council, had spent almost his entire professional career outside Ely as a software engineer before returning in retirement. Both endorsed a stronger city administrator, but had considerable differences regarding Ely's troubled relationship with its townships, though these did not emerge until months later.

But, even with strong support from both the new mayor and the returnee to Ely, the council's conversion of the clerk position to a city administrator failed. The causes were not so much political as a textbook case of poor "change management" with personnel. Butler proved to be an unsuccessful hire as city administrator, in part because he and city leaders failed to adequately sell the idea to city employees, or in some respects to even inform them of what was going on. Instead of a city bureaucrat leading economic development efforts, the city's administrator was being consumed by issues of human resources management.

The first flashpoint was a disciplinary action that involved a rare case of Hegman's management of his department being called into question, not long before his retirement. In late 2005 Butler, with council support, suspended Hegman and a senior employee under his supervision for five days following the unauthorized expenditure of $7,400 on activities that included the changing of locks at City Hall.[71] The benign explanation – Hegman had taken the action following the abrupt refusal of an existing locksmith vendor to do any further business with the city of Ely – would have likely been accepted in past years, but now the city was attempting a far more formalized way of doing business. In February 2007, following a written reprimand from Butler to Jackson due to the latter's unauthorized discussion of merit pay with union officials, the issue of formalization came out into the open again, dominating a council meeting, though Jackson's grievance was rejected.[72]

However, it was a controversy over a minor hire that doomed Butler in the end. The appointment of a janitor became a summer-long controversy after the council split, four to three,[73] on the hiring decision, at once showing the extent to which they were still in practice involved in minor decision-making as well as the continuing disagreement over basic policies at City Hall. Some councilors objected to the job going to a Twin Cities resident, given the shortage of secure and stable jobs in Ely. Amid several public meetings and threats of litigation from the

Ely: Infrastructure Delivered 105

rejected finalists, the city interviewed and ranked nine candidates, but the council, this time on a four–two vote, reached the same decision.[74] Yet within two months, before the end of his probationary period, the chosen hire resigned and left town, an outcome announced in a raucous September 2007 council meeting in which Butler and then city attorney Rae Bentz were sharply criticized for giving council members inaccurate information on the hiring process.[75] Three months later the council voted six to one to terminate Butler's contract following two performance reviews.[76]

Novak, wanting no repeat of the Butler era, moved decisively toward a settlement that, given his earlier views, could be seen as realistic rather than idealistic. In January 2008 he called a joint Saturday public meeting of the city council, Ely Utilities Commission and Paul Ness, a consultant long used by the city for human resources issues, at a local hotel to discuss the future structure of city administration and management. With the management of public works, public utilities and the front office at City Hall now all vacant and the city having to retain Hegman as a consultant simply to meet regulatory requirements on the electric utility,[77] action was urgently needed.

A consensus emerged around a clerk-treasurer handling city accounting, planning and zoning administration, and paperwork; and an operations director, a chartered civil engineer, to run public works and the public utilities.[78] This position was filled first, the city's consultant engineer Harold Langowski getting the job on a unanimous council vote and a strong endorsement from Ness, at a salary of $75,000 a year, $13,000 above Butler's former pay and also above Jackson's pay.[79] Three months later Terri Boese, a human resources manager for hardware store chain Home Depot who had previously served for several years as city administrator in Pequot Lakes, Minnesota, was hired at a mere $56,000, an unprecedented disparity in a situation in which the clerk had traditionally been at or near the top of City Hall salaries, status and job description.[80] Boese would remain in the position only three years, though without the controversies that dogged Butler; on her departure, Lowell briefly returned, but, on his retirement, Langowski took charge of the clerk's responsibilities as well – the closest Ely has come yet to a council-manager structure.

At least for now the question of city administration in Ely appears to be settled, albeit dependent on an administrator with qualifications ranging broadly from finance to utility management. And, although Langowski is the dominant player on managing city infrastructure and services, the city council is taking a direct lead on economic development, albeit emphasizing infrastructure, public services and financial stability more than business assistance. Enhanced city services, amenities and community broadband are on the agenda; but specific supply-side assistance to business is sporadic. The city council has also forcefully endorsed expanded mining, in spite of a significant minority within Ely opposing it – a pattern that may in the eyes of some clash with Ely's current reality but fits an old standby

106   *Ely: Infrastructure Delivered*

on the Iron Range: political lobbying of the state for support of big business projects.

Policy Outcomes, Chains of Authority and Project Delivery

Ely's recent pattern has been one of attempts to streamline the delivery of economic and community development policy, shifting it away from specific business subsidies toward general-purpose community development, and moving it as close as possible to elected officials rather than running it in a corporate manner and delegating day-to-day management and the minutiae of making business deals. The result is spartan in administrative terms: the city council handles economic development functions as a committee of the whole as well as general policy, and, administratively, the process runs through the director of operations. This is largely because, after initial successes, Joint Powers came to be seen as a failure, thus removing the rationale for a separate institutional vehicle for economic development policy. For, in the end, EADA struggled as much as the city of Ely did prior to EADA's professionalized role in economic development through the joint powers board.

Before looking in detail at the city's work on private-sector economic development, it is worth considering an example of its recent successes, with infrastructural renewal as a counterpoint in terms of comparing political and administrative processes. In contrast to its troubles with economic development, Ely's large recent output of public infrastructure, amenities and services is striking. After a new water plant, the start of the business park, electrical grid upgrades and extensive street reconstruction in the 1990s, the decade of the 2000s saw the successful delivery of around $30 million in new public infrastructure in town; a state-of-the-art reconstruction of its sewage plant, with capacity for some 2,000 residents beyond current population; a new public works garage shared with county and township governments; and state and federal projects, including the new Minnesota Department of Revenue building and new US Forest Service district rangers' headquarters, both of them owner-occupied buildings that secure a long-term future for major local employers that had previously been operating in rented office space. During the same period partners in state, county and federal governments have substantially improved the area's roads with additional investments, a process that is ongoing.

The key common factor behind all these public projects is that – unlike with most economic development projects – they had powerful outside patrons who could overcome divisions within the community of Ely. By far the best example of this is the city's $11 million sewage plant, completed in 2002. This project, the largest construction project in the city's history, faced as much internal opposition as economic development initiatives. In this case, the cause was the cost of the plan and distrust of the city's commission for public utilities that culminated in an overwhelming 1999 referendum vote to revoke the board's operational independence from city council control. The political atmosphere also enveloped the city's consulting engineers, Brown & Caldwell, whose inaccurate early cost estimates and high fees (more than $800,000 in 1999 alone) raised continual questions.[81] What clinched the project was forceful outside intervention. The city had already been threatened with heavy fines from discharge violations at the plant. Financial inducements for rebuilding followed; during 1999 and 2000 more than $2 million in federal grants and $3.4 million in low interest state and federal loans were committed. The region's then state senator, Doug Johnson, led efforts at the state capitol to prioritize the Ely plant and line up support. At the same time, congressman Jim Oberstar and the US Department of Agriculture's regional headquarters in Minneapolis played a key role in mediating the conflict and securing federal support, emphasizing the national importance of the wilderness area and even the drainage into Canadian territory. However, approval was a close-run affair; in the fall of 2000 the city council briefly deadlocked on accepting a construction bid and nearly derailed the entire project.[82]

Four years later Oberstar intervened again in a major Ely issue – the public works garage – along with 4th District St. Louis County commissioner Mike Forsman, a former Ely mayor, this time to provide major grant funding that resulted in the city of Ely paying for only one-quarter of what had become an $8 million project. Once again, conflict was intense, with strong support from city departments, significant public skepticism and close votes on the city council, the controversy this time being driven by the garage's proximity to the city cemetery. A city official at the time the sewage plant was finally approved cites the case as clear evidence of the importance of the government structure and of the extent to which Ely depends on "melding with the outside agencies" for its major projects.[83]

The difference between these projects and direct economic development – as in direct public-sector support for private-sector job creation – is that the latter has not seen the level of outside intervention, or in some cases force of law, that helped clinch Ely's big-ticket public infrastructure. This applies especially to annexation and the incompatibility of city and state goals for economic development; the more successful Ely Business Park has had generally higher, though not perfect, local consensus. In the area of annexation, politicians and officials from state and federal government simply are not involved.

What Developable Land? Ely and Annexation

A constant feature of debates and activity surrounding economic development in Ely is the question of land use. This is a particularly common point of dispute in US cities, on account of the extent to which unincorporated land not under the jurisdiction of any municipality still exists around them. This differs from Europe and Canada, where the norm is for most

108 *Ely: Infrastructure Delivered*

or all land to be under some kind of municipal or district council jurisdiction, and boundary changes between jurisdictions are a matter for higher levels of government. In practice, annexing new territory is a common US approach to maintaining the availability of land for development. And this question of land use has dominated the debate about annexation in and around Ely – a process slowed by Morse Township's fear of city taxes and inclination to limit development and the city's meek approach in exercising the rights it has under existing annexation agreements. After all, in the end, Joint Powers was meant to bring the city and township closer together not only in terms of generally defining community-wide goals but also for promoting development, including addressing Ely's stunted tax base and serious shortage of developable land.

The city's struggles with annexation stand out for two reasons. One is the length of time for which it has been discussed. Ely's "Orderly Annexation Agreement" with Morse Township dates to 1973, and allowed for the addition of 1,000 acres of township land to add to the city's current 1,340. Yet, in the first four decades of the agreement, only 40 acres were annexed – parts of the Beacon Hill neighborhood on the city's south fringe that were not already within city limits, and a handful of "spot annexations" of single properties – theoretically leaving 960 acres still on the table. Only in 2015 did a deal finally arise, and then only for around 50 acres of largely non-controversial though strategically situated land mostly owned by the city government. The other reason is the extent to which the city council has backed down in the face of township opposition to annexation despite speaking favorably of annexation. The township has posted stiff demands for revenue-sharing, such as replicating a 60/40 revenue split in perpetuity agreed to by the tiny Iron Range city of Biwabik and neighboring White Township, and avoiding any tax increases for existing residents who are annexed or Morse residents who remain outside the city limits. This tough line emerged after the city of Ely's refusal since the late 1990s to extend utilities to unincorporated areas,[84] a policy backlash against the Ely Utilities Commission's extension of lines to these areas without council support that had been a factor in a local referendum in 1999 revoking the EUC's operational autonomy from the council.

The reason for the city to pursue annexation was the lack of developable land, for new business and for housing,[85] and the need for more customers for municipal infrastructure that is designed to handle more than Ely's current population. Much of the land eventually annexed in 2015 was first identified in early November 2008, when city council members listed 60 acres for high-priority annexation, including potential commercial sites and the land occupied by the US Forest Service's new regional headquarters, which was requesting annexation.[86] This move followed a summer in which the council balked at Morse Township's demands for perpetual revenue-sharing from annexed land[87] and later agreed to consider unilaterally pursuing land under the Orderly Annexation Agreement.[88] However, this plan bogged down within a week of the potential sites being identified when Mayor Novak, who advocated using the agreement to force annexation, lost in the 2008 election to Skraba, whom he had in turn ousted at the polls just two years earlier.

Indeed, the political barriers to annexation are powerful both within Ely and outside it. First, there is a powerful fear of forcing the issue; for example, a city council debate on the subject in August 2008 revealed serious doubts among a majority of council members about contested annexation, despite the existing 1973 agreement.[89] Second, political opposition in the township is entrenched, especially on the town board of supervisors. Besides the aversion to taxes in the township, inclusion in city services could leave serious sunk costs literally in the ground for residents. For example, people who have recently upgraded expensive systems such as septic disposal do not want to pay for city utilities.[90] Third, there remains a strong fear – especially in the township – of the risk of overdevelopment in the area affecting the character that builds Ely's current tourist base. As one township official put it prior to the city identifying specific parcels for annexation, "We're not anti-development but we want to be very careful of how it affects things. People come here to go to the BWCA because they are looking at something you're not going to be able to find in Wisconsin Dells" (see Figure 4.5).[91]

Figure 4.5 Highway near Ely, Minnesota, June 2017
Source: Daniel Bliss.

110 *Ely: Infrastructure Delivered*

The deal finally passed by the city and township governments in 2015, to take effect in January 2016, affected 50.4 acres, mostly land on the city's southwestern boundary near the Ely-Bloomenson Hospital. This parcel, already owned by the city government, has some potential for commercial development, though upgrades are likely to be in the longer term. A small cluster of homes seeking improved utility access were also included in what ended up being a relatively modest annexation.[92] But the deal opens land in an area of critical importance of the city: the western gateway, through which State Highway 169 passes and which has long been hamstrung by the lack of potential building sites. The deal provides land for the city adjacent to properties recently vacated by the US Forest Service, city government and St. Louis County government, and now represents by far Ely's biggest new pool of potential commercial land.

Developing a Business Park in Central Ely

Ely's own strategies for land development prior to the 2010s were not oriented toward such a large single project, though the city has recruited larger employers itself. At the core of local economic development strategy of the past 30 years has been the redevelopment of old railroad and industrial land into a business park. The 1982 abandonment of the Duluth, Missabe and Iron Range Railway (DM&IR) branch into Ely – a result of the end of large-scale logging in the Boundary Waters "portal zone" east of Ely – freed a large quantity of land in the heart of the town for business development, land once occupied by the DM&IR mainline, a freight yard and a locomotive depot, without annexation or township involvement. The goal was private sector, non-retail, non-residential and preferably office or manufacturing jobs. The various successes and failures of the business park since then have strongly correlated with episodes of unity or division, respectively, on the council; disputes have arisen when prospective tenants have lobbied to change the policy to allow a wider range of enterprises.

The management of the business park was handled almost exclusively at the local level by city of Ely government. Thus, it was relatively free of the intergovernmental conflicts over policy that have often affected other economic development initiatives in the Ely area. In many respects, the policy structure and agenda surrounding the business park more resembled Ely's successful pattern of infrastructure development than it did efforts at business recruitment. The city clerk's office was closely involved with finance, the city attorney's office with land titles. The city council's committee structure included a separate committee to supervise the business park, and, in order to prevent circumvention or "venue-shopping" of the committee structure by businesses and public agencies alike, was put under the partial supervision of a "projects committee" that, from the late 1990s on, served as a clearinghouse for all city-funded infrastructure projects.

The land itself has a complicated history, as former railroad property often does. Clear title to the land took the better part of a decade to obtain, dramatically slowing the early pace of development and costing the city heavily in legal fees with contracted city attorneys Bill Defenbaugh and then Larry Klun, both lawyers whose private practices were primarily in real estate law. Furthermore, the planning for the business park got off to a poor start. The sale of private lots along the former mine pit Miner's Lake diminished the opportunity for developing parkland and fragmented a proposed trail system. The first major project, the new office building for a medical equipment venture that was occupied a decade later by Sato Travel failed spectacularly in 1989 when the principals absconded amid a fraud investigation, the mortgage payments and ownership of the building boomeranging to what was at the time a severely cash-strapped city government.[93]

The first successful venture in the business park also created controversy. From the beginning the desire for jobs comparable to those that had been lost led the city to adopt covenants on the land that restricted development to manufacturing, back-office facilities and other non-retail, non-consumer businesses. Before the process of assembling the land under municipal ownership and drafting covenants was even complete a new veterinary practice sought, and received, a variance to enable permission for a clinic in the business park. Its presence has been controversial in view of the eventual political victory of those who wanted the business park for medium- to larger-scale light manufacturing and back-end white-collar enterprises – not retail services and not small business. Nonetheless, this practice, which has now grown to five partners and is the only veterinary clinic within an hour's drive of Ely, is the longest continuous occupant of the business park.

The second successful venture in the business park bore little more resemblance to the original goals of the project than the first. Faced with a substantial vacant office building with a crushing debt, Ely lobbied its state legislators for assistance – and they did not disappoint. The vacant building was selected as one of four locations around the state of Minnesota for a new Department of Revenue venture to collect delinquent taxes, Minnesota Collection Enterprise (MCE). MCE has since become the largest employer in the business park, with the highest average staff rate of pay, the approximately 100 state employees enjoying a substantially higher success rate on collections than is typical among private contractors, along with an exceptionally low staff turnover rate.[94]

State legislators on the Iron Range Resources and Rehabilitation Board subsequently worked in both securing the future of MCE in Ely and recruiting Sato Travel when they succeeded in securing $2 million in state bonding in 1998 for a new, state-owned MCE building, thus freeing up the city-owned building for Sato to lease. MCE began construction in August 1999[95] despite a low bid that went more than $100,000 over the state's

112 *Ely: Infrastructure Delivered*

$2.2 million budget; nonetheless, state Senator Doug Johnson and the then state Representative Tom Bakk convinced the state Department of Administration to proceed anyway. In Bakk's words, it literally "cements those jobs into the community of Ely and any decision to leave would come at a serious expense to the state. My hope down the road is to try and grow the number of jobs there, especially now that the Revenue has designed a building they're comfortable with."[96]

During the 1990s two more enterprises located in the business park, much more in line with the city's original private-sector-oriented goals. In 1994 Steger Mukluks,[97] a high-end local producer of cold-weather winter footwear, relocated – with $150,000 in low-interest financing from the IRRRB[98] – from cramped quarters in a downtown store unit to a spacious new factory. The factory provided Steger with the capacity to sharply expand production, leading to a nationally distributed mail order catalog, a much larger downtown Ely store and an additional retail outlet in Jackson Hole, Wyoming. Steger currently employs around 30 people in Ely, and manufactures almost all its products locally and in house. In 1997 direct-mail marketer Irresistible Ink, since taken over by Hallmark Cards, Inc., established an office in Ely for producing personalized, handwritten bulk mail. However, unlike the other business park ventures, Irresistible Ink did not last; in 2008 Hallmark closed the Ely facility and consolidated operations in Irresistible Ink's original hometown of Two Harbors and in Duluth. The building remained vacant for several years, and was eventually leased by the St. Louis County government to relocate its offices within Ely from a school district building facing demolition.[99]

Another proposed development in the business park that foundered upon political sensitivity over the covenants would also have drawn an IRRRB subsidy. In 1999 property developer John Fedo, a former Duluth mayor and Hibbing city administrator who has since become an economic development consultant to Ely, proposed a 60-resident assisted living facility that would deliver approximately 20 jobs for home health care aides. In view of the shortage of land elsewhere in the city, Fedo lobbied for a business park lot. The IRRRB's $10,000-per-unit housing construction subsidy program would have yielded $600,000 in public support for the $3 million project, an amount Fedo said would ensure that no city subsidy was needed.[100] But, after an initially favorable council vote,[101] controversy erupted. First, another senior housing project, a market-rate rental development just outside the business park two blocks from Fedo's proposed site, was blocked (it would eventually be approved seven years later).[102] At the next meeting, council members opposed to the assisted living plan cited their (and voters') reluctance to use the business park for any kind of residential development, and tabled the ordinance for the development by a one-vote margin.[103] Within days Fedo withdrew the proposal, after canceling a scheduled appearance at a committee hearing; he signed off with a warning to the council to avoid "protectionist legislation" favoring local over regionally based enterprises.[104] Just days later, as if to reinforce the point about non-conforming land use, the city council rejected an application by a local bakery to relocate to the business park, on the grounds that it didn't want any direct retail or service business there.[105] Ultimately, a key opponent of the assisted living project – Ely's hospital – would prove a beneficiary, partnering with a private developer to build an assisted living project with IRRRB support.[106]

The failure of the apparently low-risk assisted living proposal demonstrated the political sensitivity of economic development in Ely. First, it failed even though it would have cost the city nothing. Second, political support on the council quickly evaporated in the face of opposition from citizens and the influential hospital and housing authority management. In the end, the council took the political path of least resistance – upholding the existing business park covenants – rather than taking the path that would have provided the quickest boost to the local economy and tax base. Politics and economics thus came into conflict, not synthesis.

In the past few years the largest new development in the business park has been the regional office and logistics base for Twin Metals, its project on hold at the time of publication from the federal government's 2016 decision to terminate its mining leases, a decision the company has challenged in court. The arrival of the mining firm's physical presence in the community was the result of networking; the continuation of that presence will depend on whether it can convince Minnesota regulators and politicians (still likely), US government agencies (in question) and the courts (difficult, in view of scientific evidence, statutes and case law) of the environmental safety of the project.

The business park is a major success for the community, though survey interviews from Ely leaders show frustration with the slow pace of further development since the 2000s, with Twin Metals' operations base and expansion at Steger Mukluks the only new structures since then. Against considerable odds, Ely took derelict railroad land with a legally complex title history and in the context of a weak local economy, albeit with IRRRB support, established a base of over 200 jobs. The length of time it took to develop and the blocking of the assisted living proposal demonstrate limits in the city's ability to complete the project, affected as it was by questions regarding the willingness of citizens to compromise on its original goals, and of special interests to pull for shared community needs. But the park, whose original lots are now all occupied, continues to expand, with a $940,000 project – including $540,000 from the city, $200,000 from IRRRB and $200,000 from the state Department of Employment and Economic Development (DEED) – approved in 2015 to open additional land for development.[107]

Conclusion

The progress Ely made with economic development in the private sector during the 1990s indisputably slowed in the 2000s before progress started to show again in the 2010s. In part, a weaker economy, changing trends among visitors and summer residents, and increasingly constrained local government budgets are all a factor. But the weak institutionalization and organization of governance over economic development also emerges as a factor. The many key changes in personnel at the top of city government stand out. Ely city clerk Lee Tessier's retirement in 2000; the years of dispute and argument over how to replace Tessier in the long run; the death of city attorney Larry Klun in 2006 – a key figure in the development of the Ely Business Park; and the two major changes in leadership at Ely Area Development Association and the Joint Powers Board have all had tangible impacts upon policy. Most importantly for this argument, the institutional structure that might cushion the blow from this loss of leadership is weak. Ely lacks a forum aside from the city council in which consensus on economic development and logistical support for it can build.

Nonetheless, major public infrastructure projects in the city have continued to be delivered in quantity and with success. These projects – the sewage treatment plant in 2001–2; the reconstruction of major arterial streets in 2003 and 2010; the new public works facility in 2006 – all had powerful outside patrons and standing state and federal policies to help see them through. But economic and community development depends much more on reconciling competing agendas, both within the community and between Ely, other area governments and the state. The IRRRB's $400,000 grant support for renovating office space for Sato Travel and its 120 jobs, for example, enjoyed the unanimous support of the city council and leading city officials, business leaders, IRRRB board members and agency officials. The city's generally strong condition in terms of finance and infrastructure has also boosted confidence. Fedo, the consultant who once failed to convince the city council of the value of assisted living in the business park, now is in his fourth year as the city's economic developer, and is actively pushing community broadband infrastructure as central to his strategy – an effort that so far has not been funded. The city is also helped by recent growth in the tourism sector, the increasing willingness of developers to take on renovation projects in the largely century-old downtown, and improvements in the availability of both leasable space and developable land.

The dependence of northeastern Minnesota economic development in general upon state support in the form of the IRRRB also has the effect of giving that agency veto power over local preferences. As other development efforts in the Ely area demonstrate, the region's generally weak economy has helped to concentrate state influence over community and economic development alike. In this environment, modest attempts at devolution such as the state's JOBZ tax abatement program – in which local communities get to designate, with state approval, parcels of land free of property tax and state sales tax – are not sufficient to provide local control. The key point of power is control over the stream of money coming through the IRRRB. The IRRRB's basic design is theoretically very strong; it has underwritten large volumes of needed improvements to public infrastructure while reducing the amount of money local communities spend on private business subsidies. But, as the biggest recent attempts at private economic development demonstrate, the dominance of state-level representation on the agency's board creates a serious governance problem whenever local and state agendas diverge, a problem that disproportionately affects smaller communities whose scale is not in tune with the agency or its leaders. It may well be up to Ely, then, with its internal disputes on community development policy now more settled and its tourist and retail sales base in a long-awaited recovery, to do as much as it can to influence the agency, further build internal consensus and promote its local policy agenda.

Notes

1 Projects in Ely engineered, organized or led by Mayor Grahek from the late 1960s to the end of his first period as mayor included $10 million in public housing, developments mostly for senior citizens; a new airport with a 5,600 foot runway, terminal and US Forest Service base; a major upgrade to the city's sewage plant as part of an Environmental Protection Agency experiment to see if eutrophication (choking of the lake with algae due to high phosphorous, in this case from previous irresponsible sewage disposal) of a lake could be reversed; the new community college campus, funded entirely by the state of Minnesota; expansions of the local hospital; and various smaller projects. See M. Peltier, US's newest regents represent variety of careers, backgrounds, *Minnesota Daily*, May 14, 1987.

2 Aside from his pull with Minnesota's senators and congressmen, Grahek also served on the University of Minnesota board of regents in the late 1980s and early 1990s, starting during a final three-year term as mayor.

3 Interviews 07, 08, 11, 13, 35; also interview 02 for note on Grahek's creation of the city's Storefront Rehab program, a key small business economic development revolving loan fund.

4 Ely Chamber of Commerce, Ely, Minn., named 'Coolest Small Town in America' by Arthur Frommer's Budget Travel, May 25, 2010, via PR Newswire.

5 K. Strauss, Pecha sounds off as council term draws to a close, *Ely Timberjay*, August 26, 2006.

6 Interview 35.

7 Interview 27.

8 Interview 32.

9 See A. Masloski, City sees future in an old agreement, *Ely Timberjay*, October 25, 2008. Mayor Chuck Novak, shortly before losing re-election, proposed to annex 940 acres under the 1973 agreement after Morse Township had earlier insisted on the long-term sharing of tax revenues.

116 *Ely: Infrastructure Delivered*

10 Average annual pay in natural resources and mining in St. Louis and Itasca Counties in Minnesota, almost entirely accounted for by iron ore mining, was $76,970 in St. Louis County and $67,351 in Itasca County for 2008. Sources: Bureau of Labor Statistics, series ID numbers ENU270615051011 for Itasca County and ENU271375051011 for St. Louis County.

11 Sources: Bureau of Labor Statistics, series ID numbers ENU270611051011 (Itasca County, Minnesota natural resources and mining employment) and ENU271371051011 (St. Louis County, Minnesota natural resources and mining employment), detail total employment of 4,300 annualized full-time equivalent jobs in 2001, declining to 3,791 jobs in 2008 and rising to 4,500 by 2015. Immediately prior to the collapse of LTV Steel Mining in 2001 total headcount was about 5,400 on an annualized basis. Employment temporarily declined by almost a half during the 2008–9 recession due to short-term layoffs and furloughs, but most of these workers have been called back.

12 For examples, see B. Kelleher, A bad year for mining, Minnesota Public Radio, December 27, 2001; accessed at http://news.minnesota.publicradio. org/features/200112/27_kelleherb_steel-m.

13 *Ely Timberjay*, January 13, 2001.

14 Source: National Century for Education Statistics, School district demographics system; accessed at http://nces.ed.gov/surveys/sdds/singledemoprofile.asp? county1=2711520&state1=27.

15 Sources: October 2006 interview with Tom Coombe, for 1977 data; Independent School District 696, Review and comment, for 2010 facility improvements; September 1, 2010, correspondence to the Minnesota Department of Children, Families and Learning, for current enrollment data; Independent School District 696, Board meeting minutes, September 2015.

16 Source: Minnesota Office of the State Auditor, State local government aid and total current expenditures as reported by the city of Ely.

17 Interview 10.

18 Ely had 4,923 residents in the 1980 census, 3,968 in 1990, 3,724 in 2000, 3,460 in 2010 and an estimated 3,390 by 2016.

19 See, for example, D. Bliss, Planning Commission approves Du Nord project, *Ely Timberjay*, December 19, 1997.

20 Interview 26; a local business owner cites zoning policy and increasing demand for high-end cabins as factors in the conversion of former resorts – and notes the economic impact.

21 US Department of Transportation, Passenger travel facts and figures 2015.

22 K. Strauss, Ely area festivals bright spots in so-so tourist season, *Ely Timberjay*, September 13, 2003.

23 *Ely Timberjay*, Blues Fest says goodbye to Ely, November 20, 2009. A festival organizer, Mary Cich, described the move away from Ely as "unfortunate" and attributed it to the failure of the city to provide logistical support such as permitting and available sites, calling it "a symptom of a much bigger problem for the area."

24 See sales tax data from the Minnesota Department of Revenue: gross retail sales dropped from $103 million in 1998, more than double 1990 levels, to $99.9 million in 2005. Hibbing's gross sales rose during the same period from $496 million to $661 million; Duluth's, the biggest regional retail center, from $2.7 billion to $4.4 billion.

Ely: Infrastructure Delivered 117

25 Both the IRRRB and Minnesota's Department of Employment and Economic Development were significant shareholders in Duluth Metals and each lost around $284,000 after the decline in share price; however, officials say that stock warrants carry far more upside investment opportunity and lower risk than the alternative of lending money to mining firms. See J. Meyers, IRRRB, DEED lost big bucks on Duluth Metals stock, *Duluth News Tribune*, January 31, 2015; accessed at www.duluthnewstribune.com/news/ 3669036-irrrb-deed-lost-big-bucks-duluth-metals-stock.

26 Based on 2000 census US zip code tabulation areas for 55731 (Ely) and 55796 (Winton); US Census Bureau.

27 See Minn. Statute §§469.090–469.1081. Under a 1987 reorganization of state law, Chapter 469 handles all statutes pertaining to economic development.

28 City of Ely Resolution 1993–9. In 2008 the Ely City Council additionally delegated powers conferred by the Housing Act (Chapter 462C, Minnesota Code) for making or purchasing mortgage or rehabilitation loans to finance the acquisition or rehabilitation of single-family housing by low- and moderate-income persons and families or making or purchasing loans to finance multifamily housing developments or their rehabilitation. See City Ordinance 2008–212, adopted April 2008.

29 See K. Strauss, Ely looks toward airport jobs, *Ely Timberjay*, January 3, 2004. At the time, city clerk John Tourville was negotiating with Honeywell's aviation systems division and another (unnamed) firm to set up operations at Ely Airport.

30 Based on author's calculations from Iron Range Resources Board/Iron Range Resources and Rehabilitation Board biennial reports, 1994–present.

31 State Rep. Loren Solberg (DFL–Bovey) lost in the November 2, 2010, general election to Republican Carolyn McElfitrick after 28 years in office; this was the first time a Republican had won a seat in the IRRRB service area, and therefore eligibility to serve on the board as a legislator, in more than 30 years.

32 Interview 07.

33 Interview 45.

34 Interview with Tom Coombe, *Ely Echo*, October 2006.

35 Interviews 45 and 20.

36 The Blandin Foundation was established by Charles K. Blandin in 1941 and expanded dramatically following the family's sale of Blandin Paper Company in 1977. As of the end of 2015 it managed around $360 million in assets with a remit to strengthen rural Minnesota communities.

37 See Iron Range Resources and Rehabilitation Board, Biennial report to the legislature 1997–1998, pp. 20–21, for a full description of the IRRRB/Blandin Foundation program.

38 The ICCLP operated under the umbrella of the Blandin Community Leadership Program, which has been in operation since 1985. Hibbing and Chisholm partnered together for a total of 16 years from 1987 to 2003; the Ely area's participation has so far been limited only to the ICCLP.

39 See S. Stowell, Ely opts out of Economic Development Joint Powers, *Ely Timberjay*, December 11, 2010.

40 Sources: US Census Bureau and Minnesota Land Economics (University of Minnesota). Taxable market value for Fall Lake, whose 2000 population was 584, was $356 million in 2009. Estimated median household income for 2008

118 *Ely: Infrastructure Delivered*

was $58,412. For comparison, taxable market value in the city of Ely itself was $184 million in 2009, and median household income for 2008 was $33,078. Property tax data accessed through landeconomics.umn.edu.

41 In a newspaper interview upon Henning's 2004 retirement, Morse Township supervisor Jack Willis described the Joint Powers Board as "Bill Henning's vision." "He could see things were fractured here with different groups and entities fighting. It was his vision to bring people together at one table. He has given us a great vision of what we can do cooperatively for the common good and he will be sorely missed on Joint Powers." See K. Strauss, EADA's Henning will retire, *Ely Timberjay*, May 15, 2004.

42 City of Ely land use and comprehensive plan, 2016.

43 K. Strauss, Ely signs SATO lease, *Ely Timberjay*, August 19, 2000.

44 D. Bliss, SATO begins interviewing next week, *Ely Timberjay*, July 8, 2000.

45 Interviews 10 and 27. These extensively covered the impact of broadband Internet. From 27, the following comment: "Without that I don't know how we'd ever be in business; we'd be looking at satellite dishes, I guess."

46 These 300 or so residential and business customers, mostly in remote rural areas to the southeast and west of Ely, had depended for many years on wireless phone service. GTE/Citizens predecessor Contel had provided an unreliable wireless party line, with often only one or two out of 12 group lines available at any given time; Stamford, Conn.,-based GTE, upon their 1989 acquisition of Contel, upgraded the system to individual phone lines with the IMM Ultraphone, a 2400bps-capable digital wireless device, at a monthly fee of $80, five times the fee for landline users. In an area with annual bouts of –40°F winter temperatures, the Ultraphones failed at temperatures of below –25°F, and could not support more recent fax systems that "bottom out" at 4800bps. Since the successful 1999–2001 petition to force GTE and its successor Citizens and Frontier Communications to provide standard landline service and DSL, broadband Internet has been available throughout Ely's rural hinterland, reaching locations as far as 40 miles from any significant settlement.

47 See *Business North*, Project Firefly™ in Ely receives Blandin Foundation and Iron Range Resources grants, December 19, 2007, for a full press release discussing project funding in detail.

48 T. Coombe, Project Firefly lands grant award, *Ely Echo*, October 27, 2007, p. A5.

49 Interview 20.

50 A. Riebe, Iron Range towns work together to lure businesses, create jobs, *Mesabi Daily News*, August 13, 2006.

51 M. Helmberger, Joint task force struggles with mission, *Ely Timberjay*, September 30, 2006.

52 T. Coombe, EADA preps for session with legislators, *Ely Echo*, September 23, 2006.

53 T. Coombe, EADA dealing with dissension: Henderson seeks unity, says her style may not mesh with city leadership, *Ely Echo*, January 12, 2008.

54 Interview 07.

55 T. Coombe, EADA director takes aim at mayor in meeting, *Ely Echo*, December 22, 1997, pp. 1, 8.

56 Coombe, January 12, 2008.

57 S. Stowell, Nancy Larson hired for EDA spot, *Ely Timberjay*, November 22, 2008.

Ely: Infrastructure Delivered   119

58 Larson facilitated a "goal planning segment" of the Ely City Council's annual retreat, in part addressing city budget issues, in March 2009. See Ely City Council official minutes for March 4, 2009.

59 See Councilman Mark Zupec's request for JPB executive director Nancy Larson to get involved with advising the city on a program for revitalizing Ely's public housing (Housing Revitalization Pilot Program), Ely Economic Development Authority official minutes for January 20, 2009.

60 See Ely City Council official minutes for December 2, 2008, discussing grant applications to restore a historic mine head in the city.

61 Calculation using EADA 2009 budget and based on Minnesota Department of Revenue data for township tax levy.

62 Prior to entering city administration, Tourville had worked in management for Honeywell and Medtronic, and openly touted his Medtronic connections as opening a strong possibility for economic development in Ely. See K. Strauss, Ely to be included in tax-free zone application, *Ely Timberjay*, September 6, 2003.

63 A three-year term from 1996 to 1998 inclusive; then, after charter amendment, a four-year term from 1999 to 2002.

64 See S. Foss, City council inaction leaves Ely facing another loss, op-ed commentary, *Ely Timberjay*, October 16, 2004, for an extensive discussion of the debate over institutional reorganization involving the Ely city clerk's office, and the growing possibility of it at the time of Tourville's departure.

65 K. Strauss, Ely faces big government challenges in coming year, *Ely Timberjay*, January 3, 2004.

66 K. Strauss, City clerk job description gets shakeup, *Ely Timberjay*, February 5, 2005. The lack of communication described here was directly discussed by Chuck Novak, then an Ely city council member, at a public meeting on the reorganization of city government.

67 K. Strauss, City officials work toward filling clerk position, *Ely Timberjay*, January 1, 2005.

68 S. Foss, Tourville takes Virginia position, *Ely Timberjay* (online only), November 13, 2004.

69 S. Foss, Tourville gets offer from Virginia, *Ely Timberjay*, November 13, 2004.

70 K. Strauss, Tourville gets solid job rating, *Ely Timberjay*, November 20, 2004. Discussing the evaluation, Tourville said, "I feel good about the evaluation," adding: "This obviously got too personal."

71 K. Strauss, Ely council suspends public works director, head custodian, *Ely Timberjay*, December 31, 2005.

72 K. Strauss, New accountability system has its share of bumps, *Ely Timberjay*, February 24, 2007.

73 S. Stowell, Residents, councilors call Ely city hiring process into question, *Ely Timberjay*, June 9, 2007.

74 S. Stowell, Council hires new custodian in another split vote, *Ely Timberjay*, August 11, 2007.

75 S. Stowell, Hiring problems won't quit, *Ely Timberjay*, September 29, 2007.

76 S. Stowell, City administrator contract terminated, *Ely Timberjay*, December 8, 2007.

77 Former public works director Ken Hegman holds a master electricians' license – and Minnesota law requires municipal electrical utilities to have at least one master electrician on staff or working as a consultant.

120 *Ely: Infrastructure Delivered*

78 S. Stowell, City and EUC tailor two job descriptions, *Ely Timberjay*, January 19, 2008.

79 S. Stowell, Council makes choice for operations director, *Ely Timberjay*, March 1, 2008. Langowski, a former manager for Ely-based highway contractor Louis Leustek, Inc., was reportedly the only applicant in the entire field with a degree in civil engineering.

80 S. Stowell, New clerk-treasurer in town, *Ely Timberjay*, June 28, 2008.

81 D. Bliss, Sewage drains city finances, *Ely Timberjay*, April 29, 2000.

82 K. Strauss, Vote on sewage plant delayed until election, *Ely Timberjay*, October 21, 2000. See also D. Bliss, Pond may not meet standards, *Ely Timberjay*, October 28, 2000, in which claims made by sewage plant opponents about alternatives were strongly criticized by a variety of federal and state regulators and wastewater treatment industry sources.

83 Interview 20.

84 K. Strauss, City, Morse Township, moving fast toward annexation, *Ely Timberjay*, May 27, 2006.

85 Interview with Tom Coombe.

86 S. Stowell, City determines first land parcels for annexation, *Ely Timberjay*, November 1, 2008. Commercial sites included land adjacent to a former county maintenance garage as well as a site being evaluated for a hospital expansion.

87 A. Masloski, Ely–Morse annexation hits a snag, *Ely Timberjay*, August 9, 2008.

88 S. Stowell, City sees future in an old agreement, *Ely Timberjay*, October 25, 2008.

89 S. Stowell, City retools proposal for annexing township land, *Ely Timberjay*, August 23, 2008.

90 S. Stowell, Sewer extension requires annexation, *Ely Timberjay*, July 31, 2009. A survey of residents on Brisson's Point, just west of Ely, found a fifty-fifty split among them as to whether they wanted city water and sewer (the area already received city electricity).

91 Interview 45.

92 Ely City Council, Regular meeting minutes, July 21, 2015. This contains a full copy of the resolution including tax distribution arrangements between the City of Ely and Town of Morse governments. See also Minnesota of Administrative Hearings, Docket number OA-101-4, request received January 14, 2016, decision rendered January 26, 2016.

93 Interview 22.

94 See M. Helmberger, Ely touts successes for Governor Pawlenty, *Ely Timberjay*, October 25, 2003. Ely MCE office director Bob Maidl noted that, in a 1995 contest with eight private collection agencies, the MCE office had beaten them all, and estimated that the center recovered $10 for every dollar spent in office costs and salaries.

95 D. Bliss, Revenue building "within days" of construction start, *Ely Timberjay*, August 14, 1999.

96 *Ibid.*

97 Steger Mukluks' name originally comes from the former husband of owner Patti Steger: the polar explorer Will Steger, who co-led (with Ely resort owner Paul Schurke) the first unresupplied expedition to the North Pole in 1986, and whose expedition effectively provided the fledgling company with its first big client.

98 See Iron Range Resources and Rehabilitation Board, Biennial report to the legislature, 1993–1994.

99 S. Stowell, New options for city buildings, *Ely Timberjay*, January 15, 2010.

100 D. Bliss, Ely Revenue building delayed, assisted living moves forward, *Ely Timberjay*, July 10, 1999.

101 *Ibid.* Council voted six to one, with only Jerome Debeltz opposed. Debeltz, who at the time worked for Ely-Bloomenson Community Hospital, which was planning its own assisted living development, failed to recuse himself from the vote.

102 See D. Bliss, Washington Street land sale defeated, *Ely Timberjay*, June 19, 1999; and Strauss, February 5, 2005 (referring to federal loan guarantees for the rental project).

103 The first reading of the required ordinance to allow the Fedo development was tabled, three to two, with council members Debeltz, Ed Steklasa and Mayor Lolita Schnitzius voting to table, and council members Paul Kess and Dan Przybylski voting to support the ordinance. Two other council members, Terry Anderson and Roger Skraba, were absent. See *Ely Timberjay*, July 24, 1999.

104 See M. Sweet, Go-ahead given for first phase of Ely Revenue building upgrades, *Ely Timberjay*, July 31, 1999.

105 See M. Sweet, McCrea's wants Ely business park lot, *Ely Timberjay*, August 11, 1999, p. 1.

106 See T. Coombe, Assisted Living on a fast track: Spectrum moves toward construction, three buildings set to be up by July '08, *Ely Echo*, November 17, 2007.

107 See Iron Range Resources and Rehabilitation Board, Meeting minutes, May 12, 2015.

References

Eisinger, P. K. (1988). *The rise of the entrepreneurial state: State and local economic development policy in the United States.* Madison, Wis.: University of Wisconsin Press.

Proescholdt, K., Rapson, R., & Heinselman, M. L. (1995). *Troubled waters: The fight for the Boundary Waters Canoe Area Wilderness.* St. Cloud, Minn.: North Star Press of St. Cloud.

5 Hibbing, Minnesota

The Evolution of Activist Development

The city of Hibbing may be best known across the United States for having more than its fair share of the nation's pop culture icons (see Figure 5.1). It is the childhood home of Bob Dylan, the birthplace of former Boston Celtics star and Minnesota Timberwolves general manager Kevin McHale, one-time baseball home-run king Roger Maris, and Charles Manson prosecutor Vincent Bugliosi, and the place where Greyhound started its first bus route. Within Minnesota, it has a broader and sometimes notorious reputation in politics and in economic development. Long the Iron Range's largest city, it is the home of a giant opencast iron ore mine, seven miles long and as much as three miles wide, that combines the historic and still productive Hull–Rust–Mahoning pit, designated a National Historical Monument in 1966 for its huge share of America's high-grade iron ore in the Second World War, with the more recent Hibbing Taconite pit. Politically, it conjures up an additional set of images. The home of Minnesota's longest-serving governor, Rudy Perpich (in office from 1976 to 1979, and again from 1983 to 1991), Hibbing has had an outsized influence on state politics for a city that peaked at just over 21,000 in population, anchoring the Iron Range in its traditional role as an area whose huge election turnouts would roll close statewide elections, notably Perpich's political comeback in the form of his upset 1982 primary win. In this stronghold of organized labor and big employers, that influence has been heavily wielded on behalf of Democrats over the past 70 years. There are also negative stereotypes: hardball politics; the economic boom and bust that goes with any mining town; and the catastrophic recession of the early 1980s, which delivered the area a setback from which it has yet to fully recover. Here is the context of big-ticket economic development policy and its gamut of successes and failures, most notoriously with a chopsticks factory promoted by Perpich that never successfully produced chopsticks.

That Hibbing has made considerable progress over the years on economic development is often lost not only on people elsewhere in the state but even among the city's own residents. In 2007 the city took the step, unique among this group of cases, of hiring a branding consultant to

Figure 5.1 Fourth of July parade on Howard Street in Hibbing, late 1940s
Source: Hibbing Historical Society.

improve its image – a campaign aimed at residents and local businesses as well as the outside world.[1] But both the aggressiveness and the concern over self-image that this move implied were symbols of a change in policy that had been in train for almost a decade. Still another turn came in 2010, when, in the aftermath of the massive mining industry layoffs that accompanied the Great Recession, voters turned out the existing administration and its approach of a corporatized, public–private partnership in economic development in favor of more direct city council involvement, greater transparency and a broader community development agenda. Those results have been mixed, with those who lost the 2010 election expressing concerns that economic development has been blunted, those who won, along with Iron Range Resources and Rehabilitation Board (IRRRB) officials, suggesting the new approach is also paying dividends, and with many long-term trends continuing to be in evidence. The previous administration's commercial and retail development policies have continued, and, while the town's only mall continues to decline as of 2017, standalone retail development has strengthened and a long-awaited goal of a new conference hotel has been fulfilled.

124 *Hibbing, Minnesota: Evolution of Activist Development*

Recent History: A Reputation for Failure, an Effort to Reform

If one were to ignore politics, or arbitrary boundaries or the organization of government, and look instead at control factors, Hibbing would look remarkably like Ely were it not for the fact that it is bigger. The city faces many similar challenges: sub-par personal income; the out-migration of youth; an aged population; a relative lack of college-educated individuals, or jobs that require a four-year or graduate degree; and considerable dependence on cyclical industries. And what Hibbing has that Ely does not – a major iron mine and extensive manufacturing in its city limits[2] – is offset at least in part by other factors, such as a weak tourism sector and a generally lower proportion of white-collar employment (see Table 5.1).[3] Indeed, Hibbing depends heavily on boom-and-bust employment sectors such as the iron mining industry, and has carried the additional burden of a highly visible political reputation in the region and even the state for dysfunction and policy failure.

Hibbing's image problems with economic development are closely connected with the city's flailing efforts in the 1980s, which mirrored many across northern Minnesota, to combat a wave of unemployment and business failures. In the 1960s and 1970s, with the boom in taconite mining, central St. Louis County, reaching from Hibbing on the western boundary to Babbitt 70 miles east, had some of the highest median incomes in the state of Minnesota. When the collapse of the US steel industry in the 1981–82 recession effectively furloughed the taconite industry as well, it

Table 5.1 Comparison of Ely and Hibbing industrial-sector profiles

Occupational category (percentages of total employment)	City of Hibbing	City of Ely
Agriculture/forestry/fishing/mining	9.0%	6.4%
Construction	7.0%	6.6%
Manufacturing	10.4%	3.1%
Wholesale trade	2.8%	1.3%
Retail trade	12.0%	18.8%
Transportation/utilities	5.1%	5.1%
Information	0.9%	0.4%
Finance/insurance/real estate	5.7%	2.6%
Professional services	7.4%	8.0%
Education, health and social services	23.7%	17.7%
Arts, recreation, hotels, restaurants	8.1%	19.7%
Other	4.8%	4.5%
Public administration	3.0%	5.6%

Note: Non-mining activities in the agriculture/forestry/fishing/mining category account for 0.3 percent in Hibbing, 0.8 percent in Ely.
Source: American Community Survey, 2015 data, table S2403, Industry by sex for the civilian employed population 16 years and over.

Hibbing, Minnesota: Evolution of Activist Development   125

profoundly affected the Range cities, whether or not they still had active mining (long-distance commuting has been a fact of life here for several decades). Mechanization during the recovery ensured previous production levels could be reached with only around a quarter of the employees.

Perpich, the state's last Democratic governor for 20 years until Mark Dayton's narrow 2010 victory, was closely involved with efforts to trigger economic recovery. In 1982, with the recession slamming Minnesota, Perpich won an upset victory in the Democratic primary in September, and then six weeks later easily dispatched incumbent Republican Al Quie (to whom he had lost four years earlier in the devastating Democratic defeat known as the "Minnesota Massacre"),[4] and back in office he pursued a highly activist economic development policy. Perpich oversaw major successes in the Minneapolis–St. Paul metro area but often struggled, despite strenuous efforts, to find answers for rural Minnesota. He eventually picked up the media sobriquet "Governor Goofy" for his malapropisms, off-the-cuff remarks and occasionally eccentric ideas about economic development, which included support for bringing the Winter Olympics to Minnesota.[5] If nothing else, he and his IRRRB staff were as committed to the wellbeing of the community and its surroundings as they were associated with missteps.

Hibbing's reputation suffered further as it became the site of one of the most notorious of Perpich's projects, a prominent and expensive failure of economic development policy in which his IRRRB[6] commissioner, Gary Lamppa, was also deeply involved. This was the board's ill-fated attempt to land for the Range a business that aimed to bring North American mass production ingenuity to an Asian cottage industry: chopsticks manufacturing. Canadian timber producer Lakewood Industries had the idea of filling demand in the fast food utensils market in east Asia by at least augmenting the small-scale manufacturers of chopsticks that dominate that market with the mass production of chopsticks from the wood of northern Minnesota's aspen forests, an ideal raw material for the product. The company found a willing partner in Lamppa, who saw the market opportunity: the promise of at least 95 new jobs and strong advance product sales.[7] But the plan failed miserably when automated equipment in the plant that awkwardly straddled the definitions of "cutting-edge" and "experimental" failed to produce usable chopsticks in production quantities (a high percentage of them were splintering, including many that passed automated quality control). By the time the project was abandoned, in July 1989,[8] Lakewood Industries summed up every stereotype of economic development on the Iron Range: big budget, grandiose vision, abject failure. It was costly to the reputation of Hibbing and the Iron Range, in the words of Minnesota Public Radio reporter Bob Kelleher being seen statewide as a "poster-project" for the IRRRB's failures,[9] and seen locally as an example of how economic development funds were easily wasted.[10] Most importantly, it was an expensive mistake; it took with it some $5 million

126 *Hibbing, Minnesota: Evolution of Activist Development*

in taxpayer funds, and the factory built by the IRRRB for Lakewood has since had several short-term tenancies punctuated by periods of sitting vacant.

Boondoggles are not the only reputation Hibbing has in economic development. Other incidents besides Lakewood include a past pattern of sharp-elbowed competition for new projects with neighboring cities,[11] skepticism about the effectiveness of economic development,[12] fierce protection of local retailers against outsiders[13] and unseemly shenanigans on the city council. But worse was to follow. In 1992 leaders of the city employees' local union sued Mayor Jim Collins, city clerk Ray Sogard and city council members Frank Modich and Steve Saban over serial violations of the Minnesota Open Meeting Law, due to their repeated addition of unrelated agenda items to meetings that were ostensibly closed to discuss a labor dispute. The state Supreme Court's decision in that case in June 1994 disqualified all but Modich from public office (the first time that public officials in Minnesota had been disqualified for illegally closing meetings) and forced interim appointments to serve through the fall general election.[14]

Even with a largely new city council, a favorite son could not make a major development deal happen due to what a Hibbing survey respondent described as "too many people involved, not enough of them willing to make the deal work."[15] A fractious dispute on the council over business subsidies in 1997 and 1998 led Hibbing native Jeno Paulucci, the owner of frozen food processor Luigino's and former CEO of R. J. Reynolds (to which he had sold an earlier business in the 1960s), to pass on the former chopsticks factory as a location for his nationally marketed Michelina's frozen food brand in favor of a heavily state-subsidized facility in West Virginia.[16] Perhaps the city's then economic development director, Duane Northagen, summed it up best in a December 2007 hearing on a new initiative to "rebrand" Hibbing for marketing the city as an economic development haven. "Hibbing's brand is our reputation; it's what people say about us both inside and outside our city lines," the minutes of the meeting state. "Hibbing's current reputation could use some work, both internally and externally. The city's reputation clouds that perception of being a truly great city both in our citizens' minds and in greater Minnesota."[17]

But by this point, in the mid-2000s, Hibbing had changed its whole approach to economic development. Simply considering such a strategy as "branding," with its connotations of commercialization, commoditization and concern over public image, demonstrated how far city leadership had already moved away in practice from this past reputation. By the time Northagen made his successful case for branding, in 2007,[18] the city had systematized economic development policy in a proactive and technocratic manner, not unlike the approach favored by professionals in the field. Perhaps the most visible example has been the city's aggressive push during the 2000s to promote retailing, including extensive market research, providing city-owned land at below cost to chain retailers, rezoning residential areas for retail, marketing nationwide at industry trade shows and even including neighboring cities formerly seen as rivals in their research and marketing efforts. The city's interventionist economic development policies have also assisted expansions by locally owned manufacturing employers that have helped offset substantial job losses from the 2001–2 recession. Two firms, heating and cooling component manufacturer L&M Radiator and oil pipeline manufacturer Iracore International, have more than doubled in size, supported by Hibbing's own industrial loan fund, the Economic Development Special Revenue Fund (EDSRF), but also by low-interest financing from state funds.

The city has even dabbled, with IRRRB backing, in speculative development in recent years. The Hibbing Economic Development Authority (HEDA) and the city council enthusiastically supported the construction of an office and light industrial building in 2007 at Chisholm-Hibbing Airport's[19] (now Range Regional Airport's) aviation services business park, the Hibbing Airpark. This project proved more of a marathon than a sprint. The building was authorized in 2006 and ready for use in 2007, but not until 2013–14 did the buildout and expansion of DMR Electronics, part of heavy engine re-manufacturer Detroit Reman, occur, backed by $7.5 million in direct IRRRB loans in 2012 and 2013 in addition to the $1.625 million loan to the airport authority to build the shell in the first place in 2006–7.[20]

Delays apart, Hibbing was, in the late 2000s, meeting its own policy goals on economic development and in the process delivering positive results for citizens and satisfying key community leaders. The murkier but more important question in Hibbing is how closely this major progress on building consensus and delivering economic development, often assisted by the IRRRB, is linked to institutional organization and reform at City Hall. This point was amplified when Mayor Rick Wolff unexpectedly lost his bid for a third term in 2010 to a mineworker and union official with no previous elected experience, Rick Cannata, who campaigned on skepticism about existing policy and promised a more consensual but also more open process. The result, much like events in Ely, appears to have been connected with public concerns over the effectiveness of city government and community development, with Cannata's multigenerational roots in the community possibly also a factor. For one thing, incidents in economic development that stained Hibbing's reputation, whether failing to deliver policies or trying to deliver policies that failed, did not cease with major changes in city government, such as consolidation with the surrounding township in 1979 or the emergence of the city's economic development authority separate from the city council. And the success of the mid-2000s in delivering economic development came to an abrupt halt with the Great Recession.

Some key parts of the process in Hibbing have consensus support and have been retained under Cannata and city administrator Tom Dicklich, appointed in 2011 after the contract of the previous administrator, Brian

128 *Hibbing, Minnesota: Evolution of Activist Development*

Redshaw, was not renewed. Part of this may be related to the personalities involved; the low-key and locally raised Dicklich, whose father, Ron Dicklich, was a long-time Democratic state senator and briefly Hibbing mayor in the mid-1990s, made a sharp contrast to the more vocal and staunchly conservative Redshaw, who was from Iowa. In any case, the continuity of the policies is evident. This includes HEDA's institutional stability and access to capital, such as loan assistance to businesses and the long-term relationships with local manufacturers. Even the new policies of the mid-2000s – notably the retail market analysis and recruitment initiative – have had broad enough political support[21] to stay in effect.

Hibbing's Economic Development: An Established Process, an Economy that Fits State Agendas, but Consensus Is a Challenge

In terms of its mechanisms for formulating and delivering economic development policy, and public policy in general, Hibbing differs from Ely in several key respects. Hibbing fits the model of an "adapted city" in terms of moving part-way toward a more streamlined and centralized management structure. It has a more deeply institutionalized process for handling economic development, a simpler committee structure than Ely and a steady rate of output in terms of private-sector economic development. But Hibbing also has an important advantage beyond its control: its economy – far larger than Ely's, in reflection of its greater population – better fits regional and state agendas for economic development in terms of both scale and function. The IRRRB's board structure, with mostly legislators backed by larger labor unions, has a majority of politicians with ties of some kind to labor in the mining industry and its support services, both of which sectors are heavily represented in Hibbing. Particularly important to note is the nature of Hibbing's economic development policy outcomes, which have arisen either from recent initiatives with broad political support[22] or from long-term, well-rooted relationships with local business.

With regard to institutions, leadership, local and intergovernmental processes for delivering policy, and results, Hibbing's governmental configuration can be summarized as follows. First, overall city governance is relatively traditional: Minnesota's statutory standard plan weak mayor-council government, with a directly elected mayor, no home-rule status, five council members each elected from a single ward, and an elected city clerk. Not only is there no city manager, there are no at-large council members either. (The city has obtained legislative authorization for, and approved a change to, a modified form of Minnesota Optional Plan A, a weak mayor-council government with an appointed clerk, four ward members and two at-large members, to take effect for the November 2018 election).[23] But, second, much of the city's economic development function has been delegated away from the political pressures of an elected council, an arrangement that has been stable for a generation through major political change.

HEDA sits separately from the council, including only three representatives from the city council (the mayor, clerk and one ward member) among its seven-person membership, and has jurisdiction over the EDSRF, whose purpose is to assist private employers with capital investment. Additionally, the Chisholm-Hibbing Airport Authority (CHAA), a six-member joint powers board with the neighboring city of Chisholm that supervises Range Regional Airport on Hibbing's southeast side, also undertakes economic development activity due to the large amount of land under its control and synergies with the airport itself.

Closer examination reveals further provisions in Hibbing's governance structure that, in practice, tend to establish continuity in public policy and lower political conflict. A city administrator supervises general services and infrastructure; and a public utilities superintendent supervises electrical, water, sewage and steam heat services[24] and works with HEDA on managing economic development projects and business recruitment. Although Hibbing has not made a full transition to a council-manager system of government, day-to-day decision-making is in practice more delegated than in Ely due to the substantial power held by HEDA, CHAA, their respective executive directors and the city administrator. Thus, the city council is more policy-oriented in matters related to economic development, and less preoccupied with day-to-day management. In practice, the Hibbing council exhibits more consensus than Ely too, in line with findings in the public administration field of lower levels of conflict within municipal government associated with "reformed" government (Folz & French, 2005; Nelson & Nollenberger, 2011).

But this level of reform did not, on its own, appear to produce significant change; it seems to have been more of a prerequisite. Changes in policy have been gradual and did not fully emerge until several years later, especially after the 2002 election. That election brought a slate of leadership in city government that shared similar ideas on economic development: Mayor Wolff, a strong advocate of interventionist economic development policy; and increasing consensus. But, when Wolff lost his bid for a third term in office, the responsibilities of HEDA and CHAA did not significantly change. The clear implication is that these institutions within Hibbing government have helped to produce a public policy characterized by consistency with gradual, but steady, trends toward more proactive economic development and even cooperation with neighboring jurisdictions on big-ticket infrastructure projects (despite notable failures).

Hibbing city government has one further advantage over Ely. Although both cities draw heavily on state aid for local government operations, Hibbing's local property tax levy entered the current era of declining state aid at a much lower level per capita than property taxes in Ely. Part of the story was a lower rate of spending on infrastructure and economic development than in Ely during the 1990s and 2000s (though that has recently changed), and resulting lower debt, with the city's Moody's

130 *Hibbing, Minnesota: Evolution of Activist Development*

rating improving steadily from Baa1 in 1998 to Aa3 by 2012. In any case, Hibbing had more room than Ely to adapt to the substantial cuts in state support during the 2000s.[25] Hibbing's tax levy for 2000 of $3.5 million[26] was around double Ely's despite the city having approximately five times the population, giving the city more room to adapt to the abolition of HACA (Homestead and Agricultural Credit Aid) and reductions in Local Government Aid under the Pawlenty administration. Even in 2006 and 2007, the peak of the economic cycle, Hibbing's levies were $4.5 million and $4.9 million, respectively, out of a total 2006 budget of $15.6 million and 2007 budget of $16 million, making for a modest property tax burden and continued substantial state support despite heavy cuts in aid.[27] Almost a decade later spending had dropped significantly in inflation-adjusted terms but intergovernmental support played a stronger role. Total spending in 2016 of $17.4 million, approximately four times that of Ely or around 20 percent lower on a per capita basis, was supported by almost $8.1 million in LGA, a property levy of just $3.75 million, almost $2.2 million in taconite aid (which has long substituted property tax on the area's mines), $249,000 for licenses and permits, over $2.05 million in charges for services, $456,000 in earmarked intergovernmental support for police, fire and community development and over $612,000 in other categories, including fines and rents.[28]

Governance of Economic Development in Hibbing

In economic development, administration and governance in Hibbing differ from Ely in some respects. First, most key decisions are not made entirely by council members, as the statutory EDA, the Hibbing Economic Development Authority, sits separately from the council and includes both council members and private citizens. Although CHAA makes decisions regarding the airport outside HEDA's jurisdiction, and the city council's oversight, HEDA's recommendations in recent years have in practice almost all been accepted. While some Hibbing and regional officials speak longingly and enviously of Ely's strengths, for example in areas ranging from public infrastructure to large-scale and long-term support for the arts, they speak proudly of their own success in the long-standing pattern of technical and financial support for local businesses that has survived multiple political changes on the city council.

Second, Hibbing's intergovernmental relations are far less complicated than Ely's. Locally, Hibbing annexed a vast surrounding area in 1979, the 173 square miles of Stuntz Township, becoming by far Minnesota's largest city by land area, and at a stroke removing most of the geographical political fragmentation, physical constraints on tax base and the shortage of developable land that bedevil Ely. Its current land area of 186.4 square miles is 68 times that of Ely. This has had a bigger impact in local Hibbing politics than in relations with other municipalities, but there are

Hibbing, Minnesota: Evolution of Activist Development 131

still notable successes with neighbors, such as joint administration of the city airport with the city of Chisholm and joint electricity generation from renewable sources with the city of Virginia.

Lastly, Hibbing also has an advantage over Ely in terms of its relationships with state leaders. Its economic structure and larger scale better fit the economic development agenda of the region's all-important state legislators and IRRRB than Ely. Its taconite mine, Hibbing Taconite, jointly owned by ArcelorMittal, Cleveland-Cliffs and US Steel, is one of the biggest recipients of IRRRB grants, and Hibbing also benefits from agency expertise in assisting several local manufacturers.[29] This is an important factor in view of what one survey respondent described as the attempt of state agencies including the IRRRB to "centralize control of a number of functions, only to the detriment of the cities and counties."[30]

The role of HEDA in city government, the role of geography in economic development since the 1979 annexation, and both local and state intergovernmental relations represent an apparently stable institutional settlement that clearly influences policy outcomes. The city council, while it oversees HEDA's activities, mainly concerns itself with city administration and services. But it also takes a role in community development and infrastructural initiatives, such as the recently successful push to renovate Hibbing's centralized steam heat utility system, the bid to provide a regional water and sewer network with neighboring cities and a joint venture in renewable energy with the nearby city of Virginia that will see both communities provided with electricity generated from burning waste wood.

The council also serves as the city's intermediary on community development projects with the IRRRB, submitting grant and loan applications and ranking projects such as street improvements and infrastructure. Thus, the city council, along with the public utilities commission, handles intergovernmental relations on public services. But the council's role in handling economic development is more limited. When required to do so by state law, it serves as the fiscal agent for economic development loans and handles necessary rezoning for new projects, supervising the Planning and Zoning Commission in the process.

Economic development operates under HEDA as the statutory economic development authority, but HEDA has more autonomy than a typical EDA, taking full advantage of the flexibility in state law on how an EDA is configured.[31] Hibbing's EDA is configured with particular attention to enabling the authority to work efficiently and at arm's length from the electorate. Unlike its counterparts in other Iron Range cities, including Ely, HEDA's membership is not coterminous with that of the city council. Rather, the authority's membership includes both citizen members and city council members, operates independently of the council for purposes that do not require access to zoning power or the general fund and works in conjunction with its own full-time executive director.

132   *Hibbing, Minnesota: Evolution of Activist Development*

Hibbing's EDA therefore plays a major role in policy formulation. This manifests itself in several ways. First, HEDA controls a significant financial resource. The EDSRF account balance, its principal source of capital for business assistance, ranged in the 2000s from around $800,000 to over $1.1 million and reached almost $1.6 million by the end of 2016, with total outstanding loans in the $400,000 to $600,000 range.[32] HEDA's decisions regarding this fund, which is used to originate "economic development loans" and enable businesses to secure matching private backing such as bank loans, are independent of the city council. Second, it is the primary point of contact for a wide range of economic and community development activity, including the provision of office and factory space, recruiting new businesses and developing affordable housing. Third, it can set its own agenda and initiate policy. It has used this capability to sharply accelerate Hibbing's push to expand retail development. HEDA, rather than the city, made the December 2008 application for $150,000 in funds from the IRRRB's recently constituted Community Business Partnership Program, which provides grants to the many Range cities that have low-interest loan programs for storefront renovations and expansions.[33] Additionally, the city of Hibbing's share of the $40,000 market research study involved with the retail policy, the Retail Market Analysis Study of Hibbing ("Retail-MASH"), was commissioned and paid for directly by HEDA,[34] and public hearings were organized by the consultants working in conjunction with HEDA in October 2006 just a month after the contract was placed.

HEDA's autonomy is also demonstrated by its status as a major landlord and property developer in Hibbing. It owns more than two dozen office and factory buildings, ranging from the Airpark Spec Building[35] (a speculative office and light industrial development near the main airport terminal that stood vacant for several years after its construction until buildout for its tenant in 2013) to the building on Hibbing Community College's South Campus that was vacated when Reptron Electronics, a circuit board manufacturer that was locally owned for many years, closed down. HEDA, rather than the city council, also manages Hibbing's bid to provide public-sector support to expanding the supply of family-oriented housing. In this case, an IRRRB program goes directly through HEDA rather than the city council[36] – the IRRRB's policy of offering subsidies of up to $10,000 per housing unit for new construction – in line with state statutes that give cities the option of enabling an EDA to assume the functions typically handled by a public housing authority or directly by a city council.

The Special Role of Hibbing's Geography

Hibbing's institutional organization marks several important contrasts with Ely, but it is not the only factor affecting the city's abilities to originate

Hibbing, Minnesota: Evolution of Activist Development 133

and deliver public policy. Hibbing's civic geography is also unique, in that it includes the vast majority of the surrounding area that is economically tied to the community, as opposed to having tightly drawn boundaries beyond which lie areas of fragmented governmental responsibility. In 1979, in a deal brokered in part by city clerk Pat Garrity (Hibbing's city clerk from 1974 to 1990, 1994 to 2002 and since 2006), the city of Hibbing undertook the biggest annexation in Minnesota history, absorbing 173 square mile Stuntz Township and in a single stroke becoming Minnesota's largest municipality by land area. The city's elimination of at-large council seats, unusual in a smaller town, stems from this massive annexation. Under the current population distribution, three seats are entirely within the former town-site, one is split between former Hibbing and former Stuntz and one is almost entirely within the former township. The former Stuntz Township is effectively guaranteed representation on the city council but denied the possibility of controlling a majority.

This reconfigured political geography has had direct effects on economic development. Major assets such as the airport and the Airpark are well within the post-1979 Hibbing city limits, and therefore do not require cooperation among governments on land use and zoning. The vexed question Ely has faced of whether to extend city utilities outside corporate limits does not apply here as it does in municipalities with boundaries that are more typical of US standards. Rather, Hibbing effectively applies city planning, land use and infrastructure management over an area at least a third of the size of a typical Midwestern county and comparable to that of many small town or rural district authorities in Europe. The city controls land at the airport not merely as a developer and owner but also as a zoning and taxing authority; using the same powers, it has undertaken infrastructural development in the rural area, such as expansion of the sewer and water system, without having to negotiate with township governments.

Lastly, expanded political geography broadens the pool of leadership in Hibbing. The business leaders of the community mostly live within the city limits, in part because living outside them entails a substantial commute. Therefore, they can, and do, participate on city boards and commissions that typically require city residency. In contrast, many Ely business leaders live in the unincorporated townships or even beyond, giving them little influence on the city committees where key decisions take shape. While the city charter allows for non-residents to serve on boards and commissions so long as they do not form a voting majority, the general practice has been for most such appointments to be on boards and commissions that provide services in conjunction with or located in neighboring townships, the primary examples being the Ely Library Board (which is partly funded by township revenues) and Ely Airport Commission (with Ely Municipal Airport being in Morse Township).

134 *Hibbing, Minnesota: Evolution of Activist Development*

Governance of Economic Development with Hibbing's Neighbors

Hibbing has not historically been known for its cooperativeness with neighboring communities, a fact community leaders acknowledge.[37] Several survey respondents complained that the city had an insufficiently regional outlook on both economic development assistance to business and community development schemes such as housing and infrastructure. Even today, long memories ensure that the city's reputation among other Range cities remains somewhat questionable. One example is the critical news coverage that greeted Hibbing City Council's 2008 decision to effectively kill the IRRRB's latest bid to expand the region's fiber optic network;[38] Hibbing's central position in the network ensured that the project stood or fell on its approval rather than that of the IRRRB.

Not all the ambitions for cooperation on infrastructure management have been fulfilled. The city of Hibbing co-founded two major joint powers boards that aimed ambitiously to tackle electricity generation and sewerage disposal, respectively, on a regional basis rather than a local one. One, the Central Iron Range Sewer and Sanitary District (CIRSSD), would have produced a partnership between Hibbing, Chisholm, Kinney and Buhl, as well as Balkan and Great Scott Townships, to rebuild the area's sewer system as a single regional entity. The goal was to replace failing sewer plants in the smaller communities with connections to Hibbing's two plants, both of which were being enlarged anyway. Hibbing's pivotal initial role in CIRSSD was enabled in part by the Stuntz annexation, meaning the public utility could directly connect all bordering communities without crossing any township territory or having to undertake any new annexation, while also accessing rural areas of the city that previously lacked utilities. But CIRSSD now has proceeded without Hibbing, leaving the smaller communities to build their own plant, due to intense opposition to the original scheme by Hibbing residents who live near one of the city plants. These opponents, known as the "Down Winders," feared increased air pollution and bad smells from the increased volume of sewage and also pointed to the risk of cost overruns, and started aggressively lobbying the city council in fall 2008. By the following spring, council support for the project had collapsed, and at the end of April 2009 the council voted unanimously (with one absent member) to leave CIRSSD.[39]

However, regional cooperation has grown in other areas. The Laurentian Energy Authority (LEA) is a cooperative venture with the city of Virginia 20 miles east of Hibbing that, for the first time, gives these two municipal utilities home-owned power generation capacity through biomass electrical plants that run on discarded pulp wood from the timber industry. Both utilities already provide sewerage, water supply, electrical distribution and even central steam heat for the many homes and businesses in both cities that lack their own furnaces. Now they are in an $80 million joint venture to fuel cogeneration of electric power in both cities, having bought out another company's contract to provide renewable electricity to statewide utility Xcel Energy. The project was at first supported through utility bills in both cities and by major grant funding from the IRRRB and directly from the state of Minnesota. But, in 2013, the project received a further boost when the Minnesota legislature passed price parity regulations requiring Xcel to pay equal rates to all three of its biomass providers (Laurentian and two others in the Twin Cities metropolitan area)[40] as well as requiring Xcel to reimburse LEA for fuel costs for delivering biomass to the Hibbing and Virginia plants and preventing it from charging LEA for "costs which were not actually and reasonably incurred" by Xcel.[41] This change is estimated to have saved Hibbing and Virginia ratepayers $1.4 million a year.

Although CIRSSD eventually proceeded without Hibbing, the cooperation that led to the formation of CIRSSD itself arose from an institution – the Central Iron Range Initiative – that included the same municipalities as members, and that has itself participated in economic development. CIRI proved to be the vehicle by which Hibbing, in early 2007, included its neighbors in the Retail-MASH initiative, despite having explicitly "gone it alone" until that point. HEDA's unanimous vote authorizing a regional Retail-MASH included both long-time advocates and earlier skeptics of regional cooperation.[42] For the city that once chased away the local branch of department store chain Herberger's to nearby Virginia in a futile attempt to protect a local retailer, this represented a dramatic change in policy, in outlook and in institutional capacity and confidence.

The CIRI involvement in the retail study is notable because Hibbing had, until then, tended to avoid cooperation with its neighbors in recruiting and retaining private business, to the point that several survey respondents still complained the city was uncooperative, "not a team player" in economic development policy. The "Hibbing first" outlook played out during the recruitment of a major Northwest Airlines reservations center, when the city of Hibbing simply quoted one general hospital on the airline's questionnaire for inventorying local services and amenities – Fairview Range Medical Center, in Hibbing – while Chisholm, without a hospital in the city limits but promoting the area's regionwide resources as assets, quoted two: Fairview and also Virginia's municipally owned Virginia Regional Medical Center.[43] Chisholm landed that reservations center, with some 300 jobs, and it has survived numerous corporate restructurings and downsizing efforts as well as the merger of Northwest with Delta Air Lines.

In an interesting postscript, the city's airport, which for many years has been jointly managed by the Chisholm-Hibbing Airport Authority, which includes representatives from the city of Hibbing, HEDA and the city of Chisholm, has been the subject of a regional shift in marketing that may reflect the lessons of the airline call center project. The IATA code on your checked baggage tag still reads "HIB" but the title "Range Regional

136　*Hibbing, Minnesota: Evolution of Activist Development*

Airport" has replaced "Chisholm-Hibbing Airport" on all public documents and mentions of the facility, as well as on the terminal building.

But Hibbing's economic development efforts have a more intriguing feature as well. They do not necessarily follow the perceived imperative of building the tax base. The city has no local option sales tax, and, under Minnesota law, no realistic option for getting one; and the emphasis on landing "good-paying jobs" is more reminiscent of a community that depends on local income taxes than a Minnesota municipality that draws upon property taxes and state aid (Pagano, 2003). Rather, it is more generally oriented toward local political preferences, which means boosting the job base and improving the supply of amenities in the community. This is most visible with Hibbing's aggressive push to recover its former status as a major regional retail center, as well as its close cooperation with the IRRRB on industrial development.

The State's Role in Hibbing Economic Development

The state of Minnesota is an integral part of economic development policy in local government throughout the Iron Range, and Hibbing is no exception. Where Hibbing stands out, however, is in the level of activity it shows in making use of state programs. One such example is the state-designated tax breaks under the Job Opportunity Building Zones program during the Pawlenty administration. This program, almost ignored in Ely due to the lack of a suitable project despite JOBZ designation for both the Ely Business Park and airport, has been applied at several sites in Hibbing.

But even here the impact of JOBZ was limited. The eligible acreage under the JOBZ program was limited compared to the Illinois enterprise zone program, the program ended at the end of 2015 after only 12 years in use, and governance was by the individual city, not by a geography of the city or cities' choosing, as in Illinois. Five locations in Hibbing were designated under JOBZ: the undeveloped portions of North Hibbing Industrial Park; a site on the Beltline highway that includes a disused elementary school and the now closed Central Campus building of Hibbing Community College (which recently developed a new campus); the undeveloped portion of the Airpark, the aviation services business park at Range Regional Airport; and the former Reptron Electronics property neighboring the Airpark, now partly occupied by the metal fabricating firm Cast Corporation. Only the Cast property saw employment growth clearly attributable to the JOBZ program, with the 14 positions representing a net increase of six over its previous staffing level in Buhl.[44] Applications for JOBZ designation involving L&M, Iracore and aviation services provider TNT Airworks came after projects had already been committed.

The principal successes in economic development arising from state government aid have been from more traditional grant and loan programs from state agencies, primarily very strong support from the IRRRB in

Hibbing, Minnesota: Evolution of Activist Development 137

Hibbing's case. Furthermore, Hibbing's funding is more tilted than Ely's toward economic development projects as opposed to general infrastructure, due in part to its applications and needs more closely fitting the agency's agenda. Besides the millions in rebated production taxes every year that go to Hibbing Taconite along with the other taconite producers, Hibbing has enjoyed consistent success in getting IRRRB grants. Today's IRRRB economic development grants tend to be smaller than the ill-fated support of Lakewood Industries but the agency is still a major player in economic development in this, the largest town in the agency's service area and among the most driven by mining, and in Hibbing recent grants and loans from the IRRRB include the following:[45]

- Grant assistance of $150,000 in 2009 from the Community Business Partnership Program, a new IRRRB program to support cities that provide low-interest loans for retailers to renovate and/or expand their businesses; Hibbing's Storefront Loan Program is the principal beneficiary.
- A grant of $1.16 million from the IRRRB's Forest Industry Assistance Program to subsidize the Laurentian Energy Authority's purchases of waste timber to fuel biomass electrical generation plants serving Hibbing and Virginia. Laurentian Energy Authority is a joint partnership of the two cities.
- The demolition of more than 30 disused buildings in Hibbing, as well as nearby Chisholm and Coleraine, in 2008, under a long-standing IRRRB program for removing blighted structures.
- A total of more than $4.7 million in production tax rebates in 2007 and 2008 to Hibbing Taconite, earmarked for investment and upgrades in the facility, and $793,000 for a tailings pond spillway and $99,000 in 2012 for mine-pit shore reclamation; a further $3.6 million in funds for improvements in 2013 and 2014.
- $400,000 in grants in 2007 and 2008 to help pay for the infrastructure for two new housing developments, a 28-unit assisted living complex and a new development containing 14 townhouses, and a further $200,000 in the 2011–12 biennium toward a $5 million project for a 30-unit senior development.
- $37,500 for a fiber-to-the-premises (FTTP) project for Internet service upgrades, in 2007.
- $150,000 for a building housing snow removal equipment at Hibbing Airport.
- A direct, low-interest loan of $835,000, covering the entire cost of the new speculative office building at the Hibbing Airpark, in 2007.
- A $1.5 million "participation loan" (a loan with equity privileges for the IRRRB) helping to leverage bank financing for an $8.8 million project by Industrial Rubber, Inc., to expand a plant with 86 employees by another 20 positions.

138   *Hibbing, Minnesota: Evolution of Activist Development*

- A $4 million direct loan to the Laurentian Energy Authority, supporting LEA's $62 million project to build biomass power generation stations. During the 2007–8 biennium Laurentian received a total of $8 million (the city of Virginia's share being the other $4 million), more than two-thirds of the total IRRRB lending activity for the biennium.
- $250,000 toward a half-million-dollar project in 2012 to provide solar power at the Hibbing Public Library.
- $400,000 toward hanger remodeling at the airport, around 13 percent of total cost.
- $950,000 in 2013 and 2014 toward redevelopment of Highway 169 in Hibbing to improve commercial access.

The IRRRB's activity thus dominates the economic development scene in Hibbing, as it does elsewhere on the Iron Range, in part through the sheer variety of its entrepreneurial initiatives. But, thanks to city and state programs working in tandem, other players in Hibbing assume considerable influence. The approximately $1 million in operating capital controlled by HEDA works to support manufacturing industry in the city, in some cases in conjunction with loans from the state's Minnesota Investment Fund. These programs have been key in helping two other firms, L&M Radiator and Hibbing Fabricators, to expand and/or re-equip.[46] As with the IRRRB's aggressive push at the end of the 1990s to reclaim financial support for the Hibbing plant of frozen food producer Luigino's (whose brands include Michelina's), the city keeps beneficiaries of its programs under close supervision.

The Role of Governance in Policy Outcomes: Leadership or Institutions?

This composition of Hibbing's boards and commissions enabled by its expansive city limits raises the question of leadership, and helps us to understand how the city of Hibbing has sustained such a high level of intervention on economic development on so many fronts and in ways so consistently "pro-business." As we have seen, city institutions and geography play a key a role. HEDA has a broad and powerful set of tools: considerable control of resources; board-level autonomy from elected officials; leading business owners among its membership, whose absence due to geographical exclusion is often felt in similar capacities in Ely; staff support; and a steady working relationship with the IRRRB.

But the increasing policy activism over the past two decades has been driven by changes in the city's leadership and greater public attention to economic development. The first major change occurred in 1994, when effectively half the city council was disqualified from office for violations of the Minnesota Open Meeting Law. In came former state Senator Ron Dicklich, by this time one of the top lobbyists at the Minnesota Capitol, as mayor, accompanied by Pat Garrity, the veteran of the Stuntz Township annexation, in a return to his former city clerk's office. Dicklich's stay at City Hall was short-lived, his intention simply to be a caretaker followed through. But Hibbing's approach on economic development from this point became steadily more proactive and interventionist, a fact hammered home by the events of the past several years. Whereas the city's approval of Walmart in 2000[47] involved little more than the necessary permits after private developers took the initiative,[48] the development Walmart's arrival triggered ensured future city involvement would become more active,[49] as it did with the courting of home improvement chain Lowe's.

The council continued to become ever more activist on economic development despite changes in the mayoralty and an unexpected hiatus in the Garrity clerkship. The manager of Hibbing's Social Security Administration regional office, Rick Wolff, was elected mayor in 2002 on a strongly interventionist economic development platform. Garrity's unexpected loss that year to Jeff Young was reversed at the next election (2006), and their disagreements over planning issues appear to have had more to do with process than goals. Neither Young's activism nor Garrity's more cautious approach substantially deviated from the underlying trend toward a greater degree of activism in assistance to business and planning to support the local economy. In any case, the clerkship apart, the main pattern of recent years in Hibbing, especially since the 2002 election, has been the near-unanimity on the city council and on HEDA around the city's economic development policies.[50] Officials have pursued and often delivered expansions in skilled blue-collar employment, retailing and affordable housing in a sustained and aggressive way, while abandoning the city's long-standing pattern of aversion to regional cooperation in order to increase the value and spread the risk of major infrastructural development.

Hibbing's record on economic development policy in recent years thus stands as the most visible reminder among these cases that institution-building is a necessary condition for successful economic development policy, but not a sufficient one. Strong and well-embedded local institutions, HEDA above all others, have proved to be a vital conduit in the diversification of economic development. HEDA has played an integral role in providing the necessary capital for local manufacturers to secure themselves and grow, and it plays a leading role in the strategy for developing retail as well, ranging from assistance to local property developers to recruiting new stores.

Admittedly, Hibbing has already had these institutional and administrative tools for decades. To broaden Hibbing's economic development policy beyond the IRRRB focus on large-scale manufacturing and mining took a major change of leadership. But, once that change had occurred, it survived further turnover in city politics. Hibbing had long been a small-c conservative community in which one's status was determined by the number of generations the family had lived there. In contrast, the Hibbing

140 *Hibbing, Minnesota: Evolution of Activist Development*

City Council of most of the 2000s constituted a pro-development coalition of what old-timers derisively call "packsackers" with multigenerational locals who own small businesses. Today's Hibbing City Council, as of 2017, includes locally raised current or retired business owners, a union millwright, a law enforcement officer, a union official mayor and a council member who directs the nonprofit Hibbing Foundation. Through all this change, the entities most charged with economic development, HEDA and the airport authority, have continued to provide direct assistance to businesses. The agenda has not so much changed as broadened, with recent city support for a new hotel and affordable housing. The hotel, a Hampton Inn with expansive meeting space, opened in 2016 with city subsidy; the affordable housing represents an intervention of a kind not nearly as extensively used in the past in Hibbing as in other parts of this region.

Policy Outcomes: The Case of Hibbing Retailing

The positive turnaround in Hibbing's local reputation and the region's planning record has not gone unnoticed by the public and by community leaders. Survey responses, meeting minutes and newspaper coverage all indicate that the city of Hibbing's success in setting and then reaching economic development goals during the 2000s not only dramatically improved but was seen to improve. Success, as far as it went, produced support for a policy agenda that even the 2008–9 recession and the ensuing 2010 election did not reverse. In this respect, it is also notable that goals have been set, and reached, as much according to preferences within the community as according to traditional, supply-side patterns of economic development policy, a trend that the 2010 election if anything reinforced.

Nowhere is this clearer than regarding retailing. Hibbing's push to boost the retail sector has no specific value for the city in terms of tax base beyond the taxability of improvements to property. Besides the continuing refusal of the state to grant permission for local option sales taxes even under the extremely limited circumstances under which they are allowed, the city of Hibbing has, in contrast to Ely, barely even discussed the matter. But the concept of a vigorous retail sector as an amenity has proved to be a powerful motive for citizens. In meetings, in newspaper reports and in public hearings on Retail-MASH held in the fall of 2006, two things emerge: the strong desire of citizens for more local retail choices and the strong intentions of local politicians and community leaders to ensure that those choices become a reality.

HEDA's independence gave it the ability to set an agenda and accelerate policy change. But unlike the industrial economic development loans program, supported by HEDA's own operating capital, direct assistance for retail store improvements requires the financial support of the city council through the Storefront Loan Program, which was reactivated at HEDA's December 2005 meeting after a seven-year hiatus with support from the

Hibbing, Minnesota: Evolution of Activist Development   141

city's general fund rather than a devolved fund. In contrast to its Ely counterpart, Hibbing's program has – apparently for want of other applicants – largely operated in support of one company over the past four years. Lees Rentals and Development, owned by local businessman Rich Lees, has developed two new strip malls near the Beltline Highway and renovated several commercial buildings in downtown Hibbing. But a $40,000 loan – double the typical limit storefront loans – helped a local Chinese restaurant that had outgrown its previous location to secure bank financing for renovating a long-vacant downtown store unit, a large former ACE Hardware store that had ended up in city ownership and proved difficult to sell on.[51] Nonetheless, loans proceeded at a relatively small volume until June 2009, when $122,000 in storefront loans toward six different renovation projects were approved at a single meeting, along with a $100,000 economic development loan to Lees Rentals toward the redevelopment of a former garage.[52] Six months later Lees got its sixth HEDA loan, this time toward renovating the downtown building formerly used by a local cosmetology school.

Hibbing's shortage of retail was not a situation the city was historically accustomed to. Like other Range cities, Hibbing had a vibrant downtown, full of retail businesses, many of them Jewish-owned.[53] As the largest community on the Iron Range, Hibbing was also a regional center for retailing. Duluth, which now dominates regional retailing, did not gain its super-regional mall or box retailing until the 1970s. Instead, the primary retailers in each market were local; Duluth had Glass Box and Hibbing had Feldman's Department Store. But these independent retailers were vulnerable, and, one by one, they were bought out – Glass Box in the 1990s by Des Moines, Iowa,-headquartered Younkers (which itself was absorbed by York, Pennsylvania, chain BonTon Stores) – or went out of business.

The city of Hibbing went to considerable lengths in an unsuccessful attempt to protect Feldman's from collapse. When St.-Cloud-based Herberger's, an upper-middle-market department store chain that was eventually also acquired by BonTon,[54] wanted an edge-of-town store to replace its city center location, it was rebuffed as a threat to Feldman's and downtown.[55] Some lost ground was recovered when Hibbing's Iron Gate Mall secured J. C. Penney, another refugee from downtown, as an anchor tenant, but the regional prize of Herberger's went to Thunderbird Mall in Virginia. By 1998 Virginia had a third more taxable retail sales than Hibbing despite having only just over half the population. Both Hibbing and Virginia seemed like marginal shopping draws compared to Grand Rapids, which had almost double Virginia's retail sales despite having fewer people still, thanks to its recruitments of box retailers (see Table 5.2) and a more populated catchment area (Grand Rapids has since outgrown Virginia in population). Grand Rapids is still the only city in northeastern Minnesota other than Duluth to have both Target and Walmart, but lost

Table 5.2 Taxable and gross sales in Minnesota cities, 1998–2015

City	Taxable 1998	Taxable 2005	Taxable 2015	Gross 1998	Gross 2005	Gross 2015
Ely	$39.6m	$38.2m	$45.7m	$104.0m	$99.9m	$109.2m
Hibbing	$129.4m	$147.9m	$194.1m	$496.2m	$661.5m	$750.8m
Virginia	$147.9m	$184.7m	$175.4m	$371.4m	$475.1m	$524.4m
Grand Rapids	$221.2m	$217.1m	$252.5m	$1,122.8m	$802.6m	$979.2m
Duluth	$872.3m	$1,448.3m	$1,316.7m	$2,736.5m	$4,401.1m	$4,969.3m
Minneapolis	$7,205.5m	$6,860.2m	$7,688.0m	$23,461.0m	$20,944.5m	$25,262.3m
Bloomington	$1,454.6m	$2,089.4m	$3,219.0m	$4,921.4m	$8,677.2m	$11,187.6m

Source: State Department of Revenue, Minnesota sales and use tax statistics, 1998, 2005 and 2015.

Hibbing, Minnesota: Evolution of Activist Development   143

business sales with the buyout of hometown paper manufacturer Blandin Paper Company by Finnish multinational UPM-Kymenne in 1997.

However, Hibbing started to turn its retail sector around by the early 2000s. Walmart had long wanted an Iron Range store and was unfazed by the area's strong union tradition. Having first failed to get the city of Mountain Iron to approve a tax increment financing (TIF) district for a store (it eventually opened a store there anyway), Walmart then turned to Hibbing, where the firm seized the opportunity to buy a site at the junction of two major highways, next to Iron Gate Mall. In terms of expanding the retail sector, this was a case of infrastructure and location winning out over incentives, for Walmart received no financial assistance from the city. But Walmart's arrival changed the game for policy and economics alike; indeed, several respondents view it as a turning point in local and regional perceptions of the city as a place to shop and a node for growth.[56]

Hibbing's recruitment efforts for retail businesses started to grow steadily from this point. In 2005 the council approved the below-market-rate sale of a rough piece of city land next to the community's main cemetery and across the highway from Iron Gate to Lowe's, for a large new store development. In another clear sign of the council's intentions, it unanimously overturned a planning and zoning commission recommendation against rezoning the last remaining residentially zoned lots along the Highway 169 Beltline – which enabled Walgreens to buy out homeowners and build their first Iron Range store as part of a major regional expansion. The trend of retail sales during this period showed growth in Hibbing catching up with other regional retail centers including Ely, Virginia and Duluth.

At this point, HEDA intervened to build a more systematic approach to recruiting retailers. First, the board decided to prioritize strip mall development, and two companies, national strip mall developer Oppidan and local firm Lees Rentals and Commercial Development, got support from HEDA for new projects. Oppidan was eyeing a site across Minnesota Highway 73 from Walmart that required a sewer extension; HEDA paid for the extension to the property line.[57] Lees Rentals successfully applied for a series of storefront loans toward two strip mall developments (Lees would later also secure substantial storefront loan funding for several downtown projects). Among the newcomers to the community in this wave of development were branches of Caribou Coffee, NAPA Auto Parts and Radio Shack. This new climate boosted unsubsidized development too. Notably, another major retail expansion, a doubling of floor space to over 70,000 square feet by local hardware store L&M Fleet Supply as a direct response to Lowe's, was *not* subsidized by the city, as no application for city support was even made. Lees Rentals continued with its rapid pace of building redevelopment, supported by almost $300,000 in city financing by the end of 2009.[58]

144   *Hibbing, Minnesota: Evolution of Activist Development*

Table 5.3 Taxable sales per capita of selected cities, 2005 and 2015

City	Tax base per capita (2005)	Population (2005 est.)	Tax base per capita (2015)	Population (2015 est.)
Ely	$10,728	3,558	$13,480	3,404
Hibbing	8,919	16,582	11,990	16,387
Virginia	20,769	8,895	20,451	8,578
Grand Rapids	19,975	10,869	22,717	11,117
Duluth	16,863	85,889	15,305	86,030
Minneapolis	17,694	387,711	18,746	410,116
Bloomington	24,772	84,347	37,820	85,114

Source: State Department of Revenue, Minnesota sales and use tax statistics, 1998, 2005 and 2015.

Lees and other property owners were able to attract chain tenants in part because of the Retail-MASH market research study commissioned by HEDA. This was first rolled out in June 2006, when HEDA's board agreed for the authority to serve as the "fiscal agent" for the project – in other words, responsible for authoritative decision-making on behalf of all those funding it. Requests for proposals resulted in placement of the contract in September with MapInfo (now owned by Pitney Bowes Software), at a cost of $40,000. Additionally, HEDA opted to hold "community visioning" hearings itself, moderated by board members and representatives from Hibbing Community College – information it passed on to the consultants. The feedback from these hearings was clear. Residents wanted local services, they wanted to be less dependent on the hour-long drives to Duluth or Grand Rapids, they wanted more national chain stores and they were ambitious in terms of the chains they wanted to see in the community, with Costco and Staples among the most frequently mentioned.[59]

MapInfo's principal recommendation, issued in February 2007, was for the city to dramatically step up marketing efforts aimed specifically at retailers. The firm suggested Hibbing could support between 130,000 and 260,000 square feet in additional retail space, with the biggest needs in general merchandising. Since then the city of Hibbing has regularly sent delegations of city leaders to conferences of the International Council of Shopping Centers in a bid to further this process. This burst in activity in the mid-2000s has survived the Great Recession (though progress has been slower subsequently), with Lowe's, Walgreens and others all continuing to succeed, and with notable results; Hibbing has registered a larger percentage increase in retail sales than any other major Iron Range retail center, and a larger percentage increase than Duluth or Minneapolis. This means that, at least in percentage terms, retail sales growth in Hibbing is outpacing that of the regional centers that are supposed to be increasing their concentration of business at the expense of small towns. It is an

Hibbing, Minnesota: Evolution of Activist Development   145

outcome that offers hope to any small community trying to boost its own regional profile in retail.

Meeting Goals on Industrial Employment

Hibbing's policies for boosting employment are centered around a close and long-term relationship between HEDA and private-sector employers that also involves workforce training at Hibbing Community College.[60] Nonetheless, in the industrial sector, Hibbing has an advantage through having several well-established businesses in the city that fit the IRRRB agenda of manufacturing jobs, as opposed to Ely's more strongly tourist- and service-oriented economy. Home-owned businesses, including Hibbing Fabricators, oil pipeline lining manufacturer Iracore, which merged with another Hibbing firm, Industrial Rubber Products, in 2008, and heating and cooling systems maker L&M Radiator, all have long-standing relationships with HEDA and are stable or growing. Iracore added 40 positions in 2006 with both city and IRRRB assistance;[61] Cast Corporation relocated to Hibbing from Buhl, also with city and IRRRB assistance, leasing a disused former electronics factory, after outgrowing its original facility;[62] and DMR Electronics saw a large increase in the volume of its work (warranty repairs on automotive components)[63] after years of a close working relationship with HEDA and Hibbing Community College on workforce training.[64] Retail has expanded strongly in conjunction with an increasingly formalized policy of heavily promoting Hibbing as a retail center.[65] The city's biggest vulnerability is the highly cyclical nature of mining, given Hibbing Taconite's role as the city's second largest employer after Fairview Range Medical Center,[66] putting these vendor firms in a vulnerable position from time to time.

Following policies through public minutes – for example, supporting the steady expansion at L&M Radiator or Iracore, or the progress and development of retail promotion and the market research and marketing associated with it – shows how HEDA operates independently of the council on most matters, and, above all, the extent to which it can move quickly to seal deals with private employers. Take the example of L&M Radiator, a company that exports its Mesabi brand of modular truck engine radiators worldwide. L&M drew public-sector support for an ambitious expansion that saw the company double in size between 2004 and 2006 to reach around 170 jobs in the city.[67] The city of Hibbing's portion of public-sector financing of L&M's expansion was provided entirely through HEDA, with additional support for worker training to alleviate a chronic shortage of skilled welders directly from Hibbing Community College. Of note is the waiving of the usual rules regarding the size of the loan and Hibbing's ownership guarantee requirement. L&M received a $100,000 loan toward an additional $3.1 million expansion in September 2006, double the usual city economic development loan limit for a single project. As for the ownership

146 *Hibbing, Minnesota: Evolution of Activist Development*

guarantee, a city requirement aimed at maintaining stable and preferably local ownership, L&M received its waiver on the grounds of its long history in the community. In HEDA, these were approved on a voice vote without debate.[68] On a city council (or an EDA that consists entirely of the city council membership and meets before or after the council meeting, as is the case in Ely), such a move could have been controversial. Only the portion depending on state funds – the loans from the Minnesota Infrastructure Fund – required city council approval and management (the same is true for IRRRB grants, which must be applied for by the city council).

HEDA has been similarly supportive of Iracore, which makes pipeline linings primarily for the oil sands industry in Canada. However, the creation and expansion of Iracore also required state assistance. The September 2006 HEDA meeting saw similar assistance to Iracore to that rendered to L&M, but it can be put into perspective considering that the HEDA decision occurred the day after the Iron Range Resources and Rehabilitation Board had approved a $1.5 million low-interest loan for Iracore.[69]

Conclusion: Local Initiative and State Agendas

Hibbing differs from Ely in three key organizational respects: its institutional development, its political geography and its functional compatibility with state policy in what remains a relatively centralized process for economic development policy-making. Nonetheless, these structures did not trigger immediate changes in policy; in the longer run, they simply enabled them. The reform of Hibbing government took place over decades, building an autonomous economic development department with its own working capital, though this entity subsequently had its staff support reduced; annexing Stuntz Township, and thus bringing resources and leadership within the city limits without overturning the majority of voters within the previous city limits; and electing leaders who took a more interventionist approach to economic development. Additionally, the compatibility of Hibbing with the IRRRB's mission is visibly beneficial to its policies on economic development, a fact that makes itself clear through both the archived minutes and newspaper records and the survey interviews with community leaders.

First, it is worth pointing out that Hibbing's active spending on economic development is low: less than one percent of the city budget, according to the 2009 financial statements, and around five percent when off-budget items such as revenue bonds and tax increment financing are considered. The real money and power in economic development policy in Hibbing lie with HEDA, whose own working capital of over $1.5 million is deployed to help locally owned, skilled blue-collar employers leverage far greater resources from banks. HEDA initiates grant application processes with the IRRRB and makes loans independently of the city council; it also plays a major role in managing city TIF districts. But it is not entirely

Hibbing, Minnesota: Evolution of Activist Development   147

insulated from political or leadership conditions. State economic development grants require city council endorsement, as do key land use decisions, including the completion during the 2000s of the rezoning and reallocation of the land along the Beltline Highway into retailing. Significant as HEDA's institutional role is, the council's forceful interventions on behalf of Lowe's and Walgreens, the latter involving unanimously overturning a unanimous planning commission recommendation, sent a powerful political message.

Second, the inclusion of Stuntz Township's territory represents a reconfiguration of the city's geography and political leadership that brings considerable assets on board. A remarkable portion of Ely's key business leaders live outside the city and therefore are excluded from most boards and commissions, while the approximately $1 billion property tax base of Morse and Fall Lake Townships is out of the city government's reach. The presence within Hibbing's city limits of Stuntz, or, rather, the council ward that was once the township, brings leadership (for example, active membership in city boards and commissions), a modest amount of tax base (though not nearly as much as the Ely area townships would for that city) and ready availability of developable land. Hibbing's ambitions for regional infrastructure came about in part because it directly borders neighboring cities without having to reconcile with township authorities that might favor a smaller scale approach to development; the exit from CIRSSD resulted from political conflict within Hibbing.

But the third point, Hibbing's economic compatibility with the 70-year-old pattern of the IRRRB, is more a matter of what you might call "place luck." Hibbing's good "fit" to state political leaders' agendas on economic development results from an economic tradition whose historical functions and expertise are still functioning; it is an easier context in which to practice economic development (Abu-Lughod, 2000). The IRRRB's first mission, financially speaking, has been returning production tax monies for targeted investments in the taconite mines themselves, giving communities with active iron ore mining such as Hibbing an advantage for the agency's funds over other parts of the Iron Range. Compare this with Ely, where IRRRB support for CWTSatoTravel and apparel manufacturer Steger Mukluks (a major grantee in 1996–7) stands out as unusual, simply because there are few other private-sector manufacturing and service businesses in Ely that fit the agency's prioritization of larger-scale business, manufacturing and mining. The IRRRB funds Ely has received have mostly been for community development: rebuilding streets and infrastructure, assisting with school construction and establishing a broadband network (which itself was crucial in recruiting CWTSatoTravel). In Hibbing, on the other hand, a host of employers have received IRRRB assistance in both successful and failed projects – Lakewood Industries and Reptron Electronics among the failures, L&M Radiator, Iracore and of course Hibbing Taconite among the successes.

148   *Hibbing, Minnesota: Evolution of Activist Development*

There are some ongoing setbacks in Hibbing. Downtown remains a shell of its former self despite extensive city and IRRRB efforts at improving infrastructure, landscaping and atmospherics; it lacks the tourist trade that characterizes Ely's downtown, and has not been prioritized over edge-of-town development by the city government. Several survey respondents also look enviously at Ely's success in arts and cultural promotion as well, regarding it as an example for the region. Nonetheless, the continuity of the city's long-term business relationships is striking, and has yielded clear and beneficial results.

And it is on that note that perhaps the most important lesson from Hibbing emerges from the standpoint of institutional capacity. Hibbing, through its organizational arrangements for managing economic development policy, its expanded local geography and its economic function, makes for an easy client for the all-important IRRRB. The Hibbing Economic Development Authority's autonomy, deal-making authority and relatively broad membership all help. The resources at HEDA's disposal also enable the authority to move at short notice to provide support to both retail and industrial businesses that need governmental assistance as collateral for much larger-scale bank loans. Furthermore, HEDA's nimbleness and working capital combine to provide a model that Ely could well copy, despite the awkwardness with which Ely fits into the IRRRB mission. But the question remains: what might things be like if Hibbing and other Range cities were freer to pursue their own mission, through either better service to small business from the IRRRB, or devolving its power and resources? It is to that end that we continue to Sterling and Rock Falls, Illinois, to see how economic development operates in a context of more local autonomy and a higher proportion of locally generated revenue, but with city governments having to weigh the risks posed by a weaker safety net from the state.

Notes

1   See official minutes of Hibbing Economic Development Authority, December 12, 2007. HEDA executive director Duane Northagen outlined a proposal for "re-branding" Hibbing for marketing the community to itself and to prospective businesses, and at that meeting the HEDA board agreed to hire North Star Destination Strategies of Nashville, Tenn., a firm that had already been hired by nearby Grand Rapids, Mich., on a $70,000 contract. The result was "Hibbing: We're ore and more."

2   Hibbing and Ely's occupational profiles are close in terms of extractive industries (mostly mining, which in this region provides jobs requiring similar skills to, and offering better pay and conditions than, manufacturing) but diverge strongly in manufacturing and tourism. The following data showing the percentage of local jobs in each category compare the city of Hibbing (including all annexed areas) and the 55731 and 55796 zip codes to encompass Ely and surrounding townships. Source: US Census Bureau, 2000 census.

Hibbing, Minnesota: Evolution of Activist Development 149

3 Managerial, professional and related employment accounts for 31.4 percent of the Ely-area workforce and 26.5 percent of the Hibbing workforce.

4 So-called because the Democrats lost the state House of Representatives, the race for governor and both US Senate seats in the elections, which included filling the Senate vacancies left by Hubert Humphrey's death and Walter Mondale's accession to the vice presidency, amid a bitter split between the labor union and progressive/liberal wings of the state party and urban and rural voters over industrial, environmental and social policies.

5 Curtis L. Carlson, chairman of the Minnesota Tourism Economic Recovery Commission, in its report, dated February 11, 1983. The report noted a request to the Twin Cities to consider a bid to host the Winter Olympic Games.

6 Note: the Iron Range Resources and Rehabilitation Board was renamed twice under Governors Jesse Ventura and Tim Pawlenty prior to reverting to its original name under Governor Mark Dayton in 2011. During this time the agency was known as the Iron Range Resources and Rehabilitation Agency and then simply Iron Range Resources; the board was referred to under Governor Pawlenty as the Iron Range Resources Board.

7 *Time*, Trade: The chopstick connection, December 8, 1986; accessed at www. time.com/time/magazine/article/0,9171,963018,00.html.

8 *Wall Street Journal*, Chopstick factory closes after picking up big debt, July 20, 1989.

9 B. Kelleher, After the mines: Troubles at the IRRRB, Minnesota Public Radio, December 7, 1999.

10 See Hibbing survey interview 30. The respondent noted significant local political fallout from the failure of Lakewood.

11 Referenced in interview 43: see also interview 54.

12 Interview 54.

13 Interview 51.

14 Decision rendered by the Supreme Court of Minnesota in Claude *v.* Collins, June 30, 1994, 518 N.W.2d 836. Case record accessed at http://scholar.google. com/scholar_case?case=8889463020790168580. During a labor dispute, officials were found to have held illegal closed-door meetings on several issues not pertaining to the dispute, including the sale of a city-owned building, administrative reorganization and privatizing a wastewater treatment plant. In all, one meeting was held that was entirely improperly closed; four others were held in which items not eligible for being discussed in closed session were added to the agenda.

15 Interview 19.

16 *Duluth News Tribune*, Duluth-based Luigino's builds food processing plant in West Virginia, November 8, 2002.

17 HEDA, December 2007 meeting, official minutes.

18 Hibbing's aim with branding was to create an identity and a marketing approach that reflected both the city's traditions and its current diversification strategy. More information on the branding project, "Hibbing: We're ore and more," is available at the NorthStar Destination Strategies website at www. northstarideas.com/community/CityBrandingStudy-HibbingMinnesota.htm.

19 Chisholm-Hibbing Airport is the only airport among the cities in this study that has scheduled airline service, though Ely Municipal Airport also had it in the past.

150 *Hibbing, Minnesota: Evolution of Activist Development*

20 *Hibbing Daily Tribune*, IRRRB OKs loan to CHAA for spec building, October 11, 2012; IRRRB board meeting, August 8, 2013, minutes.

21 The support was shown by unanimous votes on HEDA in June and September 2006 in support of the retail initiative, and strong citizen support at an informational meeting that took place at Hibbing Community College on October 21, 2006 (observed by the author) to assess strategy for recruiting retailers and potential chains in local demand.

22 Both the Retail Market Analysis Study of Hibbing (Retail-MASH) and support for Iracore and L&M Radiator received unanimous support – Retail-MASH from HEDA at its June and September 2006 meetings, and Iracore and L&M from both HEDA and the city council in 2006 and 2007. Rezoning for another retail project, a Walgreen's store that was the Iron Range's first, was approved unanimously by the city council, overturning a unanimous planning and zoning commission recommendation.

23 K. Grinsteinner, City Council OKs legislative request for government modifications, *Hibbing Daily Tribune*, March 27, 2016; K. Grinsteinner, Council to discuss ward system modification, *Hibbing Daily Tribune*, December 14, 2016; SF3131 Amendment 2, 89th Minnesota Legislature, 2016, amending Minnesota Statutes 2014, §216B,2424, subd. 5a; Laws 1949, ch. 422§2.

24 Hibbing Public Utilities offers direct steam heat from a central plant to commercial and residential customers, enabling them to do without furnaces in their buildings. This type of utility, common in the former Soviet bloc but rare in the West outside institutional settings, is also offered in Virginia, Minnesota.

25 Interview 19.

26 See the official minutes of the regular meeting of Hibbing City Council for December 20, 1999.

27 Source: Minutes of the "Truth in Taxation public hearing" and regular meeting of the Hibbing City Council, December 5, 2007. Spending years correspond to the previous levy year due to levies on a calendar year and spending on a July 1–June 30 fiscal year.

28 Minutes of the regular meeting of the Hibbing City Council and "Truth in Taxation public hearing," December 2, 2015.

29 For example, the IRRRB bailout of Mesabi Drill in Chisholm in 2003 resulted not only in the survival and rebranding of the company as Minnesota Twist Drill but in a doubling in workforce from 45 to 90 in an industry that has been heavily impacted from outsourcing to China. See interview 65; see also www.ironrangeresources.org/business/successstories/mntwist.

30 Interview 19.

31 2009 Minnesota Statutes, section 469.091.

32 Based on HEDA monthly statements in minutes from 2005 through 2015. The fund typically originates loans of up to $50,000, though if HEDA agrees to waive rules this cap can be increased.

33 Minutes of the regular meeting, HEDA, December 2008.

34 Minutes of the regular meeting, HEDA, September 2006.

35 Based on commercial real estate listings from Northland Connection, a public–private agency designed to enable prospective businesses to find appropriate property and public assistance.

36 See, for example, HEDA minutes from October 2008 and November 2008, regarding approval of subsidies for the Forest Heights Townhomes

Hibbing, Minnesota: Evolution of Activist Development   151

development, and September 2009, debating the sale of city-owned land to Summit Development Corp. for an apartment development next to the city's municipal cemetery.

37 Interviews 19, 43, 51, 53.

38 See, for example, M. Helmberger, Range fiber network death blow, *Ely Timberjay*, July 26, 2008.

39 K. Grinsteinner, Hibbing ditches sewer district – votes unanimously to opt out of CIRSSD, *Hibbing Daily Tribune*, April 30, 2009.

40 2016 Minnesota Statutes, Chapter 216B, 216B.2424, §§5a, Biomass power mandate. The relevant legislation is SF521, originated as HF623, and posted on May 17, 2013, 88th legislative session.

41 State Representative Carly Melin, House approves Rep. Melin's Laurentian Energy Authority Bill, press release, May 8, 2013.

42 The vote was taken at HEDA's February 2007 regular meeting, as noted in official minutes.

43 Interview 51.

44 Minutes of the regular meetings of HEDA for January 2005 and May 2007.

45 Sources: Iron Range Resources and Rehabilitation Board, Biennial report to the legislature, 2007–2008, 2009–2010.

46 Based on monthly HEDA minutes, indicating employment levels at Hibbing Fabricators as a condition of the loan.

47 Walmart is Hibbing's third largest private-sector employer after Hibbing Taconite and Fairview Range Medical Center. The Supercenter store employs approximately 400 people.

48 Interview 51.

49 Even though a question on the Hibbing Walmart was not specifically asked, 13 survey respondents – almost half the total for the city – cited the arrival of Walmart as a key turning point in the city's retail and business development.

50 Interview 54; date was cited as a particularly important watershed, and is supported by analysis of meeting minutes.

51 See monthly HEDA minutes for March 2007, detailing the bidding process by which Hong Kong Kitchen won over two other proposals for the property. At the February 2008 HEDA meeting, authority president Marvin Vuicich thanked the owners of the restaurant for their work and described it as "just a gorgeous addition to our downtown."

52 Minutes of the regular meeting, HEDA, June 2009. Projects included four downtown retail/restaurant storefronts and improvements to a strip mall and a chiropractic office.

53 N. Epstein and R. Frankel, Bob Dylan: The unauthorized biography, Moment *Magazine*, August 2005. Jewish business owners played a key role in the development of Iron Range cities through the 1950s, with one of the last and best examples being Ely resident Abe Bloomenson's donation that triggered the construction of that city's community hospital.

54 C. Selix, Drawing the Dayton's crowd: Herberger's attracts disaffected shoppers, MinnPost, May 2, 2008, retrieved from www.minnpost.com/stories/2008/05/02/1705/drawing_the_daytons_crowd_herbergers_attracts_disaffected_shoppers. Herberger's retained its original identity even after the 2006 merger with BonTon, helping to attract disgruntled Macy's customers.

55 Interview 51.

152 *Hibbing, Minnesota: Evolution of Activist Development*

56 Interviews 17, 18, 19, 30, 31, 50, 51, 58, 63.
57 Requested and approved at HEDA's May 2006 meeting.
58 Based on author's calculations from HEDA minutes, January 2006 through December 2009.
59 Author's notes: Retail-MASH visioning session, Hibbing Community College, October 21, 2006.
60 Interviews 29, 30.
61 Source: Iron Range Resources and Rehabilitation Board. See description at www.ironrangeresources.org/business/successstories/iracore.
62 See minutes of HEDA January and May 2007 meetings.
63 Interviews 16, 58.
64 M. Arnst, Local colleges mean thriving communities, Minnesota 2020, August 20, 2008.
65 Based upon Minnesota sales and use tax data; see Table 5.2 later in this chapter.
66 Source: City of Hibbing. Employment at Hibbing Taconite was 720 as of June 2010, second only to Fairview Range Medical Center, a major teaching hospital; it averaged 731 during 2015, according to the Annual Report of the Minnesota Inspector of Mines for that year.
67 See minutes of the regular meeting, HEDA, Wednesday, September 13, 2006.
68 *Ibid.* The meeting minutes discuss the L&M project in more detail.
69 *Ibid.*

References

Abu-Lughod, J. L. (2000). *New York, Chicago, Los Angeles: America's global cities.* Minneapolis: University of Minnesota Press.

Folz, D. H., & French, P. E. (2005). *Managing America's small communities: People, politics, and performance.* Lanham, Md.: Rowman & Littlefield.

Nelson, K. L., & Nollenberger, K. (2011). I – Conflict and cooperation in municipalities: Do variations in form of government have an effect? *Urban Affairs Review, 47*(5), 696–720.

Pagano, M. A. (2003). City fiscal structures and land development, discussion paper. Washington, D.C.: Brookings Institution Center on Urban and Metropolitan Policy.

6 Sterling and Rock Falls, Illinois
Reform and Recovery?

On a warm, breezy, late spring day in 2001, the kind of day that puts the Midwest's best foot forward, Sterling Mayor Ted Aggen came face to face with the reality of the decline of American manufacturing, and received the news that would change the politics of economic development in his hometown and neighboring Rock Falls to this day. The town's largest employer, Northwestern Steel and Wire, Inc. (NWSW), was telephoning the mayor to let him know the firm was going into liquidation with the immediate loss of 1,500 jobs.[1] So abrupt was the closure that a key industrial customer of NWSW would quickly intervene to save the newest, but least labor-intensive, part of the plant. But the May 18, 2001, collapse of this firm, the crown jewel of the "five companies,"[2] the five manufacturing firms that once dominated Sterling's economy, set in train a series of events that both defied local political stereotypes and demonstrated the importance of having strong government institutions in place to intervene in economic development.

NWSW had been a local institution in every sense of the term. A large-scale manufacturer of structural steel, nails,[3] fencing and the wire used in manufacturing bedsprings, the firm had been owned by three local families, including the Dillon family of Sterling, until 1988. The company's plants occupied 740 acres of prime real estate along the former Chicago and North Western (now Union Pacific) main line from Chicago to Omaha, along the Rock River and abutting downtown Sterling.[4] The firm's employment in 1980, just after its peak, amounted to almost a quarter of the entire working-age population of the Sterling and Rock Falls area,[5] and, although it automated and reduced workforce in subsequent years, it remained mostly profitable through the early 1990s until an ill-conceived reorganization by the new owners. Much of the money the Dillons made in the steel industry continues to benefit the area to this day; the Dillon Foundation, headed by former NWSW chief executive Pete Dillon, held an endowment that by the late 2000s surpassed $60 million, and continues to hand out over $3 million in grants each year to local services and organizations such as parks, public libraries, public and parochial schools, and the Whiteside County chapter of the United Way.[6]

154 *Sterling and Rock Falls, Illinois: Reform and Recovery?*

This chapter analyzes the response of the cities of Sterling and Rock Falls to this crisis. Existing institutional organization enabled the city of Sterling to respond rapidly in terms of economic development policy; institutional reorganization over the next few years enhanced Rock Falls' response as well. In this endeavor Sterling had an undeniable advantage over its southern neighbor. The city in 2001 had not only strong leadership but also well-established institutions of governance to take on the challenge. A semi-private economic development corporation had been formed in 1980, and by 2001 it had a track record of expanding land availability for business development and incubating new businesses from within and recruiting from outside. Sterling moved to council-manager government in 1974,[7] a move an appointed official described as strong evidence of what he called "a progressive local political culture," and for many years the city council has operated as an advice and oversight board on policy, with a high level of trust within the community, and with day-to-day management decisions almost entirely delegated to city staff. Furthermore, the responsibilities of key players in Sterling economic development were already well defined before 2001. The development corporation recruited new businesses with the support of the Whiteside/Carroll County Enterprise Zone board, while the city handled land title and outside grants in the process of reclaiming brownfield sites abandoned by failed companies in order to get them ready for development.

In contrast, Rock Falls decided it needed wholesale reform of an institutional structure that prior to 2001–2 featured commission-style government, a track record of conflict within the city council, no city administrator and no economic development agency. Although the Rock Falls City Council, galvanized by the jobs crisis in 2001, quickly gave economic development policy far more attention than it had in the past, the catalyst for implementing new policy turned out to be this institutional change, including the chartering of the Rock Falls Community Development Corporation (RFCDC). For more than a decade after that point Rock Falls policy converged with Sterling, reclaiming large areas of highly polluted industrial land and exceeding Sterling's success in redeveloping riverfront property. By 2007 the results were very noticeable; in the words of one respondent in Rock Falls that year, government problem-solving was "better than what we ever have been, on both sides of the river... Both towns got smart by hiring city administrators; this is what they're trained in, this is what they went to school for."[8] A counterpart on the Sterling City Council agreed, noting about Rock Falls that "the difference between their council being run now versus 10 years ago is like night and day."[9] But yet another twist emerged in 2015 as a new mayor gained council approval to defund RFCDC, resulting in its winding up, and began working directly with consultants for much of the policy-making process.

Overview: The Background of Today's Sterling and Rock Falls

This chapter takes a slightly different form from the other case studies, since it both switches to a different state and compares twin towns within a single urban area. Sterling and Rock Falls grew up on opposite sides of the Rock River in northwestern Illinois, and one could say their economy involved finishing into consumer goods the raw material that Ely and Hibbing dug out of the ground and the steel mills of Illinois, Indiana, Ohio and Pennsylvania refined. Sterling emerged first in the years after northwestern Illinois became the last part of the state to open to white settlement following the 1832 Black Hawk War, and was incorporated as a city in 1857. The purchase of rights south of the Rock River by a local businessman led to the incorporation of Rock Falls as a separate city in 1869.[10]

Sterling and Rock Falls established themselves quickly as industrial towns. They soon moved beyond flour-milling and other processing and handling of agricultural goods into manufacturing, which quickly grew to dominate the local economy. Proportionally, employment in Sterling and Rock Falls depends more on heavy manufacturing than Minnesota's Iron Range – and it is also more vulnerable to foreign competition. Whereas there are major export markets for iron ore, not to mention foreign companies that are eager to buy into mines, manufacturing finished goods is subject to intense foreign competition, and the Sterling/Rock Falls area's 30 percent dependence on manufacturing employment, one of the highest ratios in the United States, made it particularly vulnerable (the area remains well above the national average for manufacturing employment despite the job losses).

Consequently, it is not possible to sugarcoat the depth of the 2001–2 recession or the extent of manufacturing decline in northwestern Illinois. Northwestern Steel and Wire was not only the Sterling and Rock Falls area's largest employer but also the largest manufacturer in the entire region other than the Quad Cities[11] 50 miles to the west. The economic damage caused by the decline and fall of NWSW would therefore have been substantial even without other bankruptcies and layoffs in Sterling and Rock Falls' once dominant manufacturing employers. NWSW's final collapse, in May 2001, took with it the equivalent of almost 20 percent of total employment among Sterling residents,[12] mostly jobs that afforded what was for the area a comfortably middle-class lifestyle and strong retirement benefits. Existing retirees, who by the time of the bankruptcy exceeded the remaining employees by a ratio of two to one, suffered especially; the NWSW pension scheme collapsed with the company.

But the crisis in manufacturing was spreading far beyond the finished steel industry. The closure in the same year of former Rock Falls hardware factories Parrish-Alford (see Figure 6.1) and Russell, Burdsall & Ward

156 *Sterling and Rock Falls, Illinois: Reform and Recovery?*

Figure 6.1 Aerial view of the Parrish-Alford works in Rock Falls, Illinois, 1950s. While many of the buildings in the foreground survive, most of those closest to the river have been demolished, and the area is being redeveloped for parkland

Source: Sterling-Rock Falls Historical Society.

(RB&W) added to the area's jobs crisis. All three plants required extensive environmental clean-up, remediation and asbestos removal of the prime real estate they occupied at the heart of the town. Subsequently, Lawrence Hardware collapsed, Frantz Manufacturing downsized and National Manufacturing (see Figure 6.2) was bought out by competitor Stanley Works (now Stanley Black & Decker), which outsourced the company's manufacturing to Chinese firms. At National alone, employment dropped from 1,000 to less than half that number, with remaining staff handling distribution and administration rather than manufacturing. In the aftermath of the crisis the largest remaining manufacturer in the area was Wahl Clipper, which, despite adding three factories in east Asia, continued to employ approximately 780 staff at its Sterling plant and corporate headquarters as of 2007 and has expanded subsequently to over 1,000; no other manufacturer in the area now employs more than 400 locally.

As with the Iron Range, the job losses of the early 2000s in and around Sterling and Rock Falls are obvious in employment and demographic statistics. Manufacturing employment in Whiteside County in the 2000 census stood at around 30 percent, more than double the US average and

Figure 6.2 The offices of National Manufacturing and, to the right, the abandoned factory of Lawrence Hardware in Sterling, Illinois, August 2017. The city plans to renovate the Lawrence buildings for small business use
Source: Daniel Bliss.

higher than all but a select few regions of the country. By 2007 manufacturing had dropped to 19 percent of Whiteside's total non-farm employment and by 2017 it stood at 16.6 percent, around a third higher than the national average. Actual employment numbers in manufacturing in the county dropped from 7,700 in the second quarter of 2001, on the eve of the NWSW collapse, to just under 3,500 by July 2017.[13] Overall employment levels in the county have remained relatively stable, at around 21,000 to 22,000, thanks to hiring in services, retail, wholesale distribution and professional positions, though recent years have also seen a modest uptick in manufacturing employment.

The principal successes in this recovery are almost all notable for one thing in common: local government intervention was involved. At the beginning of 2003 the updated portion of the old NWSW plant reopened as Sterling Steel, Inc., in a complex deal involving a major NWSW customer, the city of Sterling, bankruptcy trustees and a prominent Chicago attorney hired by the city government. Later in 2003 Walmart was successfully encouraged, through the promise of a city sewer extension and property tax abatement, to locate a 900,000-square-foot grocery distribution center in unincorporated Sterling Township; the facility opened in early 2006 and quickly hired almost 1,000 staff. Extensive brownfield redevelopment

158 *Sterling and Rock Falls, Illinois: Reform and Recovery?*

efforts, bankrolled by state and federal environmental grants, began in Sterling and eventually spread to Rock Falls as leaders there finally reached agreement on future goals for the blighted, derelict industrial area on their river frontage. New edge-of-town retail development, especially in Sterling, followed the extension of sewer lines and annexation.

The Illinois Way of Managing Economic Development

As with Hibbing and Ely, Minnesota, the question remains how the governments of Sterling and Rock Falls delivered on their economic development goals. Part of the story concerns implementation, especially the rapid response that Sterling's more reformed government could deliver. This is to be found primarily in official meeting minutes for the two city councils and for bodies such as the Whiteside/Carroll County Enterprise Zone management organization.

The other part of the story concerns the extent to which city officials and other community leaders have met their goals, which, as with the Minnesota cases, depends on survey interviews. Overall, the story is impressive: the Sterling and Rock Falls area absorbed crushing job losses with little increase in the long-term unemployment rate, even though the new jobs were often lower-paying. City leaders too feel broadly content with the extent to which they have met goals.

The means for delivering on reform differ somewhat from Minnesota because of the lack of need-based intergovernmental aid from the state of Illinois to its municipalities for basic operations, the greater options even non-home-rule Illinois cities have for raising revenue, and the stronger degree of localism in Illinois government and politics than in Minnesota. There are noteworthy parallels. As with Minnesota, infrastructure development has required intergovernmental grants and loans. In Sterling and Rock Falls, this means mostly utilities and brownfield reclamation, paid for with state and federal Environmental Protection Agency (EPA) grants, revenue-sharing, such as the Motor Fuels Tax, and, most recently, federal stimulus funding.

Illinois differs from Minnesota both in the funding and the organization of local government. More powers are devolved to local decision-makers than in Minnesota. In Sterling and Rock Falls this can be seen by the extent to which taxation has played a key role in improving basic community infrastructure such as streets and sewers. Funding for infrastructure increased sharply thanks to the successful coordination of sales tax referenda between Sterling, Rock Falls and Dixon in 2005, an option not practicably open for Hibbing and Ely under Minnesota law. Policy direction is more devolved too, notably in economic development. Enterprise zones in Illinois, passed under the 1982 Enterprise Zones Act, enable local governments to freely associate with one another in a binding regional entity that requires unanimous support of approved projects in which to

Sterling and Rock Falls, Illinois: Reform and Recovery? 159

distribute state-funded incentives to business. (Minnesota's JOBZ program, from 2003 to 2015, in contrast required communities to apply to the state for designation and afforded no organizational framework for neighboring cities to work together.) Despite the higher level of devolution in Illinois on economic development policy, a large array of state assistance is available. Examples of state-funded incentives include sales tax exemption, a $500 per employee "jobs tax credit," investment tax credit, low-interest loans of up to $750,000, assistance with employee training, for example at Sauk Valley Community College near Sterling, and loans of up to $1 million for new or expanding businesses.[14]

After the 2001–2 crisis and the wholesale reform of Rock Falls government, economic development policies in the two cities converged. Some of this convergence depended upon informal cooperation among city leaders, notably on the sales tax referenda. Some of it has emerged within the Whiteside/Carroll County Enterprise Zone management organization, which effectively provides a common institutional venue within which to boost economic development policy. Rock Falls, for example, saw its city council unanimously support the extensive expansions of Whiteside County's enterprise zone in 2004 and 2005, which were largely on the Sterling side of the river, most importantly for Walmart's distribution center.[15] Some of it came from the similar ways in which the cities delivered on reclamation of brownfield sites. But, on municipal infrastructure, the two towns remain far apart – and without any common governance structure. And the demise of RFCDC has been accompanied by an approach that focuses more than ever on property development, while Sterling, behind Rock Falls on riverfront reclamation, has continued its successful dealmaking for small business expansion including manufacturers.

The caveat is that, while Hibbing and Ely's city governments are approximately financial equals of each other and in some years slightly ahead of Sterling on a per capita basis despite Ely's lower median income, Rock Falls substantially lags Sterling due to the lack of revenue equalization from the state. In Illinois, there is no need-based assistance to local government, no equalization and no equivalent of the Iron Range Resources and Rehabilitation Board to allocate economic development grants on anything resembling a population formula. Furthermore, while Sterling and Rock Falls can and do coordinate economic development policy through the Whiteside/Carroll County Enterprise Zone board, the local sales taxes are separate, spurring inevitable competition for retail businesses typical of sales-tax-dependent jurisdictions (Pagano, 2003). As with property taxes, there is no state equalization of disparities in local sales tax bases in Illinois, making for a strong incentive for neighboring communities to compete with one another to enhance their tax base.

Nonetheless, Rock Falls is not entirely at a resource disadvantage to Sterling. Sterling depends on private utilities for water and electric supply, both of which are municipally owned in Rock Falls. Sterling is the only one

160   *Sterling and Rock Falls, Illinois: Reform and Recovery?*

of the four cases in this study to lack a full-service municipal utility (only sewerage disposal is municipal in Sterling), and it has faced larger rate increases from both electrical franchisee ComEd and Illinois American Water than Rock Falls' municipal utilities. Rock Falls' utilities advantage helps to further pinpoint the city's difficulties in economic development upon the inability to deliver "shovel-ready" land prior to the city government's reorganization.

As far more depends on the decisions of local leaders and on local economic bases, the role of institutional organization and leadership is more important in Sterling and Rock Falls than in the Minnesota cases, as they have farther to fall if they fail. As Illinois cities rather than Minnesota ones, they do not have the local government budget safety net that a comparable case in Minnesota has now, let alone the much stronger safety net that existed in Minnesota prior to the Pawlenty administration's sweeping cuts in Local Government Aid. This weaker level of guaranteed funding for general services puts a greater premium on building the tax base. Sterling had, and continues to have, an advantage in this respect, both from higher property valuations and higher local and shared sales tax revenues on account of having the lion's share of local retailing. But Sterling's greater level of institutional preparedness for economic disaster in 2001 arguably made a greater difference in determining how rapidly the two communities responded to their jobs crisis.

Institutions and Leadership within the Twin Communities

Sterling and Rock Falls add a great deal of value to this study in that they provide an excellent example both of contrast between institutions and, for more than a decade from the early 2000s to the mid-2010s, a trend of converging institutions and converging policies. Just as Hibbing has succeeded in doing and Ely has attempted to do with occasional success, Sterling and Rock Falls both worked hard in the aftermath of the 2001 recession to push interventionist economic development policies rather than playing the role of helpless victims. This attitude was best summed up by Sterling Mayor Ted Aggen, who recalled telling city manager Jay Wieland: "I don't want [the mill] to be a rusting hulk and just go up in weeds and trash. We will not go down the tubes."[16] Aggen set the leadership tone and raised the political trust in Sterling, and is widely credited in the community for his actions following the NWSW collapse. His counterpart in Rock Falls, Ed Mulvaney, never had the same degree of local political support but nonetheless led the city, despite considerable controversy, through wholesale reform of its government administration and its institutional means of delivering economic development.

The role of institutional organization in the two communities cannot be emphasized enough. Sterling switched from a mayor-council system to a council-manager system in the early 1970s, and since then

Sterling and Rock Falls, Illinois: Reform and Recovery? 161

has had a mere five city managers in more than 35 years. Council-manager governments are increasingly recognized for having somewhat less conflict within the council than mayor-council governments, a function of the fact that management decisions are extensively delegated and council members are free to devote most of their time to setting "big-picture" government policies and planning guidelines. In this, Sterling is no exception; minutes indicate only four divided roll call votes from 2006 through 2009 inclusive: a six to one vote for including wildflower planting in state-backed street projects;[17] defeat by three to two of an ordinance to allow convenience stores to sell alcoholic drinks;[18] a three to two vote in favor of objecting to a rate increase from a private water utility;[19] and a five to one vote on an almost five percent levy increase in 2008.[20] The city's record shows in its financial stability: even in the aftermath of the NWSW collapse it enjoyed a AAA bond rating[21] for much of the 2000s, extremely unusual among local governments, particularly covering this small a population (Sterling is currently rated A+ for general obligation by Standard & Poor's, while carrying no general obligation debt; like many Illinois governments, it now faces a significant pension liability).[22]

Council-manager governance was not the only innovation; Sterling was also at the forefront of delegating the steering of economic development policy to a public–private partnership. In 1980 the Greater Sterling Development Corporation, a partnership between the city government and local business leaders, was chartered with a remit to nurture new businesses, recruit outside businesses and retain old ones. The GSDC's leadership has persistently had strong local credibility. At the time of the NWSW crisis it was led by a well-connected Sterling native, David Barajas, Jr., whose father was vice-president of a local bank (Barajas, Jr., is now president of the same bank, Freedom Bank in Sterling);[23] upon his 2007 departure from the position, Barajas was replaced by Heather Sotelo, the executive director of the local Sauk Valley Chamber of Commerce, who has held the position since. GSDC manages key economic development policies, including initiatives to recruit business as well as a business "incubator" that provides low-cost office and warehouse space to new businesses.

Responsibilities in economic development are clearly delineated. The city government, primarily through the city manager and city attorney, handles brownfield sites such as properties left over from shuttered factories, secures state and federal reclamation grants from environmental agencies, secures clear title to the land so that it may be leased or resold to new occupants, and prepares sites for redevelopment. GSDC is the lead agency for recruiting new businesses from outside the community, fulfilling a similar role to the Hibbing Economic Development Authority and doing what in the 1990s and 2000s was the personal responsibility of the executive director of the Ely Area Development Association in Ely's system for handling economic development.

162 *Sterling and Rock Falls, Illinois: Reform and Recovery?*

Rock Falls provides an interesting contrast, because it had, as recently as 2001, no formal institutional arrangements for managing economic development policy and no agency able to handle even minor technical details of negotiations with business without a public meeting. With commission-style government, Rock Falls placed each of its eight city council members in charge of a city department, thus projecting interdepartmental divisions directly on the council. Divided roll call votes on the council were frequent. Public skepticism about government ran higher than in Sterling, according to survey respondents, even though Rock Falls in national politics has typically voted more Democratic than Sterling (in this respect, Rock Falls' much stronger shift away from the Democrats in 2016 than Sterling's can arguably be viewed as a symptom of this skepticism about government in the city's political culture).

However, in 2001–2 the political conditions were ripe for reform, and Rock Falls delivered reform rapidly.[24] The combination of the economic crisis, pro-reform Mayor Ed Mulvaney and an increasing pro-reform element on the city council resulted in major reorganization of city government within 18 months. RFCDC was chartered in late 2001, and hired its first executive director, Christian Tscheschlok, a fresh graduate of Western Illinois University's master's program in rural development,[25] in 2002. The following year, day-to-day management of most city departments was vested in the hands of newly hired city administrator Richard Downey.

Sterling's pre-existing conditions of reform and Rock Falls' reorganization had consequences for the two cities' policies. Not surprisingly, Sterling's organizational head start gave it the advantage, most visibly in brownfield development. Sterling moved immediately to reclaim the former Northwestern Steel and Wire factory site, while taking the lead on aggressive recruitment of outside business. Local politicians see even basic matters of enforcement against blighted properties as a formidable challenge.[26] Additionally, brownfield reclamation is resource-intensive, too much so for either of these cities to finance on their own. Therefore, securing the required outside grants means cities must first clear the necessary legal hurdles, including getting control of land and/or approval from property owners. While Rock Falls was working hard to reform its local institutions, Sterling was already implementing policy. Extensive applications for Illinois and federal Environmental Protection Agency funds for reclaiming brownfield sites began in Sterling in 2002, and reclamation on the NWSW site was complete by 2007.

The 2001–2 crisis also provided the political impetus for Rock Falls to reform its own administration on more managerial lines. Although the city would not go all the way toward adopting Sterling's council-manager system of government, the extent to which the city did emulate its northern neighbor was notable. Rock Falls City Council delegated substantial amounts of authority to its first ever city administrator and to civil service department heads, and the council was also closely involved in chartering RFCDC, supporting it with $100,000 a year in funding, to much support from the local business community, and thereby enabling it to have well-qualified, full-time staff.

From 2004 onward Rock Falls, which had formerly intervened very little in the local economy, pursued a similar set of policies. While the city of Sterling had secured state and federal funding for redevelopment of the NWSW property, the city of Rock Falls did the same with the heavily polluted former sites of Parrish-Alford and RB&W. While GSDC had recruited new distribution and retail businesses, RFCDC pursued new retail opportunities of its own and cooperated with GSDC and other area agencies in pursuing major distribution businesses. And, when a Mulvaney critic, alderman Richard Blanton, became mayor in 2005, the new policies on economic development were not altered but, rather, accelerated because of the greater personal support Blanton enjoyed from the city council.[27]

With the path that Sterling was already following, and that Rock Falls embarked upon from the early 2000s onward, it is not surprising that economic development policy turned to brownfield reclamation in response to the vast quantity of vacant factory sites; outside business recruitment to rapidly fill the void of employment in the community; and various measures to improve municipal revenues. In the process of implementing the response, Sterling and Rock Falls have both added further weight to the suggestion that effective institutional organization of economic development policy and process is a helpful condition for the adoption and successful completion of such policies. However, the two cities' broadly successful completion of their goals demonstrates the importance of both locally generated and outside resources in assisting these projects. Three key examples concern us here: the reclamation of brownfield sites from 2001 to 2016, as well as a newer portion of the NWSW plant in its original manufacturing function; the successful coordinated increase in sales tax rates in 2005 by Sterling and Rock Falls, along with nearby Dixon; and the recruitment of what is now one of the area's two biggest commercial employers, Walmart's principal grocery distribution facility for northwestern Illinois.

Brownfield Sites and the Story of Sterling Steel

Brownfield reclamation is resource-intensive, expensive in the money needed to make a derelict site usable again and expensive in the time and legal fees involved to clear often complicated land title problems and secure outside funding for improvements. So, it is not surprising that Sterling's organizational head start on economic development gave it an advantage over Rock Falls in terms of being able to quickly develop a reclamation plan for abandoned factories. While Rock Falls was working hard to reform its local institutions, Sterling was already implementing policy.

164 *Sterling and Rock Falls, Illinois: Reform and Recovery?*

The most significant example of this concerns the one major surviving part of Northwestern Steel & Wire: Sterling Steel, Inc. The NWSW bankruptcy had left a key customer, Fortune 500 furniture and mattress manufacturer Leggett & Platt, without a key local source for the wire it uses in bedsprings. Leggett & Platt wanted an almost new part of the NWSW plant: two state-of-the-art arc furnaces that are essential in the manufacturing process. But, to secure the plant for itself, Leggett & Platt would need assistance in claiming the facility from the bankruptcy trustees, which for the purposes of acquiring the property and reopening the factory effectively meant the city of Sterling.

The city, for its part, had a clear division of labor in which key figures in established positions of power slotted immediately into roles for dealing with the crisis. The future of the steel mill and the clearance, redevelopment and disposal of the property was a city function, and city manager Wieland's office would handle site redevelopment at the steel mill and other brownfield properties. The Greater Sterling Development Corporation, the public–private partnership for economic development then led by Barajas, would simply focus on the recruitment of new employers as well as the continued management of the city's business incubator. Community members, including labor and business leaders, would work with the city in developing a strategic plan for the NWSW site, which became the Rock River Redevelopment Project.

The largest benefit of the city's strong management and organization concerned an unusual partnership formed early in the bankruptcy process. At the behest of the city manager and city attorney, Sterling itself arranged to become the real estate broker for the bankruptcy trustee, as opposed to the more typical approach of leaving this task to a private real estate broker, and so city officials negotiated directly with potential purchasers recruited by GSDC – including Leggett & Platt. To protect the purchaser from liability for environmental reclamation under Superfund, the EPA agreed to a prospective purchaser agreement, and Leggett & Platt bought the 145 acre site at the core of the mill including the new furnaces. In a key respect, Sterling had an advantage: NWSW's pollution of this portion of its site proved to have been minimal, unlike other parts of it.

This process at the old steel mill proceeded rapidly considering the complexity involved. The city government pursued funds from the US Environmental Protection Agency's Brownfields grant program[28] and spent substantially from its budget surplus on legal representation to ensure the deal's success, hiring a high-ranking real estate lawyer, Greg Hummel, at the time a partner of Chicago-based Bell, Boyd and Lloyd and later with another major firm, Bryan Cave. The first part of the strategy was reclamation. The city secured $400,000 from the EPA's Targeted Brownfields Assessment program to evaluate the site, and eventually another $4 million was spent on the project, including $1.6 million from Sterling itself and almost $1 million from the state of Illinois, as well as $1.2 million in

Sterling and Rock Falls, Illinois: Reform and Recovery? 165

private and foundation investment and $260,000 from Sterling Township and Whiteside County.

The other part of the deal concerned the incentives and technical assistance provided to Leggett & Platt and its new Sterling Steel subsidiary by the city and its lawyers. The biggest part of the deal involved tax increment financing, as the city council unanimously passed a $4.3 million tax increment revenue bond to assist the project. The inclusion of the site in the Whiteside/Carroll County Enterprise Zone meant additional credits from property and sales taxes as well as support for worker training. The city paid for the legal services of Hummel and his firm and waived permit fees, while securing agreement from the county to waive back taxes; and both the city and GSDC picked up the cost of marketing the property.

The city clinched Sterling Steel's future in January 2003, with Leggett & Platt's acquisition of the arc furnaces that produced the wire for its bedspring manufacturing. Bell, Boyd and Lloyd won the American College of Real Estate Lawyers' "Unique Deal" award for 2003 thanks to the Sterling Steel deal, beating an aquarium in London, a business improvement district in Hong Kong and various other projects in the United States.[29]

Despite strong support for brownfield reclamation from Mayor Mulvaney, Rock Falls did not arrive at a consensus on reclaiming brownfield land until RFCDC was well established and a new mayor, city councilman David Blanton, had been elected in 2005 to fill the vacancy left by Mulvaney's retirement, in part on promises to accelerate economic development. Blanton, with a more conciliatory style, and from a business career background (Mulvaney's style and his career as a teacher at Rock Falls High School were noted by a few survey respondents as being factors that made some residents and community leaders suspicious of him, in a community with below-state-average levels of educational qualifications), had considerably greater success in enacting a set of policy goals essentially unchanged from his predecessor. The city received its first major grant funding for reclamation work at RB&W and Parrish-Alford in 2006, and the project is ongoing. Besides Rock Falls' later start on promoting economic development policy, the city faced another challenge: its brownfield sites were far more polluted than the NWSW plant in Sterling, notably including extensive asbestos contamination.

The CDC proved vital both in securing brownfield funding and in developing proposals for future land use. Having an organizational means of building a political consensus for reclaiming the mess that RB&W and Parrish-Alford had left behind was an essential prerequisite for gaining the outside funding without which Rock Falls could not afford improvements. The grant applications to the Illinois EPA and the federal EPA could not proceed until community leaders had agreed on a set of goals for the site, a process that was hammered out mostly around a vision presented by RFCDC board members and executive director Tscheschlok: a mostly residential, retail and office development on the riverfront. Although the

166 *Sterling and Rock Falls, Illinois: Reform and Recovery?*

Figure 6.3 The Rock Falls riverfront trail and Holiday Inn Express at the site of the former RB&W plant, August 2017. The trail connects downtown Rock Falls and Sterling with the Hennepin Canal Parkway, a long-distance trail maintained by the state of Illinois
Source: Daniel Bliss.

goal deviated sharply from Rock Falls' industrial past, it dovetailed with the city in one critical respect – its density. Rock Falls has a more concentrated and walkable business district than Sterling, and a successful riverfront development next to the existing downtown is expected to build upon this asset. City leaders have strongly pushed the idea of condominium and retail development that capitalizes on the area's relative popularity with retirees.

Work on the site reclamation began in 2008 after a fire gutted a major building on the site. The city of Rock Falls took involuntary possession, making it eligible for EPA funding for remediation, and gradually demolished all remaining RB&W and most Parrish-Alford buildings, removed and replaced large amounts of polluted building materials and soil and extended a city street to connect the town's east side with the business district through the former factory site. In 2012 the city began work on site reclamation to develop a new riverfront park, and in 2015 a developer built a Holiday Inn Express hotel next to a riverside walk linking a popular regional trail with downtown Rock Falls (see Figure 6.3), and other lots were placed on the market. The final city-directed phase of this project is a performing arts amphitheater built in the park in 2016 (see Figure 6.4).

Figure 6.4 The performing arts amphitheater built in the park in 2016
Source: Daniel Bliss.

This has fit a trend in Rock Falls, both under the CDC and recently under mayoral control, of promoting property development and "shovel-ready" land along with amenities. Major utility extensions on the east side of the city have been completed; farmland the city owns is leased on the basis of tenants being able to vacate for industrial development after no more than a single planting season.

In another key economic development respect, the provision of higher-quality, affordable, single-family housing, Rock Falls has led Sterling in implementing policy. As with Hibbing and Ely, the Sterling and Rock Falls area suffers from a shortage of high-quality family-oriented housing that qualifies as affordable on typical area pay scales. Addressing this clearly ranks very high on Rock Falls' agenda, with the city exceeding its neighbors in finding land for and adding new residential developments. This includes major new development on the river frontage near downtown, platting new subdivisions and an aggressive program of using state grants to fund the renovation of older single-family homes. In a four-year period in the late 2000s Rock Falls secured more than $1 million in state grants under the Illinois Single-Family Owner-Occupied Rehabilitation (SFOOR) program, providing $40,000 a house in renovation funds,[30] as well as adding a substantial new subdivision on the west side of the city that included former Mayor Mulvaney among its residents. Once again, here is a new policy that

168   *Sterling and Rock Falls, Illinois: Reform and Recovery?*

has emerged since city reorganization, though in this case the CDC apparently had no role in placing the issue on the policy agenda.

This has not been lost on community leaders in Sterling, who noted Rock Falls' lead over Sterling in promoting residential development. One respondent specifically cited Rock Falls' lead over Sterling on its plans for downtown, housing and retail redevelopment[31] and another pointed out the lead of both Rock Falls and Dixon in boosting new residential projects.[32]

Building Cooperation with a Sales Tax Referendum

In Illinois' local government revenue system, the recruitment of retail businesses is a key component of any strategy for boosting municipal revenue. This is seen throughout the state, from Chicago to some of the smallest communities with active economic development policies. The key reason retailing is so important for an Illinois municipality is the considerable leeway Illinois cities have in levying sales taxes. Home rule can mean very little if the benefits are defined narrowly by the state, if it is difficult to get without ceding council autonomy or even, to a lesser extent, if cities already have some autonomy as non-home-rule cities (Barron, Frug & Su, 2004). However, Illinois grants autonomy that is being used widely. Cities or counties – whether or not they have home rule – may levy up to a three percent local sales tax in addition to the 1.25 percent share of the state sales tax they are automatically allocated for revenue generated within their limits.

Therefore, there is a powerful political incentive to promoting retailing – an interesting contrast to Hibbing's moves in the retail sector despite the lack of revenue incentives in Minnesota. While home-rule entities may enact such a tax by a simple majority of the council or county board, non-home-rule cities such as Sterling and Rock Falls additionally require a referendum of local voters. However, the proximity of the towns and of nearby Dixon meant community leaders feared a beggar-thy-neighbor situation, in which shoppers and businesses would flee a jurisdiction with a local option sales tax for one without if at least one of the tax referenda failed. With significant retailing in all three places and excellent local road links as well as Interstate 88, political and business leaders saw the region as a single economy. The question was whether voters would view things in the same way.

City politicians and business leaders in Sterling and Dixon had little doubt of their ability to comfortably pass a referendum on the tax, a 0.5 percent local option sales tax to ride atop the 6.25 percent state tax. In Illinois' tax system, this would effectively boost local sales tax revenue from 1.25 percent to 1.75 percent given the state revenue-sharing formula, clearly establishing sales taxes on a par with property taxes as a revenue source in Sterling. But there was serious doubt over whether Rock Falls would also join in. While there was no question Rock Falls needed the tax

Sterling and Rock Falls, Illinois: Reform and Recovery? 169

money, arguably more than Sterling or Dixon, the stakes in Rock Falls were lower due to an inferior retail tax base. Initially, Sterling would see approximately $3 million a year in new funding from the tax, equivalent to almost a third of its general fund; Rock Falls would see only $800,000, equivalent to about 15 percent of its general fund.

Furthermore, the skepticism among Rock Falls' voters about supporting local tax increases was higher, tax increases for local schools were tougher to approve in Rock Falls and incumbent local politicians were voted out of office more frequently. The referendum ran the very real risk of failing in Rock Falls while passing in the other two communities, which would cost Rock Falls valuable tax revenue while potentially encouraging retail flight from Sterling and Dixon to Rock Falls.

Accordingly, in the fall of 2004, all three city councils undertook the necessary legislation for non-home-rule cities in Illinois to schedule voter referenda, which were to take place on the same day: the April local elections in 2005.[33] Community leaders lobbied intensively for passage of the tax in all three places, holding public forums and information sessions on the tax. In all three places the tax was earmarked for neighborhood streets and infrastructure,[34] rather than economic development funding; council minutes show this restriction was important for securing city council support. The culture of skepticism about giving tax money to private business showed itself even in northern Illinois, if not as strongly as in Minnesota.

The politicians' fears about Rock Falls' voters proved well founded, and their decision to coordinate the referenda is credited as being the critical factor in their success. On election day the tax passed overwhelmingly in Sterling, with 69 percent of the vote, and in Dixon, with 71 percent of the vote. In Rock Falls the tax scraped through on a 52–48 margin. Leaders in both Sterling and Rock Falls have been at pains ever since to emphasize the street projects that the sales tax underwrites, but the success of the tax is not in doubt. First, the pace of street improvements has dramatically increased in both communities. For example, in Sterling, street improvement spending of almost $1.9 million for fiscal year 2006 drew on more than $800,000 in new sales tax revenue;[35] Rock Falls street improvement projects also increased sharply for 2006.[36] Additionally, Sterling used sales tax revenue in 2009–11 for major reconstruction of its City Hall building, the Coliseum,[37] and completed Lynn Boulevard, a beltway around the north and west sides of Sterling that accesses much of the city's newer industrial property.

Retail Development in Sterling and Rock Falls

As the difficult but ultimately successful process with the sales tax referendum demonstrated, the question of often capricious differences in resources among communities is never very far away in Illinois. Sharing revenue rather than redistributing it makes for a race among towns for

170   *Sterling and Rock Falls, Illinois: Reform and Recovery?*

population, for business and especially for retailing. While Rock Falls in some respects is very competitive – it is clearly beating Sterling in new residential development, for example – it has badly lagged in retailing. The consequences of this are most clearly visible in the roughly two to one difference in sales tax revenues between the two cities. In the past Sterling has been far more effective than Rock Falls at recruiting retail business, on account of the city's proactive and controversy-avoiding approach to land use. By annexing and servicing territory on the fringe of the town while clearing much of the west side of downtown for stores with suburban-style parking and access, Sterling ensured a healthy stream of sales tax revenue. In contrast, Rock Falls' strategy for developing retailing, like its strategy for reclaiming derelict industrial land, did not emerge until after the 2001–2 recession. And, due to the lead time for securing the cooperation of landowners and, in some cases, title to land, the largest and best-located sites around Rock Falls for retailing did not finally become available until the onset of the next recession in 2007–8, ensuring it would be some time before sites are finally developed.

To a considerable extent, this has to do with the differences between the two communities from the 1980s to the early 2000s in terms of how aggressively they sought retail business. Long before the arrival of the local option sales tax, Sterling was brutally pragmatic, sprawling across cornfields to accommodate large-scale retailers and bulldozing much of its old downtown to make way for a large new grocery store and drive-in businesses. Rock Falls left its downtown business district largely intact, and, prior to its government and economic development reorganization, did little to secure edge-of-town land on the kind of scale needed for larger retailers that want big floor space and bigger parking lots.

This contrast is particularly striking due to the apparent advantage Rock Falls has over Sterling in terms of access to the highway network. While Sterling has had its own local four-lane link to Dixon since the 2000s through Illinois Highway 2, Rock Falls is more directly connected to the regional road network. Interstate 88 bypasses Rock Falls to the south, requiring Sterling residents to drive over the congested 1st Avenue Bridge and through Rock Falls to get to the highway. But, rather than brightly lit gas stations and convenience stores, the exits on I-88 mostly have the rural appearance of road junctions in jurisdictions with strict controls on development even though none exist here. Survey respondents cited the difficulty of convincing landowners to sell key parcels near two of the exits, meaning that these sites remain either undeveloped or "underdeveloped." Most of Rock Falls' industrial activity has long been near the river and close to downtown. Much of the retail activity in Rock Falls is concentrated in the downtown, in smaller businesses, or a half-mile to the south around the Illinois Highway 2/US 30 intersection. The only retailer with more than 50,000 square feet of space is an older, smaller Walmart store that does not sell groceries.

The "strip"-style pattern of large-scale retail development is to be found instead on the Sterling side of the river, especially along Illinois Highway 2, which carries traffic to nearby Dixon, and, since four-lane conversion in the early 2000s, does so with approximately the same efficiency as the interstate. Sterling developed a regional shopping mall in the 1970s and has since lined the highway with box retailers, including office box retailer Staples. Two car dealers call Sterling home – but none are in Rock Falls. The area's only enclosed shopping mall – the only enclosed mall between Rockford, Illinois and the Quad Cities – is also in Sterling, as is the only Walmart Supercenter (Rock Falls has a conventional, smaller-format Walmart) and both the area's full-service supermarkets.

In a sales-tax-oriented system of local government finance such as Illinois', this represents a serious disadvantage for Rock Falls in terms of its tax base: a 75–25 split of the area's approximately $4 million in annual sales tax revenue in favor of Sterling[38] even though Sterling contains only 62 percent of the total population of the two cities. One Rock Falls respondent noted that a single major event, such as the relocation or expansion to Rock Falls of just one of Sterling's car dealerships, could dramatically alter this balance.[39] From the mid-2000s, with the increased activism and organization of Rock Falls' city government, much of the land around Rock Falls' I-88 highway exits has come on the market and been opened up with city utilities. This was accompanied from the start by a strong pitch for regional retail business. During 2006 and 2007 downtown Rock Falls saw the addition of a new bank and of Whiteside County's first Walgreens store, at the junction of US 30 and Illinois 40, viewed as a major achievement for local economic development policy and cited by several survey respondents. The recession proved a severe setback, but, aside from the Holiday Inn Express built at the former RB&W site in 2016, the city has acquired land and rezoned around the busiest of the interstate exits, opening that area to future commercial development.

Here, as in other economic development policy areas, policies in Sterling and Rock Falls have grown together. In some regards Rock Falls is working even more proactively than Sterling. Initially the city made mistakes; one key case involved a local landowner, George Holman, whose property near the I-88 interchange had originally been identified by the city as a likely site for industrial development. Not until the city changed its land use goal for that area to retail did Holman agree to consider selling the site.[40] But eventually, in part with the increasingly close relationship between city government and the business community through the CDC, the planning became more organized. Sandy Henrekin, who replaced Tscheschlok in 2007 as executive director of Rock Falls CDC and remained in that role through 2014, proceeded to market the community at conventions of the International Council of Shopping Centers (like her Hibbing counterparts),[41] though the 2007–9 recession meant progress on this project was largely limited to raising the community's profile; this pattern of policy continues under mayoral

172 *Sterling and Rock Falls, Illinois: Reform and Recovery?*

control today. The already industrial eastern approach of US Highway 30 is earmarked for further industrial expansion with new improvements in sewer infrastructure, and substantial additional land near the I-88 interchange and along the Illinois Highway 40 retail corridor, including Holman's property, has been identified for retail and service development. With access roads and utilities already installed in both areas, there is no question that the land is "shovel-ready." A 60-acre property immediately bordering the interchange is being marketed for use for services to interstate highway users; a similar-size site to the northwest is earmarked for "destination shopping."[42] Available land in Rock Falls within the Whiteside/Carroll County Enterprise Zone now almost mirrors that of Sterling.[43]

But, overall, retailing remains weaker than in Sterling. Rock Falls' Walmart, one of the first in Illinois, remains largely unimproved since construction in the 1980s. Most importantly, the city has failed in its attempts to maintain a stable grocery store, meaning that residents must drive elsewhere, normally Sterling, to purchase basic staples. Rock Falls lost its only supermarket after the 2003 bankruptcy of Iowa grocery store chain Eagle Country Markets. Getting a new tenant for the former Eagle market was a high priority for local economic developers and the city council through 2004 and 2005, and finally realized in the spring of 2006 when a small regional chain in Rock Island, Illinois, signed a deal to lease the building from the property developer that now owned it, backed by aid from the city of Rock Falls. But the reopened store lasted just three years until closure in October 2009, and, with a discount store next door quickly snapping up the lease on the grocery store property, Rock Falls' prospects of getting its own full-service supermarket would now likely hinge on new construction.

Walmart and the Sterling Distribution Center

Economic developers like to operate on recruitment with considerable secrecy, and GSDC and RFCDC are no exception – making full use of the arm's-length relationship they enjoy with their respective city councils. But, in some cases, early secrecy results in a broader strategy that embraces other agencies and local governments. Certainly, that has been the case with the I-88 West strategy for recruiting more service and distribution-oriented businesses to Whiteside County. This strategy has its roots in November 2003, when GSDC, with the support of officials from the state of Illinois Department of Economic Opportunity, Whiteside County and Rock Falls CDC, made a huge play.

They landed one of the largest distribution facilities ever to be built in Illinois, a cold storage facility that was part of Walmart's national strategy of breaking into the grocery market. The Walmart Distribution Center, as it is referred to in almost all local records, was by any stretch a major catch. The massive facility served at its opening 136 stores in northern Illinois and neighboring states, almost 20 more than originally planned.[44] Most notable was the size of the facility: at 900,000 square feet, its scale was almost on a par with the shuttered NWSW steelworks.

For this facility, Whiteside County laid out a substantial incentives package, supported by the city governments, partly rolling out local resources and partly making use of standing incentive programs available from the state of Illinois. At the request of Walmart, the project did not use tax increment financing – and, not coincidentally, enjoyed strong support from the Sterling school district, whose tax base was, unlike the municipalities, directly affected by the location outside the cities but still inside the school district.

The county enterprise zone was extended to include the Walmart property in rural Sterling Township, thus temporarily exempting the facility from both local property taxes and local and state sales taxes for a period of 12 years; the facility's status involving an investment of more than $5 million and employing more than 200 people qualified it for a utility tax exemption from the state;[45] additionally, the city of Sterling agreed to annex territory up to, but not over, the Walmart property line for the purpose of extending a sewer line and enabling other businesses to locate nearby, a project funded in part by state grants under the Illinois FIRST infrastructure program. For its part, Walmart contributed $2.8 million in hard costs toward infrastructure upgrade, with the private franchisee for water supply in Sterling, Illinois American Water Company, contributing a further $500,000.[46]

In terms of averting an unemployment crisis, there is little doubt that intervention in economic development was a clear success. By the start of the 2008–9 recession, total employment in Whiteside County almost reached pre-2001 levels as a percentage of the county's population, despite the massive losses in manufacturing. Under the circumstances, this is no small achievement. In total, the Sterling/Rock Falls area lost approximately 3,000 manufacturing jobs during the 2000s, in an urban area of fewer than 30,000 residents. Countywide manufacturing employment, disproportionately concentrated in the Sterling/Rock Falls area, dropped from 7,700 in the second quarter of 2001 to approximately 4,700 by the second quarter of 2007. According to the Bureau of Labor Statistics (BLS), Whiteside County – almost half of whose population is in Sterling or Rock Falls – saw unemployment rise from 4.1 percent in 1999 to 7.1 percent in 2003 in the aftermath of the NWSW bankruptcy. A slow recovery to 2006 shaved that to 5.5 percent, rising slightly to a 5.6 percent average for 2007. In the 2008–9 recession, unemployment peaked at 10 percent.[47]

Thus, small manufacturing town unemployment rates approaching 20 percent, seen in similar communities in Indiana and Michigan, have not been replicated here. The reason for this has been a continued development of service and distribution industries, actively pursued by area economic developers as part of a strategy to sell the underutilized western reaches of I-88 as a major transportation asset. The I-88 West strategy

174   *Sterling and Rock Falls, Illinois: Reform and Recovery?*

emerged as a regional initiative with the support of the Whiteside/Carroll County Enterprise Zone board in the aftermath of the success with the Walmart Distribution Center,[48] amid the sense that the kinds of facilities located in and around Rochelle and DeKalb, Illinois, could easily be lured 40 or 50 miles west.[49] As Barajas put it when Walmart went beyond its original plans for expanding the distribution center, "It is obviously very important. It helps us develop momentum for the I-88 West project. It helps to add credibility to I-88 West. Developers in the Chicagoland marketplace see that."[50] More recently, this development has extended to manufacturing as well, with Sterling increasingly tending to cultivate and recruit small to medium firms in this sector.

After the initial decline from NWSW's collapse, private-sector wages stabilized. The arrival of Walmart's distribution center provided the first upward pressure on local wages in the following years. From 2001 to 2003 average weekly private-sector wages fell from $495 to $486, then rose to $589 by 2008,[51] though that still left private-sector wages two percent below 2001 levels in inflation-adjusted terms.[52] While the Walmart jobs compare favorably with other local service industry jobs, they are well behind the $20 to $30 an hour that older NWSW employees were making[53] prior to the firm's collapse. Nonetheless, as with many other rural counties, the place to work in Whiteside County remains state or federal government. State employees in Whiteside County averaged $47,515 a year and federal employees $48,781; local government employees, with an average of just $32,294, are paid comparably to the $32,628 average in the for-profit private sector.

The reward for the area from Walmart alone has been considerable. Walmart initially promised 700 jobs, and by the facility's official opening in April 2006 already had 650 staff in place.[54] The initial round of hiring at Walmart accounted for a large majority of Whiteside County's gain in average annual employment, from 28,088 in 2005 to 29,153 in 2007.[55] Today the headcount at the distribution center has surpassed 1,000, keeping pace with the largest remaining manufacturer, Wahl Clipper, and bringing it in line with Sterling's public hospital, CGH Medical Center; these are the area's three biggest employers at present. Moreover, the Walmart jobs are well above not only minimum wage but also living wage standards for the area. At $13 to $15 an hour at opening[56] and in 2017 the upper teens to around $20 an hour, they enable a manageable standard of living in an area where median single-family house prices have badly lagged the Illinois statewide average.[57] Nonetheless, they are well below the pay rates of the jobs lost at NWSW and the hardware manufacturers.

Outcomes and Conclusion

While the convergence and the increased cooperation between Sterling and Rock Falls are notable across many facets of economic development

Sterling and Rock Falls, Illinois: Reform and Recovery? 175

policy, they have not reached all areas, and in recent years cooperation and coordination have declined again. In major municipal infrastructure projects, Sterling and Rock Falls go their separate ways. The cities are working together where the state is involved, with a pedestrian and bike connection over the Rock-Falls-owned hydroelectric dam, and reconstruction of the busy First Avenue Bridge on Illinois Highway 40. But on local projects, including the most expensive infrastructure of all, sewage disposal, it is a different story, with the competitive instinct often taking hold in apparently irrational ways. In 2004 and 2005 Rock Falls and Sterling quarreled over a consultants' report that recommended a combined plant be located on the Sterling side of the Rock River,[58] with Rock Falls demanding a location on its side of the river be considered. The concept of a regional project was set aside, and instead the cities have updated their sewage plants independently – Rock Falls first, with extensive support from the 2009 federal stimulus. In northwestern Illinois, as in northern Minnesota, a challenge remains in reconciling local rivalries, project complexity and planning goals.

The implication of these communities in Illinois, a state notorious for fragmented local government and competition between neighboring cities, is that institutional reform is an important element enabling successful policy delivery. Sterling's response to the collapse of Northwestern Steel and Wire in May 2001 demonstrated speed and organizational preparedness. Within less than two years the plant's new arc furnaces were running again, thanks to the city's direct intervention to secure the property. The city also proceeded almost immediately to seek major state and federal funding for brownfield reclamation on the NWSW site, a process that was complete by 2004. With Sterling's reclamation of NWSW well advanced, Rock Falls embarked on a similar set of policies for the former RB&W and Parrish-Alford sites only after the reorganization of city government was well in train. Although the city had institutional means of pursuing such projects – through its industrial development commission – the decision to proceed with redevelopment ultimately depended upon a more united city council featuring leaders who trusted one another. The implication of survey interviews in this project is that such trust was seriously lacking prior to the reorganization.

Leadership has also helped. Mayor Blanton, who had been a notable critic of outgoing Mayor Mulvaney prior to his 2005 election, made no major changes to Mulvaney's policies, but enjoyed far greater trust from the council. It was in this improved political environment that the votes to pursue brownfield reclamation and, ultimately, riverfront redevelopment were taken. Perhaps – though it cannot be ascertained from this survey – Mulvaney had already taken too many political hits from leading the city during its far-reaching reorganization. Perhaps it took a new mayor to finally deliver the votes on economic development policies that far outstripped Rock Falls' previous efforts. After all, it takes time for healthy

176 *Sterling and Rock Falls, Illinois: Reform and Recovery?*

stability in government to emerge. Sterling respondents repeatedly praised the city's "progressive" political culture, and a few mentioned how long the organizational components of that culture had been in place. And even Blanton did not see the riverfront project through; that task fell to former city clerk William Wescott, a stronger advocate for regional cooperation in economic development than either of his predecessors, elected in 2013 along with several new council members. Ironically, under Wescott's mayoralty, Rock Falls' reorganization of the early 2000s was partly reversed and cooperation between Rock Falls and Sterling has weakened, even as Wescott and his office have actively pursued outside business with a strategy centered on development-ready property. This reversal came in spite of the successes under the CDC, with complex land reclamation and property development projects that would have been much more difficult to achieve under the previous arrangements.

One other key institutional element for economic development, building structures for cooperation between municipalities, remains compromised in both Sterling and Rock Falls. In this respect, despite the pessimistic remarks of many survey respondents, the problem arises only from city leaders, though it also dovetails with the state of Illinois' framework for local government. On the one hand, Illinois law is supportive of the specific policy goal of economic development. The county enterprise zone was at the core of the successful effort to lure the Walmart Distribution Center, a project that was able to rely mostly upon state-funded incentives and avoided the use of tax increment financing. Furthermore, the enterprise zone has provided a key means for Rock Falls in particular to expand its supply of commercially developable land, with the tax abatements involved making these sites easier for existing landowners to sell at an economic price and more attractive to prospective buyers.

On the other hand, Illinois' system of local government finance leaves a two-to-one disparity between Sterling and Rock Falls on sales tax revenue, which represents an unfair disadvantage for the already poorer Rock Falls and means the two cities inevitably compete directly for retailers. As one Sterling respondent pointed out, the loss of a single car dealership from Sterling to Rock Falls would at a stroke equalize the per capita imbalance in revenue – and deliver Sterling a major new problem as it strives to maintain its healthy finances under trying circumstances. In this context, the success of Sterling and Rock Falls in coordinating their half-cent increase in the sales tax represents an impressive feat of leadership with no formal institutional linkage. Nevertheless, by this time, the presence of the enterprise board with this successful recruitment of Walmart meant that Sterling and Rock Falls already had an institutional venue for maintaining relations beyond mutual aid in emergency services. Externally, as internally, institutional organization made for an environment in which leaders considered new policies and were often able to deliver them.

Notes

1 J. Bustos, Reflecting on his two cities: For retiring mayor, today's Sterling is much different than it was 12 years ago, *Sauk Valley News/Daily Gazette*, May 6, 2007.

2 Interview 94. The "five companies" were Wahl Clipper, a maker of electric clippers that is by far the largest surviving local manufacturer; Lawrence Brothers, a hardware manufacturer that went bankrupt in 2002; National Manufacturing, a manufacturer of hand tools that was bought out by Stanley Works and saw most local production outsourced; Frantz Manufacturing, a bearing manufacturer that is a fraction of its former size; and Northwestern Steel & Wire, now Sterling Steel, Inc.

3 NWSW made several "Sterling" branded products, including a widely available line of nails.

4 Bustos, May 6, 2007.

5 Interview 94.

6 Based on Form 990PF filing of Dillon Foundation, as reported by GuideStar Grant Explorer. At the end of October 2008 the foundation held assets of $61,507,000 and had awarded $3.8 million in grants to recipients in Illinois, mostly in Sterling and Rock Falls.

7 Interview 84.

8 Interview 69.

9 Interview 84.

10 *Sterling Daily Gazette*, July 25, 1967.

11 Davenport and Bettendorf, Iowa; and Moline and Rock Island, Illinois, where farm equipment manufacturer John Deere has long been the dominant employer.

12 Based on US Census Data. Sterling's labor force as of the 2000 census was 7,609; total labor force for the Sterling Urban Cluster (including all urbanized portions of Sterling and Rock Falls and neighboring urbanized portions of Coloma and Sterling Townships) was 14,534.

13 Source: Illinois Department of Employment Security, Economic Information and Analysis Division; and Whiteside County.

14 For a full list of local and state incentives for Rock Falls, Illinois, see the Rock Falls Community Development Corporation website, at www.rockfallsdevelopment.org/incentive_properties.html (accessed July 8, 2010).

15 Minutes of the regular meeting of the mayor and aldermen of the City of Rock Falls, October 4, 2005.

16 Bustos, May 6, 2007.

17 City council minutes, March 1 2004.

18 Ordinance 2004-04-13, April 19 2004 council meeting.

19 City council minutes, September 17 2007.

20 City council minutes, December 15 2008.

21 City of Sterling, 2007–2008 budget in brief, and City of Sterling, 2001–2002 budget in brief, among others. Standard and Poor's rating stood at AAA throughout the 2000s; Moody's raised its rating to Aaa from A2.

22 Source: City of Sterling annual financial report, 2016.

23 A. Walters, Development leader banks on new career: David Barajas Jr. helped bring Walmart Distribution Center to Sterling, *Sauk Valley News*, October 26, 2007.

178   *Sterling and Rock Falls, Illinois: Reform and Recovery?*

24 Several survey respondents in both Rock Falls and Sterling noted the speed and effectiveness of Rock Falls' reorganization. See, for example, interviews 69, 78, 80, 81, 84.

25 Interview 78.

26 Both city councils have repeatedly discussed problems about enforcement relating to residential and industrial abandoned properties. See, for example, Rock Falls City Council minutes from March 2, 2004; June 1, 2004; August 16, 2004; and April 27, 2009; and interviews 22, 24, 72, 78. Illinois law prevents a city from reclaiming legal fees in actions against delinquent property owners, and ranks a city last in order of priority in the event of a lien against the property. See Rock Falls City Council minutes from August 16, 2004, for discussion.

27 Interview 80.

28 See SRA International (2006), a report prepared for the US Environmental Protection Agency, Office of Solid Waste and Emergency Response and Office of Brownfields Cleanup and Redevelopment.

29 Sterling City Council minutes, November 17, 2003, available at http://ci.sterling.il.us/main/council-meetings/2003/111703/minutes11-17-03.pdf.

30 Minutes of regular Rock Falls City Council meetings, December 20, 2005; November 6, 2007; June 3 and 17, 2008; March 3 and 17, 2009; and June 16, 2009.

31 Interview 78.

32 Interview 94.

33 The issues involving the sales tax referendum are covered in considerable detail in official minutes of Sterling City Council's August 2, 2004, meeting, at which the April 2005 vote was scheduled (see Ordinance 2004-08-23, City of Sterling).

34 Minutes of regular Sterling City Council meeting, October 18, 2004.

35 Minutes of regular Sterling City Council meeting, November 6, 2006.

36 Minutes of regular Rock Falls City Council meeting November 7, 2006.

37 See minutes of Sterling City Council study session, September 8, 2008, for a general description of the Coliseum project.

38 Based on first-year revenue figures from the local option sales tax.

39 Interview 81.

40 Interview 82.

41 February 17, 2009, minutes of regular Rock Falls City Council meeting.

42 Source: Rock Falls Community Development Corporation. See website at www.rockfallsdevelopment.org/sites.html (accessed June 10, 2010).

43 See Figure 6.1. Sterling enterprise zone sites are relatively concentrated and include the downtown, the former NWSW site and most west and north side areas that were opened for development by the construction of Lynn Boulevard; Sterling Township's principal site is the Walmart Distribution Center; Rock Falls sites are spread throughout the city, including the manufacturing sites on the city's east side, both major highway corridors, the downtown and the major exits from Interstate 88.

44 J. Bustos, Sauk Valley jobless rate drops year over year, *Sauk Valley News/Daily Gazette*, November 1, 2006.

45 Whiteside/Carroll County Enterprise Zone management organization minutes, July 11, 2006.

Sterling and Rock Falls, Illinois: Reform and Recovery? 179

46 Finance Committee report (statement from Betty Steinert, economic development director for Whiteside County), minutes of the regular meeting, Whiteside County board, January 18, 2005.

47 Source: Bureau of Labor Statistics, using county-level data for Whiteside County. BLS data were used for unemployment data and to calculate the loss of manufacturing jobs.

48 The I-88 West initiative is discussed extensively in each of the Whiteside/Carroll County Enterprise Zone board's regular quarterly meetings from October 2006 through the end of 2008.

49 Interview 78.

50 A. Walters, Walmart to add 150 jobs, *Sauk Valley News/Daily Gazette*, January 18, 2007.

51 Source: Bureau of Labor Statistics, using county-level data.

52 US census data from the American Community Survey show a similar story on employment totals. See Table B24091, Whiteside County, Illinois, 2005–2007, American Community Survey three-year average. For data on average wages for all sizes of private-sector establishment, see Bureau of Labor Statistics series ENU1719540510 for Whiteside County, Illinois.

53 J. Hughes, Sterling the latest Illinois town to lose industry, Associated Press, State & Local Wire, June 1, 2001.

54 Whiteside/Carroll County Enterprise Zone management organization official minutes, April 11, 2006; they contain information on both the Walmart project and the expansion of the enterprise zone to east Sterling.

55 Bureau of Labor Statistics series ID LAUPA17115005, Whiteside County, Illinois. Unemployment data are not seasonally adjusted.

56 T. Appel, Savior or villain?, *Wall Street Journal*, February 24, 2006, section B, p. 1.

57 Source: City-data.com for both Sterling and Rock Falls. The median price for all categories of home in 2008 was $214,900 in Illinois, $106,595 in Rock Falls and $119,605 in Sterling; in 2000 average prices were $63,000 in Rock Falls and $70,700 in Sterling. Data accessed July 6, 2010, at www.city-data.com/city/Rock-Falls-Illinois.html for Rock Falls and www.city-data.com/city/Sterling-Illinois.html for Sterling.

58 8-04-2005 RF Public Works Committee, agenda joint sewer study discussion and recommendations.

References

Barron, D. J., Frug, G. E., & Su, R. T. (2004). *Dispelling the myth of home rule: Local power in Greater Boston*. Cambridge, Mass.: Rappaport Institute for Greater Boston.

Pagano, M. A. (2003). City fiscal structures and land development, discussion paper. Washington, D.C.: Brookings Institution Center on Urban and Metropolitan Policy.

SRA International (2006). *Revitalizing America's mills: A report on brownfields mill projects*. Arlington, Va.: SRA International.

7 Comparing Governance of Economic Development

We now turn to comparing the findings from these case studies. They should give pause to those who assume local places largely lack influence over their direction, and hope to those who seek local or state-level solutions for economic and quality-of-life problems. All four of these communities show significant economic development results from local resources: local-level leadership, institutions of governance, economic development policy and land use, as well as the utilization of state-level safety nets and/or delegation of power. A comparison of these cities shows differences at both the state and local level that affect outcomes. At the state level, Sterling and Rock Falls, Illinois, have a theoretical advantage over their Minnesota counterparts in terms of controlling the governance of economic development but a theoretical disadvantage in funding all types of public spending, and both these theories stand up to investigation. The extent to which the state of Illinois devolves control over tax breaks and other forms of assistance makes it less likely that a substantial economic development incentive will be withheld due to the differences in agendas between state and local politicians, as it has in Ely. But there is also an implied disadvantage. Illinois' devolved approach to governance, its localized system of generating sales tax revenue and its lack of any need-based general fund assistance to municipalities point strongly to the likelihood that small towns must spend heavily, perhaps excessively so and at the cost of other activities, on economic development assistance to build the tax base needed to fund basic services.

Local institutions of governance also matter. For example, Ely's long-running controversy over whether to run city government with a clerk-treasurer and department heads reporting directly to the city council or a city administrator operating as a CEO caused instability for years. Once these conflicts were settled, Ely's city council showed stronger consensus on economic development, setting a priority on shovel-ready sites for business and on property development. Rock Falls faced a greater challenge due to the scale of dereliction and industrial pollution from the shuttered RB&W works, yet produced the organizational wherewithal to deliver a successful project. Sterling's rapid response to the 2001 industrial crisis stands out

Comparing Governance of Economic Development 181

as being both impressive in its speed and the degree to which it depended on institutional readiness in city governance, including the city council and administration, and on the non-profit Greater Sterling Development Corporation. Another form of stability is evident in Hibbing's revolving loan fund for business, the Economic Development Special Revenue Fund. This fund and its governance have both survived major political changes to maintain a steady output of municipal support for local businesses, continuing relationships that are in some cases a half-century old.

These institutions of governance play a crucial role in these cities' ability to make use of the one immovable asset of every local government: land. The progress in all four cases in making better availability of land and property for business and community amenities alike has depended on better city management and a more favorable political climate. Hibbing, Sterling and Rock Falls all now have plentiful availability of land for siting new businesses, and, in Rock Falls' case, new housing as well. Even in Ely, with the most constricted geography of the four, the situation has improved with the annexation of city-owned sites on the community's western gateway close to the existing downtown. This annexation, talked about for 40 years but never acted upon until 2015, was approved only once unanimity had been achieved on the city council. These findings look at institutional capacity, leadership and the delivery of economic and community development policy, local and state intergovernmental relations and the implications of the differences in the state frameworks within which they operate. It concludes with a review of whether these communities are delivering, and are seen to be delivering, on policy goals.

How Local Institutions Deliver Economic Development Policy

The question of how institutions deliver economic development centers on how the process is configured. This includes asking how a city's process of making economic development policy is defined and delegated, and whether it is politically contested. The clear pattern in this study is that "reformed" governance in the city, such as a council-manager system, is not necessarily a prerequisite for improvements in delivering on policy goals, a pattern confirmed in large-sample quantitative research (Carr, 2015). Rather, what is needed is clearly defined, coherent and settled processes for policy delivery, whether or not a council-manager system is present. This arrangement needs to be stable, avoiding political conflicts that may derail it, and it needs to be coherent, avoiding unnecessary separations between the "steering" of defining and brainstorming policy and the "driving" of financing and implementing it. It turns out that there is no one "best" way, but that certain patterns of governance produce certain distinct results. The more delegated economic development policy is, the more it will target direct assistance to private business; the more stable it is, the more it will produce; and the more centered upon elected officials the

182 *Comparing Governance of Economic Development*

policy is, the likelier it is to address broader community-wide questions of infrastructure and public services.

The evolution of Ely in this regard is instructive because of how the apparent contradictions in its experience illustrate institutional strengths and weaknesses. The city's attempt to regionalize economic development policy in the 1990s ultimately failed in part because of an institutional and organizational weakness; the resulting joint powers board did not sufficiently connect the "steering" and "driving" functions of policy-making and implementation. Weak consensus on economic development policy within city government had even more direct consequences. Governance in Ely was in serious flux during the 2000s, with the positions of city clerk, economic developer and mayor frequently turning over. Stability emerged only when the council settled the form of city administration and revived the statutory economic development authority.[1] With greater stability came further developments in the Ely Business Park, the settling of the long-term indecision on annexation and land use and the uptick in downtown property development driven also by a strong economy. Yet Ely's pattern of public infrastructure provision bas benefited from a form of institutional strength, namely stable lines of responsibility and long-term relationships with county, state and federal officials, even when consensus has been in short supply, as with the wastewater plant reconstruction.

While the other communities in this study have had their own upheavals, all have demonstrated more consistent output of policy, borne in part from organizational stability. Hibbing's 2010 electoral turnover did not heavily affect policy, and may well have added to public trust, even though interviews in 2012 made clear that business leaders in the community were profoundly and rationally concerned at the implications of the change. In practice, the stable arrangements for delivering economic development policy have helped to drive continuity in that policy. In Sterling, council frustrations at the pace of economic development during the 2007–9 recession and its aftermath have not fundamentally changed the model of delivering economic development, with much of the project management from the private Greater Sterling Development Corporation, and support from volunteer activism through nonprofits such as Sterling Today and the Sauk Valley Chamber of Commerce. The city of Sterling continues to focus on brownfield reclamation and using EPA grants and other funding sources to remediate polluted sites. Rock Falls, once it had completed site remediation on the eastern portion of its riverfront, dissolved its community development corporation in the name of freeing up $100,000 a year for other economic development activity, and is accelerating property development while its municipal public utility rolls out gigabit Internet broadband.

Leadership also emerges as a big factor, benefiting from effective institutions but sometimes able to overcome poor ones. Coherent institutional arrangements can be considered as a necessary condition but not always a sufficient one. Sterling, for example, has only its sixth city manager since

Comparing Governance of Economic Development 183

converting to council-manager governance 40 years ago. In Hibbing, Pat Garrity, the part-time elected city clerk, has also played a substantial role in local politics since the 1970s. A trio of key officials – eight-year Mayor Rick Wolff; economic developer Duane Northagen, in his position for 15 years; city administrator Brian Redshaw, in his position almost seven years – oversaw stability for much of the 2000s, and when they were replaced the changes in direction marked more of an adjustment of efforts than wholesale reform. In the end, change since the 1994 Open Meeting Law case upended the city council has been gradual, but steady, and with a similar collection of relatively interventionist, business support policies despite several surprise defeats of incumbents over the years at the polls.

Leadership and geography can also interact with institutions of governance, especially if the membership of city boards and commissions is geographically restricted. Consider the difference between Ely's fragmented jurisdictions, Hibbing's unified, single jurisdiction and Sterling's relatively arm's-length private-sector governance of economic development. Hibbing's key business leaders live within the city's extensive limits, and are therefore eligible to serve on city boards and commissions even though few in practice run for elected office. After all, living outside Hibbing's 186 square miles means a substantial commute in most directions. Sterling's nonprofit boards are not geographically restricted, and maintain an effective relationship with city government. In contrast, many in the Ely area active in business and community affairs live outside the city limits, and most of the institutions of governance are governed by boards or committees whose membership is geographically restricted. This precludes their membership of the city council and therefore economic development authority, or of any city commissions except for the small handful that are run in conjunction with the townships. To take just one example, two of the biggest local business owners in Hibbing, property developer Rick Lees and banker Jack Ryan, have both served extensively on city boards and commissions and taken leading roles in boosting the city's economic development activities despite living outside the pre-1979 boundary; a host of comparable people in Ely, including mail order retailer and environmental activist Steve Piragis, footwear manufacturer Patti Steger, apparel manufacturer Sue Schurke, and Betsy Leustek, a local activist for better schools whose family formerly owned a highway contracting business, have been effectively prevented from serving on major city commissions other than the Ely Library Board and Airport Commission by their places of residence being just a few miles outside the city's tightly drawn limits (this is less of an issue with the governance of the school district, due to its more expansive boundaries).

Proving this relationship between leadership and outcomes is problematic, for the effect of leadership is difficult to measure. This is best seen in Hibbing, which stands somewhat apart from the other cases in that neither institutional reform nor changes in leadership immediately led to changes

184 *Comparing Governance of Economic Development*

in policy. Instead, Hibbing perhaps best proves the argument that democracy counts. Policy there has been driven by a gradual shift of opinion in the community and on the council, in part from voters turning over city government in 2002 and 2010, in part from citizen activism pushing policies such as retail recruitment. With community involvement and activism comes council self-confidence. Whereas Hibbing had deferred in the past to the Iron Range Resources and Rehabilitation Board on major projects, the city now often took the lead in setting policy and pooled its own resources with those of the IRRRB in building its own extensive relationships with local manufacturers;[2] reviving and expanding the storefront loan program for downtown business improvements several years after street improvement projects downtown;[3] and even speculative development.

Hibbing's electorate kept a close watch on results. Although Hibbing's EDA undertakes the day-to-day management of economic development, respondents to the Hibbing survey for the change in direction credit political leadership from the city council,[4] which has also received blame in the event of failures. This was evident in Hibbing's bid to rebuild its retail base, a policy change with little tax revenue benefit for the city under Minnesota law due to the lack of local option sales taxes and the dependence on the state legislature in terms of tax law, but a big benefit as an amenity to residents, and one that clearly satisfied a major political demand involving quality of life (avoiding long drives for basic supplies, or being captive to monopoly pricing).

At no time was this clearer than with the city council's unanimous decision in 2006 to overturn a planning commission recommendation and rezone as commercial the last remaining stretch of residential properties along the main local bypass highway[5] – a decision that paved the way for the Iron Range's first Walgreens store[6] in a year that saw most incumbents re-elected. Just as the city a year earlier had opted not to protect local building supply store L&M Fleet Supply when recruiting Lowe's (L&M massively expanded its store and product lines in response), now the city did not protect local pharmacies in recruiting the Deerfield, Ill.,-based giant. The city that had once declined Herberger's to protect a locally owned department store now rolled out the red carpet for national chains – with support from leaders in all centers of power. When voter concern at the economy during the 2007–9 recession turned to voter revolt, it was to the 2010 council election that they turned for a rebooting of the process.

Institutional Readiness

Institutional readiness provides another key point of comparison among these cases. Some cities can move almost immediately with activist policy once a decision has been made. These cities already have legal authority, a political consensus or simply more resources. Others may be hamstrung by lack of expertise, by lack of legal authority to make a deal or by a weak tax

Comparing Governance of Economic Development 185

base. To consider how this works, it is worth reviewing the 2001–2 recession, which profoundly affected all four of the cities in this study, more so than the 2007–9 recession, because of large-scale job losses in mining and manufacturing alike. Sterling and Rock Falls lost thousands of jobs from the collapses of Northwestern Steel & Wire, RB&W and Parrish-Alford, and Hibbing and Ely suffered from the massive layoffs in the iron-ore-mining industry that year, including the permanent closure of LTV, as the steel producers they supplied went bankrupt. The resources of all these four towns to respond to such large layoffs – NWSW alone involved 1,500 jobs in an urban area of approximately 25,000 people – was inevitably limited.

One challenge has been land use, especially in the Illinois communities. While all four communities have suffered unemployment from major business failures within city limits or, in Ely's case, within commuting distance, Sterling and Rock Falls faced the additional challenge of permanent closures of major manufacturers that left a great deal of vacant land. The contrasting, but converging, ways in which Sterling and Rock Falls dealt with more than 1,000 acres of abandoned factories within their limits provide an object lesson in the value of institutional organization backing up the delivery of public policy. Sterling had the advantage of already having institutions in place, in the form of a strong and legally well-advised city manager and a nonprofit corporation to handle economic development deals. Rock Falls rapidly adopted its own measures for policy delivery through its community development corporation, and the closure over the next few years of RB&W and Parrish-Alford created the opportunity for similar policies to Sterling. The goal was a major, ongoing transformation of the Rock River waterfront through the area.

A common set of policies thus emerged in both cities. These policies have resulted in the abatement of environmental hazards, the clearance of title to land, the provision of extensive "shovel-ready" sites for new development and the solving of long-standing problems with utility infrastructure for industrial sites in the city. Rock Falls' lesser results in business development result in part from its lateness in the economic cycle in the 2000s in resolving these problems, whereas Sterling was ready to implement policy within a matter of months. Hibbing and Ely have faced the challenge of ensuring that sites and buildings are available for new businesses to develop; not in many years has either community faced the kind of suddenly derelict sites of Sterling and Rock Falls. But, even here, with annexation in Ely and identifying locations for retailing in Hibbing, the assembling of development sites is central to policy. The management of land, local government's one immovable asset, is therefore something that appears to be clearly helped both by leaderships inclined toward proactive economic development and institutions geared to delivering it, though leadership alone can produce results if sufficiently united.

186   *Comparing Governance of Economic Development*

Lastly, financial support from the state plays a significant role in the form of specific grants and loans for economic development as well as in terms of frameworks for supporting the financing of local government. Ely and Hibbing have both extensively used grants and loans from the Iron Range Resources and Rehabilitation Board to support projects ranging from landing new businesses, such as a call center of defense subcontractor CWTSatoTravel in Ely, to business property developing, such as the publicly financed speculative building at the Hibbing airport business park. The business park in which CWTSatoTravel's facility sits is especially noteworthy because it demonstrates how even lavish state support cannot function effectively without local action; the location of the site on former railroad and mining land meant years of title work and combining of properties to make it available for development. In Illinois, state-supported tax abatements were heavily used in Sterling's successful effort to recruit the Walmart Distribution Center, which took up much of the slack in the area's labor market in 2006 and 2007; and both Sterling and Rock Falls depended extensively on state and federal grants to fund the reclamation and cleanup of the huge brownfield sites in both towns left by the aftermath of the 2001 recession.

Economic Development and Relations among Local Governments

The next question concerns where intergovernmental connections figure in the comparison. At the local level, Hibbing, after its enormous 1970s annexation, has one fewer local partner to work with. Sterling and Rock Falls must navigate a relationship with one another that features both cooperation and rivalry, with the role of local townships little mentioned and annexations generally uncontested; Ely must find common strands within a community with a strong identity yet very high governmental fragmentation.

Geographical fragmentation is a large part of this story. Ely, the city that, thanks to its fragmented political geography, depends on intergovernmental relations more than any other, remains subject to far more contestation of those relationships than the other communities. The Ely Area Development Association, Ely Economic Development Authority/City Council and the Ely area's Community Economic Development Joint Powers Board have all seen far more changes of direction in their roles than comparable agencies in the other case study cities, while the emergence of a new group, Incredible Ely, has brought a new generation of private-sector leadership. Furthermore, despite the far-reaching annexation agreement negotiated in 1973 by then Ely Mayor J. P. Grahek with Morse Township, annexation was stalled for many years prior to the 2015 agreement, with the council being unwilling to challenge the township and the township demanding concessions from the city on revenue-sharing that state local government bodies have described as extraordinary.

Comparing Governance of Economic Development   187

So, as it did with institutions and leadership, land use emerges as a point of comparison when considering intergovernmental relations too. Ely's constricted boundaries and slow pace on annexation led one city council member to complain of annexation that, among local government officials and community leaders, "I don't think anyone here can spell it"[7] – a situation that, as he noted, is a problem due to the legal limitations on the township developing land. Yet key municipal public facilities such as the airport and water intake are in the township, as are two subdivisions that draw on city utilities, giving these subdivisions, the largest in the unincorporated area, a major incentive to fight annexation and its concomitant higher property taxes. While Ely has successfully revitalized the 1973 agreement to facilitate a new subdivision and expansion of commercially developable land to the west of the city, local leaders have never broached the idea of full amalgamation with Morse or annexation of Morse in the manner of Hibbing's late 1970s annexation of Stuntz. Two key differences between Morse and Stuntz are the cause of this being kept off the table. First, Hibbing city utilities are likely to eventually reach most of the habitable area of Stuntz Township, while there is no such prospect for Morse; and, second, far more than Stuntz Township in the 1970s, Morse Township has a huge tax base of approximately $600,000 per year-round resident, more than 15 times that of the city, that it wants to protect from city taxation and whose often isolated houses are ill-suited for centralized municipal utility service.[8]

These divisions complicate infrastructure management as well, reflecting the increasing importance of good infrastructure in effective economic development. As one Ely respondent put it, "They [the employers] have come due to infrastructure, not due to city recruitment."[9] Ely's relationship with higher levels of government has been highly effective, as its steady production of new public infrastructure attests. But all four communities have faced challenges in providing infrastructure on a regional basis – especially with regard to wastewater treatment and sewage disposal. Sterling and Rock Falls failed to reach agreement on a new sewage treatment plant, resulting in both cities going their own ways; Hibbing backed out of a regional deal with its neighbors due to protests from neighbors who feared air pollution from the increasing use of a nearby sewage plant; and Ely's annexation troubles have, among other things, severely restricted the expansion of utility lines beyond existing city limits, with the consequence that many rural residents near the city limits continue to depend on septic tanks.

State government can be a complicating factor in intercommunity relations, whether or not power is centralized. The smallest towns are especially vulnerable. State policy must be effectively scaled down to local needs, and Ely, as the smallest community in this study, has proved to be the most vulnerable to this situation. The $4 million set-aside of taconite tax revenues earmarked for the Ely area during the 2006 legislative session,

188 *Comparing Governance of Economic Development*

already mentioned several times in this study, is unique among these cases. In none of the other three cities is such a prize off-limits due to a difference in outlook between city and state officials. And the state officials in this case are powerful, especially Ely's state senator, Tom Bakk, an Iron Range Resources and Rehabilitation Board member, state Senate Taxes Committee chairman prior to 2012, and then state Senate Democratic leader. Bakk's vision from 2006 – getting Ely, Tower (22 miles away), Babbitt (17 miles away) and Bakk's hometown of Cook (more than 40 miles away) to agree on a single project of "at least 200 jobs" – would be optimal for Hibbing or either of the Illinois cases, where 200 jobs would nicely complement other larger employers. For Ely and its dispersed neighbors, 200 jobs are equivalent to double the largest current private employer in the area. In Sterling and Rock Falls, this could very well be a local decision, as the land being eyed by a business for expansion or development would simply be added to the local enterprise zone and gain eligibility for state-supported tax incentives. But the power granted by Illinois to municipalities to levy certain local taxes, especially sales taxes, can raise the level of conflict among communities.

The State Framework for Local Governance

Institutional structure at the state level also influences outcomes, but not necessarily in the way expected. The considerable safety net provided by Minnesota for its municipalities, even after the deep cuts in Local Government Aid from the conservative Pawlenty administration, has a clear and obvious effect in enabling even the most tax-poor of these cities, Ely, to provide a full set of public services and facilities and competitive salaries for city staff. Repeated interventions on Ely's behalf by both state and federal politicians have also helped to secure major new public facilities, including a state-of-the-art sewage plant and a new public works garage shared by the city, county and townships, that would otherwise have been far beyond the ability of city taxpayers to pay for. Indeed, Ely, despite having lower median household income than Rock Falls, Illinois, and a lower per capita tax levy, has a substantially higher per capita general fund budget.[10] And little wonder: even in 2008, after six years of steady cuts in LGA, Ely continued to receive over half its municipal general fund budget from the state of Minnesota. The "flypaper effect" holds true here; there is little doubt that LGA is ensuring a basic level of solvency for the municipal public sector in rural Minnesota. Minnesota's more centralized approach carries with it an advantage for cities seeking some room for maneuver in terms of how they choose their economic development policies; the Minnesota cases, including Hibbing, with its strong policy track record, spend far less on business assistance than their Illinois counterparts.

Three qualifying points remain, regardless of how the legislature and governor choose to alter state aid. The first is that the major infrastructure depends upon the approval and support of all relevant higher levels of government. Even a strong federal patron will not suffice if, for example, required matching funds from the state are not forthcoming. This is particularly noticeable in Ely, where a high level of output of new infrastructure has been a bright spot in an otherwise cloudy picture on economic and community development. For example, the survey results – not to mention the frequent coverage in newspapers – suggested that arguably Ely's greatest unfulfilled goal in economic-development-related infrastructure is improvements to Minnesota Highway 169, the 1950s-era two-lane highway that serves as its primary connection to the outside world. For ten years a local task force including representatives from Ely and Tower met regularly to keep the project alive and to define key safety goals on a road that has one of the highest fatality rates in Minnesota. In 2005 Congressman Jim Oberstar secured a $20 million earmark to provide federal support for the project, but the Pawlenty administration persistently refused to produce its $4 million share.[11] After a major change in state policy under the Dayton administration to provide the state's share, and fortuitously low bids, the project finally began in 2017.

The second is that, in all these cases, there are strong local political pressures to limit cannibalization of other local governments whose tax base may be involved even when state law allows for aggressive strategies. Tax increment financing, one common tool for economic development, has fallen out of favor in these towns. Neither Ely nor Hibbing has expanded TIF districts during the period of the study; the last new one in Ely was defined in 1995 for a new hotel on reclaimed mine land overlooking Shagawa Lake, a Holiday Inn SunSpree Resort (since defranchised and renamed Grand Ely Lodge). Replenishment of revolving loan funds for storefront improvements in Ely and Hibbing has been limited. In Sterling, even Walmart specifically ruled out a request for tax increment financing for its distribution center,[12] instead seeking tax incentives that did not involve imposing upon the school district. And, in both Sterling and Rock Falls, the financial cost of the business of economic development has been shared wherever possible with state and federal authorities.

Third, state control of local government on economic development spending affects how much money is spent and how it is spent. In both the Illinois cases, local spending on economic development is enormous compared to Hibbing and Ely. This difference applies despite the apparent reluctance of all four cities to use tax increment financing for economic development. Consider Minnesota: Ely during the 2000s provided around $70,000 a year, its share of funding for administration of economic development through the Joint Powers Board, out of an annual general fund budget of just over $3 million, with the expiring TIF districts for the Grand Ely Lodge hotel and the Ely Business Park generating another $150,000 a year to service their debt. This general level of spending on economic

190   *Comparing Governance of Economic Development*

development, a little over five percent of city revenues, has continued in the 2010s. Hibbing provided a mere $111,000 in direct economic development funding from a general fund of more than $15 million in 2009[13] while TIF revenues from long-standing improvement districts round out a total share similar to Ely.

In contrast, Sterling's economic development spending from taxes, though it is organized through funds other than the $10.2 million general fund, is very substantial. The huge Rock River TIF district, consisting of the 800-acre former steelworks, alone spent almost $579,000 in captured revenue in 2007–8, mostly on environmental remediation (which continued through 2016); with the downtown business district TIF adding a further $411,000 and bond payments on the extension of Lynn Boulevard NW, a scheme designed almost purely to access new business sites, using $239,000 in local sales tax revenues (a further substantial source of economic development spending, the $352,000 budget of the Sterling Industrial Development Commission [SIDC], which underwrites much of the Greater Sterling Development Corporation's activities, is sourced from non-tax revenue such as land sales, rentals and outside grants).[14] In Rock Falls economic development spending accounted for almost 10 percent of baseline revenue in 2008 and 2009 of approximately $5.7 million per year,[15] including $100,000 for the administration of economic development through Rock Falls CDC; $5,000 to support marketing of I-88 West (monies that in Sterling are including in the SIDC budget); $117,500 in mostly retail-oriented tax incentives, including support for the ill-fated supermarket project;[16] and $332,200 for demolition and cleanup at RB&W and Parrish-Alford.[17] In 2009 Sterling thus spent more than $1.2 million in locally generated revenue, including TIF revenues, on economic development; Rock Falls around $550,000, all of it locally generated without resort to tax increments. Clearly, the more fluid arrangements in Illinois and the greater dependence of cities upon capturing business tax revenue has an effect when it comes to aggressively pursuing economic development. Spending on economic development remained similar through the early and mid-2010s even though goals had evolved. Rock Falls, with the largest policy changes of the four during this time, moved in 2017 to add municipal gigabit Internet to its utility services, a project that could see the city's public utility issue up to $13 million in bonds.[18]

These state-level contrasts are in many respects bigger than the local contrasts within each state. Consider Ely and Hibbing. Ely's considerable dependence upon state support is one factor. Although Hibbing and Ely have apparently similar property values, Hibbing has a higher tax capacity than Ely – albeit still low compared with Sterling, Illinois – and, in any case, Minnesota's need-based approach to LGA narrows the difference. Ely's relatively high property values are offset in the calculation of property tax capacity by low income as follows: total market value (TMV), as defined by the Minnesota Department of Revenue for the purposes of property taxes, is $39,184 per person, based on a 2016 estimated population of 3,390 and TMV of $132,834,142. The corresponding figures for Hibbing are a per capita TMV of $39,867, based on an estimated population of 16,093 and TMV of $641,585,272.[19] Ely's weaker income base has often limited the community's ability to tax itself; an estimated median household income of $36,059, as opposed to Hibbing's $43,831.[20] Under Minnesota's local government finance system this disparity is offset with LGA as follows: Ely received just over $2.1 million in LGA, or $623 per capita, while Hibbing received $8.1 million, or $503 per capita.[21]

Thus, despite a lower tax base and slightly higher per capita public spending, Ely ends up with similar residential taxes to Hibbing, with median residential real estate taxes of $765 for mortgaged properties and $847 for mortgage-free properties in 2015, as opposed to Hibbing's $780 and $763, respectively.[22] The most significant difference between Ely and Hibbing is on commercial taxes, due to factors entirely beyond both cities' control. Ely's unusually high commercial property values given the weakness of the local economy – values driven by the tourist and second-home orientation of the town – make for considerable pressure on the city's business tax base, though this has abated in recent years. The overall outcome is a slight difference in per capita local spending – Ely spending more than Hibbing – but a commercial property tax base in Ely that by Minnesota standards is stretched.[23]

In Illinois, a facet of state-level policy continues to drive the biggest local-level difference between a pair of cases, the contrast in sales tax revenues between Sterling and Rock Falls. More than a decade after the two cities approved their local option taxes Sterling continues to enjoy a considerable advantage due to its car dealerships, regional mall and a local monopoly on supermarkets. Local option and state shared sales taxes yielded approximately $4.05 million for Sterling in 2016 but only $2.03 million in Rock Falls, 50 percent of Sterling's sales tax revenue for around 60 percent of Sterling's population.[24]

How These Communities Deliver on Economic Development Goals

A final point of comparison is to be found in the survey interviews themselves. Sterling and Hibbing leaders were far more satisfied with their situation on policies, structures of governance and leadership than those in Ely and Rock Falls. Sterling, where contestation of management over economic development policy is but a distant memory, showed the highest ratings; Hibbing, with little contestation of policy on today's council or in its government, was not far behind. Surprisingly, Rock Falls registered closely to Ely, even with the survey having been taken almost six years after the reorganization of its local government was complete – an outcome I attribute to leaders' concern at the slowness of achieving economic development

192 *Comparing Governance of Economic Development*

policy results, not just the organizational preconditions for results. Rock Falls had the misfortune to see its changes in land use policy take effect at the end of an economic cycle rather than the beginning, resulting in a further long delay before the city saw tangible benefits.

But what the survey results do not show well is the story of convergence between Sterling and Rock Falls economic development, told in policy decisions, official meeting minutes and, for more than a decade, increased cooperation between the two communities, despite periodic failures. Leaders in Sterling and Rock Falls, despite clear evidence of competition and distrust, agree more closely on policy with one another than leaders in the city of Ely area with the surrounding townships that identify as part of the same community. The main barrier to full trust between the two communities appears to be fear that those on the "other side of the river" will be unreceptive to cooperation.

It is worth considering when the principle element of cooperation between Sterling and Rock Falls, notable as an exception to the rule, was mutual aid for fire coverage. While Sterling and Rock Falls now cooperate on a variety of issues, particularly through the Whiteside Enterprise Zone, even mutual aid has become a contested point in and around Ely. A heavily forested area of high wildfire risk that depends on good fire coverage cannot attain the same degree of institutionalized intergovernmental cooperation with a single community as two neighboring towns with a long-standing rivalry and issues with mutual trust.

How do these cities compare in delivering policy? All four have proud achievements to point to, even over the past decade. Sterling (with Rock Falls playing a supporting role) takes the prize, by landing over 1,000 jobs in a single project from Walmart's wholesale distribution arm while successfully reclaiming the derelict Northwestern Steel and Wire site, saving 300 jobs in a state-of-the-art facility and opening up hundreds of acres of brownfield for new development, with the goal of Sterling mayor Skip Lee that Sterling will also open public access to its side of the riverfront. Rock Falls overcame a once dysfunctional approach to economic development by getting itself ready for when economic conditions eventually do improve, while expanding upon a successful pattern of promoting residential development. Hibbing successfully expanded its base of skilled engineering jobs and took major steps toward a long-term goal of restoring itself as a regional retail center, both seen as key steps in diversifying the mining-dependent local economy. Ely continued to heavily overhaul its public infrastructure, developing a new public works garage jointly with other area governments, including the county and Morse Township; delivering a handicapped accessible City Hall renovation and new library building in 2015; and pursuing an aggressive program of street reconstruction.

But Ely stands as an outlier from the other cases in two key respects. First, although the city successfully delivered its City Hall and library upgrades

Comparing Governance of Economic Development 193

on its own, many of its biggest achievements have depended upon forceful intervention from higher levels of government. The wastewater plant and public works garage both depended on county- and congressional-level intervention, and, even then, Mayor Roger Skraba did not survive re-election from his own spending of political capital for the latter project. And, when state and federal leaders have differed from those in the community, as with the $4 million set-aside in 2006, project goals have not been realized. Left on their own, local leaders struggled to agree on annexation, management of economic development policy and a strategy for lobbying the state for greater taxing power, and saw a decade of instability in city administration before finally achieving greater consensus on governance and policy. Perhaps Ely's best achievement has been the maintenance of major tourist events, notably the Blueberry/Art Festival, which draws some 45,000 visitors into the community on the last weekend of July. The city has a pattern of extensively supporting these special tourism-oriented events with in-kind services, even during times of budget stress; for example, as the city was budgeting for 2003's severe cuts in LGA, a suggestion to charge the Ely Chamber of Commerce for services provided to the Blueberry/Art Festival failed even to make it to a council vote.[25] On the other hand, controversy and complications with consistently delivering pro-tourism policies are rarely far away, as the 2009 loss of a promising new blues festival to Grand Rapids, Minn., demonstrated, and as the city is now experiencing with the conflict between proposed copper-nickel mining and environment-dependent tourism.

A complicating factor in Ely is trust. Despite high rates of voter turnout in local, state and federal elections, the expressed level of trust in government in the survey data here is poor, even as trust and participation in private organizations is high. Ely has thriving nonprofits, such as the Northern Lakes Arts Association, which has over 1,000 members – an impressive feat considering the Ely area's population – and funds a large array of arts at a high level; youth social service agency Ely Community Resource; and an array of youth sports programs, among many others. The weak trust in government was exemplified in the 2000s by the community's relationship with its schools, persistently criticized over budgeting and management. In November 2005, following newspaper publication of data showing Ely's above-average teacher salaries and benefits by small school standards,[26] an excess operating levy referendum was defeated. The November 2006 election saw the narrow passage of a larger excess operating levy for the school district that officials had suggested was essential for the district to maintain its independence and avoid going into statutory operating debt, but the winning margin was more than accounted for by the city of Ely's 4th precinct, which, with an average age of just 24 years (versus 40.8 for the city as a whole),[27] includes many Vermilion Community College students, the majority from outside the local area.[28] In 2010 a further school funding initiative for repairs

194   *Comparing Governance of Economic Development*

to the school's aging buildings was resoundingly defeated, showing once again the difficulty of convincing an older community to make future-oriented but potentially risky investments in infrastructure. But, as economic conditions improved, so did community support; in 2016, even as Elyites were voting for Donald Trump for president by a seven percent margin, the 2006 excess levy for school operations was successfully extended for another ten years by a resounding 67.3 percent "Yes" vote, while the three available seats on the school board drew a full field of six candidates contesting them.

Trust can go some way toward explaining the circular arguments that characterize Ely politics on relations among its local governments, notably the thorny questions of annexation and fire coverage, as well as the city's rejection of council-manager governance. But, once again, it highlights the importance of organization, for trust is interfering with the city's ability to begin effective reform. And organization, whether generated organically within the community or enforced from above on special projects, appears to be the common thread – even more than funding – that determines whether economic and community development projects get delivered.

Notes

1 The constant calling for a more regional approach with significant private-sector leadership has been by Roger Skraba, mayor for 2005–6 and again for 2009–12 and the losing candidate for mayor in 2002, 2006 and 2012; opposing him, with an administrative approach more centered in Ely city government, was Frank Salerno (elected mayor in 2002 for the 2003–4 term) and Chuck Novak (elected mayor in 2006 for 2007–8 and elected in 2014 and re-elected in 2016).

2 See HEDA minutes, September 2006. L&M, which began business in 1957, was requesting a $100,000 HEDA loan and a $150,000 state Minnesota Investment Fund loan that required a city guarantee, in order to leverage more than ten times that amount in bank financing for an expansion.

3 See HEDA minutes for December 14, 2005. The program had been suspended in 1999 due to becoming "overextended" – at the time of a major infrastructure and streetscape project on Howard Street, the city's main downtown commercial street.

4 This is evident in several survey responses; see, in particular, surveys 19, 54, 56.

5 See survey 19; as the respondent put it, "Government's role is to make sure you create the right environment, and I think we've done that. Example: Walgreens; the vote on the council sent a signal."

6 See K. Grinsteinner, Hibbing awaits Walgreens, *Hibbing Daily Tribune*, October 30, 2006.

7 See interview 07.

8 Source: Minnesota Department of Revenue, League of Minnesota cities, Total market value data.

9 See interview 02.

Comparing Governance of Economic Development   195

10 See Table I.1. Ely's average per capita general fund revenue is almost identical to Sterling and Hibbing, and far above Rock Falls, despite the fact that the city's per capita levy is less than Rock Falls.

11 See B. Erzar, It's time for safety improvements on the Tower to Ely segment of Highway 169, Letter to the editor, *Ely Echo*, August 15, 2010.

12 See survey responses from Sterling.

13 City of Hibbing consolidated financial statement, 2009.

14 City of Sterling, Illinois, Budget in brief, 2007–08.

15 City of Rock Falls, Budget document 2009–2010.

16 *Ibid.*, item 10-01, Administration.

17 *Ibid.*, item 10-12, Public property.

18 P. Eggemeier, "Rock Falls moves ahead with broadband plan: Mayor focuses on seizing opportunities in State of City speech," saukvalley.com, February 21, 2017.

19 Source for TMV data: League of Minnesota Cities, Minnesota market value and tax capacity, March 2006. Source for population data: US Census Bureau, July 2005 estimate.

20 US Census Bureau, American Community Survey five-year estimates, 2015.

21 Minnesota Department of Revenue, 2017 Certification, City LGA amounts for 2017.

22 Source: City-data.com pages for Ely and Hibbing, Minnesota: www.city-data.com/city/Hibbing-Minnesota.html and www.city-data.com/city/Ely-Minnesota.html (accessed October 29, 2017).

23 Ranger GM (a dealership of all GM brands) in Hibbing, and owner of Mike Motors (GM and Chrysler brands) in Ely, paid higher real estate taxes during the 2000s on the Ely dealership than the Hibbing one, even though the Ely dealership is significantly smaller. According to the St. Louis County Auditor database, Hilligoss Partnership's taxes for 2007 were $16,173.60 on the parcels that comprise Mike Motors; Hilligoss Chevrolet's taxes for 2007 were $14,220.36 on Ranger GM; both properties are approximately five acres, but Ranger GM is on a much more heavily trafficked highway, has a much larger showroom and service facility and has substantially higher sales. Several Ely survey respondents raised significant concerns about Ely commercial property taxes; there were no comparable complaints in Hibbing.

24 Sources: 2016–17 City of Rock Falls budget; 2016 Sterling budget-in-brief. Unlike in Minnesota, the lower-income community of Rock Falls sees less in state aid than Sterling for the simple reason that per capita retail spending within Rock Falls' city limits is lower than in Sterling.

25 See *Ely Timberjay*, Ely balances budget – barely, December 7, 2002.

26 See *Ely Echo*, Insurance benefits issue clouds school referendum vote Tuesday, editorial, November 7, 2005. For 2005 Ely ranked third in teacher salaries out of 181 school districts in Minnesota with fewer than 1,000 students in grades K through 12, while contributing an average of $12,587 per employee for family health coverage, 87 percent above the state average.

27 US Census Bureau, 2000 census data.

28 Although county and state residency data from the Minnesota State Colleges and Universities system is not readily usable due to incomplete reporting, Vermilion's total enrollment of 714 – or more than 350 per class year – is more than the entire K-12 enrollment of the local school district, requiring

196 *Comparing Governance of Economic Development*

Vermilion to make up most of its numbers with out-of-area recruiting. More than 21 percent of Vermilion students are from out of state, according to fall 2006 enrollment data. Note that it is no longer possible in Ely elections to make this distinction, as the four precincts were combined into one after 2008 to save money on election administration.

Reference

Carr, J. B. (2015). What have we learned about the performance of council–manager government? A review and synthesis of the research. *Public Administration Review*, 75(5), 673–689.

8 Conclusion

The comparison of these cases suggests that institutional frameworks are influencing decision-making on economic and community development by setting boundaries that leaders operate within. They are driving it in ways that are distinct among each of these cases and sometimes also distinct from the kinds of economic policies that would be expected by small but activist city governments seeking to expand their revenue base and in the throes of capture by out-of-town business. The activism these structures have helped to enable include enhancing the conventional policy of boosting a community's economy and tax base by attracting capital from outside and substituting alternative models such as assisting existing local businesses, meeting public demand for better infrastructure or downgrading economic development as a policy priority. These differences have occurred despite the logic that suggests the smaller, weaker and more localized a unit of government is, the more it is a creature of market economics rather than political action and organization. Even in these small towns, the institution of government and its politics and organization remain factors besides economics in influencing policy decisions, even about economics.

The frameworks provided by state government are an important component of this. The Minnesota safety net enables local governments to be more selective about the businesses they assist because of the assurance of basic services it implies, while Illinois devolution has enabled municipalities to customize economic development assistance. The dilemma lies in the downsides to each approach. Minnesota's revenue and policy centralization, at least on the Iron Range, scales economic development policy to a level that is politically relatable to state politicians, a situation that can serve medium to large towns and cities well but is not easily scalable to smaller towns; Illinois devolution intensifies competition among neighboring towns and elevates economic development spending to the point that it may well cannibalize other government services. And neither state has combined more devolved decision-making with a centralized fiscal safety net – an outcome that merits further inquiry about whether such a combination is even politically possible or likely in the United States.

198   *Conclusion*

I chose to study small, rural and relatively remote communities in order to find the cases that face more theoretical constraints from economic trends and their lack of financial resources and tax base. If local government can influence their economies and community development through organizational means as well as deploying resources, that implies an important role for city councils and citizen decision-making in almost any setting. It means that organization and citizen involvement count as well as resources. The lesson implied from Ely, Hibbing, Sterling and Rock Falls is that even unfavorable circumstances – in this case, loss of tax revenue, constrained demographics, high rates of underemployment, an undereducated workforce and constrained municipal budgets – do not preclude government from enacting meaningful solutions to at least some aspects of these problems. But resources and institutional support from the state always help to provide additional policy choices.

Communities with less in the way of direct assistance to business and putting a higher proportion of their resources and administration into basic infrastructure are actively choosing a different policy approach. Rock Falls, according to survey respondents, has long been ahead of Sterling in terms of implementing public policy to boost the availability of affordable, single-family housing, and its riverfront redevelopment has heavily emphasized community space. Likewise, Ely – even when it has been spurned by the IRRRB and the state legislature on business assistance – has continued to win IRRRB funding and Community Development Block Grants for improving streets and utility infrastructure and subsidizing new housing, both single-family and apartments, both market-rate and "affordable."

These considerations cast local institutional capacity in a new light. If local places have these resources, they still need a means of turning them into results. Strong institutions of local governance help them do this in both the Minnesota and Illinois systems. This is more likely to happen when institutional roles are clearly defined and not heavily contested in local politics – in other words, when there is an individual or collective body clearly in charge of a policy or policies and empowered to develop and implement policy. This reveals itself in the speed by which governments can respond to the problems under their jurisdiction, especially problems involving land use; in terms of the extent to which elected boards set policy while delegating management to staff; and in terms of a local government's ongoing ability to deliver policy. In the end, this helps to reduce collective action problems. A smaller and well-organized and relatively homogeneous group tends to punch above its weight. In the same way, if there is an agreement among policy stakeholders as to where the agenda affecting that policy is supposed to be set, and where that policy is to be supported organizationally and financially, and who is responsible for carrying it out, that policy has a decent chance of success even if identifying the material resources proves to be a struggle. On the other hand, a large, unorganized and diverse group tends to struggle. A collection of such groups may be

Conclusion   199

unable to agree on anything, and may have no incentive to do so unless they belong to a larger arrangement that imposes standing obligations on each participant. If the agenda-setting process is poorly defined, different boards and commissions may clash over jurisdiction. If the responsibility for carrying out decisions is poorly defined, especially in a mayor-council government, a likely result is clashes among council members who share managerial responsibility as well as policy responsibility, or clashes between the council and city staff.

Institutional Stability and Leadership

Coherent institutional and governmental structures also help to foster coherent leadership. They provide a forum in which agreement can emerge among community leaders, and a structure and continuity in the event of rapid change, such as the retirement or death of a key leader or a major outside shock such as the loss of a key local employer or natural disaster. Incoherent institutional and governmental structures, in contrast, are at risk of negative change when a good leader leaves the scene or disaster strikes. Yet, even without a strong organizational structure for delivering policy, good leadership still has its benefits and still can accomplish positive achievements.

We have seen these phenomena at work here. Consider the two Illinois cases. Sterling was ready to tackle economic crisis, partly because of the experience and stability among senior city staff and the clearly defined roles for the city council, city staff and economic development corporation. Rock Falls soon began to build the kind of capability in economic development it already had in other areas such as housing. At the same time the two communities were cooperating, with other Whiteside and Carroll County municipalities, through the local enterprise zone board, spawning the successful Walmart recruitment and agreement on a more generalized strategy for attracting distribution and retail employers. But, when it came to changing local taxes in a way that did not result in beggar-thy-neighbor competition among cities, there is no existing organizational structure. It took progressive and proactive leadership, and informal contacts among community leaders from different cities, when Sterling, Rock Falls and Dixon, in Lee County outside Whiteside's enterprise zone, cooperated on coordinating local sales tax referenda in 2005 to achieve a half-percent sales tax increase across the region and fill long-standing gaps in funding for public infrastructure.

It is useful to consider the role of internal institutional stability by briefly discussing examples of its role in larger cities. Clearly, in small, relatively homogeneous ones, continuity helps the cause of effective government, and insulates these cities from the shocks of changes in officeholders. On the other hand, the largest cities in the United States tend not to vest staff with the levels of institutional authority found in Sterling or even Rock

200 *Conclusion*

Falls and Hibbing. Instead, they tend to employ strong-mayor systems with the idea of bringing government closer to the voters, especially when class and racial divides by neighborhood run deep – a goal that has revived a trend toward mayor-council governance in larger cities in recent years for this very reason.[1]

And, not surprisingly, the big mayor-council cities are not immune from the negative effects of a change in personality in a key leadership role. Consider the spotty transition Ely suffered in the aftermath of Grahek's legendary role as mayor. It is, in a way, reminiscent of a far larger machine-politics city with powerful leaders and weak municipal institutions, Chicago, which suffered extreme instability at a time of considerable economic crisis in the aftermath of Mayor Richard J. Daley's death in 1976; with bitterly contested mayoral primaries in 1979 and 1983; and another round of infighting following Mayor Harold Washington's death from a massive heart attack in late 1987. Just as in Ely at that time, institutional power was centered in the mayor's office, and, when that was vacated, the power was contested.

State Frameworks and Local Preferences: Implications

The role of the state is also impactful, and deserving of further research, but a discussion of the broader implications of this role is needed here. The history of local government in the United States is full of forceful interventions by state government, ranging from establishing institutional frameworks to blocking local policies and actions (Eisinger, 1988; Sbragia, 1996). It should not be surprising to find a contrast between policy outcomes in a centralized state with a public finance safety net and those in a relatively decentralized state that avoids redistributive public finance. The decentralized system of public finance in Illinois encourages local intervention in the economy by making local tax bases more sensitive to business recruitment, particularly retail, and by providing state resources in economic development that are devolved and locally allocated. The Illinois approach to revenue-sharing, with its positive correlation to retail sales and population, is the opposite of a redistributive system; it grants even non-home-rule cities more latitude to set sales and property taxes than the strongest home-rule governments in Minnesota. Even the distribution of state tax breaks is partly decentralized, through the Enterprise Zones Act. At the same time, failure to recruit retail businesses means failure to build sales tax revenue; failure to recruit people means failure to leverage shared state income tax revenue; and failure to raise local sales taxes on retail means a missed opportunity for additional revenue.

This approach incentivizes aggressive economic development efforts. And, on the evidence of these communities, it is doing just that. For example, even in the depth of the Great Recession, Sterling spent an

Conclusion 201

amount equivalent to 12 percent of its general fund on economic development in 2009, Rock Falls approximately 11 percent,[2] both more than double the proportion spent by Hibbing and Ely,[3] and more even than Ely during its late 1990s peak of tax increment financing activity on the former mining and railroad sites in the heart of the town. These funds do not include the Illinois-funded incentives to Walmart, whose big distribution project helped during the manufacturing recession of the 2000s to maintain the type of population and sales base so essential to an Illinois municipality's tax base – in the process preventing the kind of population exodus seen on Minnesota's Iron Range during the taconite layoffs and automation of the 1980s. The delegation of authority in Illinois meant that local economic developers could develop their own recruitment strategies (such as I-88 West's emphasis on distribution industries leveraging the transportation network) more thoroughly than in Minnesota. The lack of need-based assistance also means that doing nothing is far less likely to be a practical option; it creates the risk of a punishing local residential property tax burden that could drive residents away.

The Minnesota system, at least since the early 1970s, has handled matters very differently (Berg, 2012). Until the 2001–3 rollback of parts of the Minnesota Miracle, the state relied on using redistributive equalization of local property tax bases to ensure similarly high levels of public infrastructure and services across the state. Even after school funding largely ceased to be means-tested on the basis of local tax capacity and instead came directly from state sales and income taxes regardless of the wealth of the local district, the redistributive principle remained for municipalities – and school instructional funding was now entirely removed from the property tax. Local Government Aid in Minnesota reached $526 million in 2009, its highest in inflation-adjusted terms since the 2003 cuts,[4] with poorer rural communities continuing to receive a substantial share due to their weak property tax bases;[5] after a further dip in 2010 because of a combination of budget cuts and recessionary drops in revenue, LGA was once again restored approximately to 2009 levels by 2014.

Economic development is even more directly influenced by the state, especially on the Iron Range. The principal incentive is to pursue the types of economic development that the IRRRB and the Minnesota Department of Employment and Economic Development (DEED) and their legislative partners will support. When Ely and its fellow small towns in northern St. Louis County lobbied against that incentive in 2006, funds set aside from taconite revenues ended up unspent. The caveat is that aid and taxing power is always dependent on the state, and sometimes varies sharply from year to year. Aid was cut during the 2003 legislative session and again in 2004, rose significantly in 2006, was held constant in real dollars for the next two years and rose sharply again in 2009[6] before an attempt by Governor Tim Pawlenty to reduce 2010 LGA by 40 percent through "unallotments" was thrown out by the courts. It was cut again for 2011 by

202   *Conclusion*

approximately 10 percent from the 2009 baseline,[7] only to be raised after voters delivered Democratic–Farmer–Labor (DFL) Governor Mark Dayton a DFL-run legislature in 2012. Levy limits have led to stop-start changes in property taxes. After 20 years of continuous levy limits following the Minnesota Miracle tax reform of the 1970s, limits were taken off at the end of 1992, only to be reimposed on three further occasions: 1998–2000, 2002–4 and 2009–2011.[8]

In Illinois, the state's use of such power over local government is limited, but the non-redistributive nature of revenue-sharing means that tax-poor Rock Falls, for example, cannot move into a financially competitive position relative to Sterling unless it lures a major retailer such as a regional shopping mall or a car dealership – hence the large amount of land that has been made available for such a purpose. The ongoing disparity between these two communities is evident, in the built environment and in financial statements. But even greater inequalities than between Rock Falls and Sterling exist in more urbanized areas of the state, where the difference in commercial tax base between neighboring suburbs isn't the difference between a large Walmart and a small one but, rather, the difference between a major shopping mall and almost no business tax base at all. For example, in the tax-poor south Chicago suburb of Harvey, a largely minority working-class city with a heavy dependence on residential taxpayers, the 2016 composite property tax rate averaged 24.226 percent of taxable value (one-third of the property value under Illinois law; the average reflects variations between parts of Harvey that are in different school districts); in Schaumburg, a middle-class suburb with few overlapping governments and a large retail sector and sales tax revenues, the 2016 tax rate was a mere 9.547 percent throughout the village limits – despite the considerably better-funded public services there.[9] In contrast, a comparable community to Harvey in Minnesota, such as the northern Twin Cities suburb of Fridley, can provide services comparable in many respects to more prosperous suburbs.

What this means overall is that in Minnesota, and especially in the Taconite Assistance Area (as well as the Metro Council area of Minneapolis and St. Paul, which uses similar provisions to the TAA under the Fiscal Disparities Act), a city's revenue base is not inherently constrained by the lack of economic development in the way that it very well could be in Illinois; TAA communities in Minnesota are less prone to economic shifts and the exit strategies of businesses than their Illinois counterparts. The fact that Hibbing and Ely both enjoy per capita revenue slightly better than Sterling and considerably better than Rock Falls is notable because both cities have much lower property tax bases and rates and lower per capita incomes than either of these Illinois cities. Small rural Minnesota towns – and poor first-ring big city suburbs – use LGA and the proceeds of revenue-sharing to maintain a basic standard of services they otherwise could not afford.

Ideally, from the standpoint of a local government representing communities such as these, there would be a safety net for general services by the state *and* the authority to levy local taxes of choice and deploy state-backed tax incentives, in isolation or in standing institutional arrangements with other local governments of its choice. However, this combination does not exist in either of these two states; the question is whether it could politically exist anywhere. As they are, the balances of power in Minnesota and Illinois have some political stability, as they have engendered at least some satisfaction with state government among the leaders in all four communities (though the recent intensification of Illinois' pension crisis is not covered in this survey). The most noteworthy objections were raised in Ely, because of the extent to which its more small-business-oriented economy clashes with state-level policy agendas. Determining the connections between revenue-raising authority and state safety nets for local government and state centralization of policy-making is a promising avenue for further research.

But, paradoxically, state centralization does not necessarily limit local policy choices. This research suggests that the safety net in Minnesota, especially in its iron mining region, encourages forms of economic and community development that are less closely coupled to the maintenance of a tax and revenue base than those in Illinois. Hibbing's efforts with retail development demonstrate this possibility in action. Retailing is an odd economic development choice for the city given the lack of access of Minnesota municipalities to local sales taxes, yet much easier to explain given the evidence of strong public support for building retailing as an amenity and the dissatisfaction with Hibbing's existing retail choices raised in community surveys. It also represents a diversion from Hibbing's pattern of working closely with the IRRRB and the state of Minnesota on industrial, large-unit employers. Second, gearing the retail initiative to recruiting chains breaks with a long-term tradition of protecting locally owned businesses. In other words, Hibbing's retail market analysis and recruitment are less driven by the motive of municipal revenue enhancement than they are about raising the profile of the city with its neighbors and providing a valuable amenity to residents of the Hibbing area who would otherwise have to drive an hour or more each way for basic goods and services.

Partnerships among governments are another big part of building economic development policy and bargaining power, attracting the attention of businesses and higher levels of government and moving away from beggar-thy-neighbor policies. In this regard, the two states present an interesting paradox. Illinois provides a weaker safety net to local government and incentivizes beggar-thy-neighbor policies in retailing due to its handling of sales tax revenue, but gives local governments more tools to organize for themselves and cooperate with one another. Minnesota provides an extensive safety net to local governments but with the limitations of relatively centralized policy-making and a patchwork approach to building

204   *Conclusion*

partnerships among local governments. For example, Laurentian Energy, the biomass power generation project of the Hibbing and Virginia public utilities, has received extensive state funding, while Ely's Community Development Joint Powers Board is struggling with economic development; but only at the individual municipality level can these locations even apply for state-backed economic development incentives, taking the form in Minnesota of the JOBZ tax abatement program and of grants or loans.

Conventional Wisdom and Small Towns

What does this all mean? The story told here, of leeway for state and local governments to pursue organizational means of adding value to what they do and better reflecting local political choices, is at odds with a conventional wisdom in which local governments are viewed as pawns. But it is very much in the mainstream of research that indicates the importance of political choice (Ramsay, 2013; Savitch & Kantor, 2002). Viewed as models of social production, of collectively producing things of value (Stone, 1989), the municipal, county and state institutions that govern economic development emerge even in small, remote towns as entities that underpin stability, assist continuity, provide technical expertise and serve as forums in which leadership can nurture and leaders can find a common purpose.

Here, we see – even in some of the smallest towns – the organization of government playing a useful role, or, alternatively, serving as an impediment to progress. This is the power not only of decision-making but of the decision-making process. What processes, what forms of governance, what types of institutional arrangements – whether of regulatory power or funding – promote a higher volume and a more consistent pattern of decision-making? In an age in which funding is already tight in these small communities and becoming extremely limited in municipalities of all sizes, do these arrangements add value to public policy independently of the availability of money? Decision-making, despite the material risks it may carry, despite the costs it may impose, despite the possibility it may induce integral parts of the tax base to leave the community, is freer than many believe, especially if it is of a regulatory nature rather than involving substantial spending. Sometimes it simply requires political will, and building power through the institutions that come with better organization and more effective government is also an effective way of building the consensus that helps to build political will.

It is worth considering that, in some respects, these small towns have tackled problems and delivered results that have challenged much bigger cities. Comparing one of these cases, Sterling, with examples from larger cities can help to illustrate the value of having the appropriate city agencies in a state of readiness for economic change. Dereliction on the scale that Sterling faced when Northwestern Steel and Wire collapsed in 2001 often takes decades to resolve, even when the city in question is large and has the

Conclusion   205

financial and organizational wherewithal to tackle it. For example, much of the site of the former Baltimore & Ohio railroad station in downtown Chicago remains vacant, more than a half-century after the station closed, surrounded by high-rise apartment buildings and overlooked by North America's tallest building. The cooling towers at the Blackburn Meadows power-generating station near Sheffield, England, the "Tinsley Towers", outlasted the plant by so many years that they became something of a local landmark with their own preservation lobby, despite occupying prime property estate next to a major highway interchange.[10] Even New York and London found the task of reclaiming and redeveloping the former dock-lands near both downtowns after shipping lines relocated elsewhere to be a project strung out over decades, not years (Fainstein, 2001).

In this sense, these small cities hold a lesson for all. Municipalities every-where face challenges of development and land use, and, in European and North American countries, challenges of reclaiming the dereliction left behind by manufacturing. First, almost all municipalities, even large, demographically diverse, economically vibrant cities, face increasing finan-cial problems from challenges ranging from cuts in shared revenue from states to the costs of handling change in their schools, be it growth or contraction. Second, organizational challenges abound. Mayor-council versus council-manager governance is an ongoing controversy, pitting questions of democratic accountability against administrative stability. Municipalities compete with one another, especially if heavily fragmented or incentivized to do so by tax law. And these problems are to be found in cities and towns worldwide.

Consider tight finances, increasingly a ubiquitous problem. All four of these communities have performed well with financial management, yet all four, especially those in Illinois, face funding constraints. Property taxes are no longer the center of revenue that they once were; none of these cases bring in even half their general fund revenue from local property taxes. Cuts in LGA in Minnesota resulted, in Ely, in the end of 24-hour dispatcher coverage at the police station and City Hall; the number of city employees has dropped by a third since the late 1990s. There are similar situations in major cities. Clayton County, Ga., opted to discontinue its entire transit system effective March 2010 due to an $18 million budget deficit, almost half of which was accounted for by the buses.[11] Bus service there was not restored until county residents voted four years later to take Clayton County into Atlanta's MARTA (Metropolitan Atlanta Rapid Transit Authority) system. Chicago took the drastic step of privatizing its parking meters for a lump sum that yielded far less than what the lessee is projected to make in revenue over the term of the franchise.[12] Overall, state governments had to close budget gaps of $117.3 billion for fiscal year 2009, $174.1 billion for fiscal 2010 and $97.3 billion for fiscal 2011, according to the National Conference of State Legislatures.[13] Additionally, regression analysis indicates that local governments were unable to offset declining

206 *Conclusion*

aid from state and federal sources with revenue increases of their own, due to the multi-year decline in the housing market and therefore property tax revenues (Chernick & Reschovsky, 2017). These deficits are not isolated incidents. Evidence from research and data on local government finance indicate they are structural (Osborne & Hutchinson, 2004). Assuming current spending and revenue patterns and counting employee health benefit and retirement costs, state and local governments would run constant operating budget deficits until the late 2050s, according to GAO's late 2016 update on state and local government finances.[14] More and more, the small town financial reality is becoming the national reality.

Consider organizational challenges. The type of geographical fragmentation of government seen in and around Ely, Minnesota, reprises a common theme for metropolitan areas almost everywhere in the United States, and even to a certain extent in other countries, such as France, that have high levels of fragmentation in their local government.[15] It also applies to policies that overlap with economic development but are not necessarily a subset, such as transportation. In a certain sense, Ely's Community Economic Development Joint Powers Board attempted to do for economic development what metropolitan planning organizations (MPOs) do for transportation policy in larger cities: a steering body that produces good ideas, but is short of resources and statutory power, limited largely to the abilities and duties of the staff that work for it, and with few direct achievements to its name. Like Ely's Joint Powers Board, MPOs are not the entity that delivers the result. They are a reminder that the separation between institutional organization and resources is a challenge in other policy areas besides economic development and other settings besides small towns.

Final Words

These theoretical problems are of vital importance to our democracy, because they are central to the question of whether the local governments that manage these communities can effectively fulfill the wishes and needs of their citizens. We live in a market economy of great global interdependence, precarious political – and therefore democratic – influence over economic problems, and public dissatisfaction over both the performance of government and the long-term economic decline in terms of access to good pay and job opportunities. It is inevitable that towns such as these will be politically driven to fight and compete hard for economic opportunity. As one Ely survey respondent pointed out, "I think there's some effort that can be made from within to solve the problems, but I was in Duluth two or three months ago driving around and had a talk radio show on, and what they were talking about in Duluth was: 'Isn't it sad so many high school students can't get a job and leave Duluth because the economy isn't good, and couldn't we get more jobs in to build the job base?' You could have

Conclusion 207

substituted Ely in that, so the competition for that company is intense; the line is ten miles long."[16]

What is not inevitable is that communities such as these will fail to achieve critical goals in economic and community development. All four of these cities have scored victories and delivered major developments at various points during the scope of this study, and not only with the type of corporate welfare that is often held up as characterizing economic development policy. The recent development of Ely's public infrastructure, Hibbing's judicious use of revolving working capital and amenity-oriented economic development, Sterling's successful preservation of its general level of employment despite huge manufacturing job losses and Rock Falls' resolution of its long-standing problems with the availability of land for new development – all of these demonstrate points of success in tough environments for public intervention and funding in these relatively tax-poor cities. But, in every single one of these examples, the successful functioning of institutions of government was critical to the outcome. Well-defined and empowered institutions of government, where they were present, "greased the wheels" of development and cut through what otherwise might have been personality conflicts, or the inability of elected and appointed officials to align resources for a project.

Intergovernmental frameworks also can help with exercising these democratic choices. Cooperation among local governments proves valuable – if it involves sufficient resources to make a difference, and if it appropriately matches governments to the geography of an economic problem. Individual political representatives – county commissioners, state representatives, members of Congress – have a role to play, not only in representing their communities but also in directly helping these communities to agree upon and fund acceptable solutions. And the states' traditional role of holding great influence over local government remains undiminished. States can build, devolve, control, block or destroy local initiative. They can provide need-based assistance, or allow local places to sink or swim. They can delegate policy-making to local communities to craft appropriate solutions for themselves, or provide standardized, one-size-fits-all economic development policy that may be appropriate for some communities and inappropriate for others.

The question of whether discrete political units – even states, let alone cities and municipalities – can, within these constraints, still deliver the economic results needed or wanted by their electorate goes to the core of questions of self-determination and citizen choices. The implication of the findings here is that the challenges that face communities such as these are not entirely structural in nature, and arguably not beyond their control. It is a finding of considerable importance for democracy, because it means that politics, and therefore the involvement of citizens, still matter in shaping economies to local needs, and that such politics and involvement, where constructively organized, can make a difference

208   *Conclusion*

to development outcomes even where money is short. The effective politics and governance that institutional capacity helps to enable, and that we are often too quick to discount, have a role to play at all levels of government in opening more policy choices that benefit people and communities, whether or not they are part of groups favored by today's economic systems and trends.

Notes

1 Source: Strong Mayor-Council Institute. Among cities with a population over 100,000, nine – Tulsa, Okla.; St. Petersburg, Fla.; Fresno, Calif.; Sioux Falls, S.D.; Oakland, Calif.; Spokane, Wash.; Hartford, Conn.; Richmond, Va.; and San Diego, Calif. – have moved from council-manager to mayor-council governance in the last 20 years; only two – El Paso, Tex.; and Topeka, Kan. – have moved in the other direction.

2 Based on 2009–2010 financial statements for Sterling and Rock Falls; Sterling spent $1.3 million on economic development, including almost $600,000 in revenue from the tax increment district around the former steelworks and around $300,000 on programs such as the business incubator funded through the Sterling Industrial Development Commission and managed by the Greater Sterling Development Commission; Rock Falls spent approximately $550,000 of $5.7 million in general revenue, with by far the largest component on brownfield remediation and the long-standing annual allocation of $100,000 to the administration of Rock Falls Community Development Corporation.

3 Based on city financial statements. Amounts vary from year to year, especially in the Minnesota cases, where economic development spending can drop farther still in years without local matches for IRRRB grants.

4 Source: Minnesota House of Representatives, Research Department; Local Government Aid by city. Accessed at www.house.leg.state.mn.us/hrd/lgahist. asp.

5 Source: *Ibid.* On a per capita basis, LGA in Ely rose from $370 to $518 between 2004 and 2009; LGA in Hibbing rose from $369 to $542 over the same period; and in Minneapolis from $216 to $229, a slight decline after considering inflation. Eagan, the Minneapolis suburb formerly represented in the legislature by Governor Tim Pawlenty, has received zero LGA during this period.

6 Source: Minnesota House of Representatives, Research Department, Local Government Aid lookup. Accessed at www.house.leg.state.mn.us/hrd/lgahist. asp.

7 B. Swenson, Coalition of Greater Minnesota Cities: Make LGA an election issue, *Bemidji Pioneer*, July 27, 2010.

8 Source: Minnesota House of Representatives, House research, Levy limits. Accessed at www.house.leg.state.mn.us/hrd/pubs/ss/sslvylmt.htm.

9 Source: Cook County, 2016 tax rates report. Accessed at www.cookcountyclerk.com/tsd/extensionsandrates/Pages/default.aspx#reports.

10 The plant closed in 1980; the towers were not imploded until 2008.

11 R. Fausset, Clayton County loses vital bus service, link to Atlanta, *Los Angeles Times*, April 1, 2010.

12 See Office of the Inspector General, City of Chicago, Report of Inspector General's findings and recommendations: An analysis of the lease of the city's parking meters, June 2, 2009, p. 2.
13 See the National Conference of State Legislatures' State budget update: March 2011; and Jonas (2012).
14 See the Government Accountability Office's State and local government outlook: 2016 update, GAO-17-213SP.
15 France has more than 36,000 units of local government – a comparable number per unit of population to Illinois, which has more local government units than any other US state.
16 Ely survey 15.

References

Berg, T. (2012). *Minnesota's miracle: Learning from the government that worked.* Minneapolis: University of Minnesota Press.

Chernick, H., & Reschovsky, A. (2017). The fiscal condition of US cities: Revenues, expenditures, and the "Great Recession." *Journal of Urban Affairs, 39*(4), 488–505.

Eisinger, P. K. (1988). *The rise of the entrepreneurial state: State and local economic development policy in the United States.* Madison, Wis.: University of Wisconsin Press.

Fainstein, S. S. (2001). *The city builders: Property development in New York and London, 1980–2000.* Lawrence, Kan.: University Press of Kansas.

Jonas, J. (2012). Great Recession and fiscal squeeze at US subnational government level, Working Paper no. 12/184. Washington, D.C.: International Monetary Fund.

Osborne, D., & Hutchinson, P. (2004). *The price of government: Getting the results we need in an age of permanent fiscal crisis.* New York: Basic Books.

Ramsay, M. (2013). *Community, culture, and economic development: Continuity and change in two small southern towns* (2nd edn.). Albany, N.Y.: State University of New York Press.

Savitch, H. V., & Kantor, P. (2002). *Cities in the international marketplace: The political economy of urban development in North America and western Europe.* Princeton, N.J.: Princeton University Press.

Sbragia, A. M. (1996). *Debt wish: Entrepreneurial cities, US federalism, and economic development.* Pittsburgh: University of Pittsburgh Press.

Stone, C. N. (1989). *Regime politics: Governing Atlanta, 1946–1988.* Lawrence, Kan.: University Press of Kansas.

Appendix
Survey Questionnaire

1. First, tell me a little about yourself and your involvement in the community.
   a. What do you do for a living?
   b. What public office do you hold and what are the major functions of it with regard to civic, community and economic development?
   c. What community and civic groups are you involved in?
   d. In what other ways are you involved in the civic and economic development of the community?
2. What major problems are you and others in city government and economic development most occupied with these days?
   a. In what order of importance have you listed them?
   b. What change has there been over the past five years in the problems that those concerned with community development are paying attention to? Why do you believe that change has taken place?
3. What are the most important development projects currently taking place in your community?
   a. Economic development projects such as business recruitment and retention and business-oriented infrastructure?
   b. Community and civic projects including general-purpose infrastructure, public services and cultural and civic resources such as libraries, the arts, city buildings, etc.?
4. To what extent do you believe the problems facing the community can be solved within the community?
   a. How effective at solving problems is local and state government, especially your local city government? Explain.
   b. How effectively involved in solving problems is the private sector, especially your local chamber of commerce and local businesses? Explain.
   c. Do the public and private sector effectively work together in the community?
   d. In what ways are local economic development efforts making a difference? How much do they depend on (a) market conditions and (b) higher levels of government?
   e. What about support from the nonprofit and foundation sector in your community or regionally?
   f. What about support from and cooperation with the local school district and local community colleges, and, if applicable, local and state four-year institutions of higher education?

Appendix: Survey Questionnaire 211

g. It has been suggested that there is such a thing as "civic capacity" that helps cities better and more responsively deliver community and economic development. Specifically, this "civic capacity" is said to include broad private-sector support of public–private partnership in development, a city government with adequate ability and tax base to "get things done," good relations with other governments, and a citizenry that trusts in both public and private organizations and above all in where its tax money is going. How do you believe your community scores on civic capacity?

5. In what way is the community mobilized or organized to solve problems?
   a. What institutions (e.g. city departments, CDC, county, state) are available to solve problems and what are their responsibilities?
   b. Are these institutions generally effective or ineffective? Do they have formal power or at least significant influence or do they merely serve as forums or talking shops?
   c. Are these institutions well coordinated or not?
   d. To what extent do they depend on individual personalities, or do they survive changes in personnel well?
   e. In what way could they be made more effective?
   f. How involved are the schools and area colleges?
   g. How effective is city, county and township government?
   h. How effective are state agencies and state government?
   i. What could and/or what needs to be done to make potential stakeholders more engaged on an ongoing basis?
   j. Would greater engagement from stakeholders, in particular on a more formal and ongoing basis, be a benefit, of neutral effect or a disadvantage regarding getting things done? Please elaborate.

6. If not within the community, can these problems be solved:
   a. Through better and more formalized relations with surrounding governments (cities, townships), for example joint powers boards or special-purpose governments, or a reorganization of existing government (e.g. cities, townships, sewage districts, etc.)?
   b. Through stronger support from and better relations with county government (Illinois) or regional agencies (Minnesota)?
   c. Through stronger support from and better relations with state and federal government?
   d. Only through a significant change in market conditions brought about by changes in federal and state regulation – e.g. restrictions on international trade, changes in land use policy on "sprawl," changes in transportation policy?

7. I would also like to ask you about some specific civic and economic development projects or issues in your community and how you believe they were handled...
   a. Hibbing: retail development on the Beltline (including Lowe's, Walmart and pre-existing developments such as Irongate Mall); beautification of the downtown; renovation of educational facilities, including Hibbing High School and HCC [Hibbing Community College]; aid to Northwest Airlines; aid to Hibbing Electronics.
   b. Virginia: retail on US 53 (including Target and Thunderbird Mall); stabilization of the downtown; civic infrastructure including the steam plant; renovation of educational facilities; recruitment of business outside the steel industry.

212 *Appendix: Survey Questionnaire*

    c. Sterling: downtown development, including reclamation of abandoned or run-down buildings; the north Beltway and associated business parks; recreational projects from both the public and private/nonprofit sector; performance of educational institutions in the community, including Sterling High School and Sauk Valley College; maintaining manufacturing in the former Northwest Steel & Wire facility; the local sales tax referendum; the Walmart Distribution Center.

    d. Rock Falls: mobilizing community support for active economic development; the local sales tax referendum; retail development, including development that makes use of land accessible to I-88 and US 30; the Walmart Distribution Center; constraints posed by the lack of a unit school district.

8. Is there anything else you think I might be interested in?

Index

abandoned properties, Illinois limitation on local government enforcement 178

agenda-setting: alignment between economic and political geography 27; alignment between state and local government 27, 32; economic development policy-making 26, 99, 191–194, 199; framing of political debate 26; inclusion of politically popular policy items 30; institutional influence on 26; relationship between state and local government 99, 128–131

Aggen, Theodore "Ted" (1930–2010), Sterling, Ill. mayor 153, 160

Alaska, policy on local sales taxes *see* local option sales taxes: state role in

Anderson, Wendell (1933–2016), Minnesota governor (1971–76) 9

annexation 21, 92, 120, 131, 139, 181–182; complication of tax revenue sharing 115; contested 108; as economic development policy tool 86, 95, 107–110, 133, 158, 181, 185; effect on leadership *see* political geography; effect on municipal revenue 170–171; effect on political fragmentation 21, 107–110, 131, 133–134, 186; Ely, internal disputes over 95, 108–109, 193–194; Ely, Minn., and Morse Township 8, 86, 92, 95, 107–110, 120, 181–182, 186–187, 193–194; governance and 22, 133–134; Hibbing, and decision to adopt ward-based council seats 133; Hibbing, Minn., and Stuntz Township 7–8, 130, 131, 133, 134, 146, 147, 186; as infrastructure

development tool 134, 158, 187; lack of support for from higher-level government 107; for Sterling, Ill., Walmart Distribution Center 173; and supply of land for development 108; utility extension for 110, 158, 173, 187

Antofagasta plc, Chilean–British mining firm 91

arts, support for, as economic/community development strategy 89, 90, 148, 166

Atlanta, Ga.: as example of reforming urban governance 23, 75; infrastructure as economic development tool 70; transit as example of intergovernmental agreement 205

attractiveness, of a city for economic development 3, 30, 32, 50, 64, 90

Bakk, Thomas M. "Tom" (1954–), Minnesota state representative (1995–2003), state senator (2003–) 99

Barajas, David, Jr., economic developer and banker, Sterling, Ill. 161, 164, 174, 177

Begich, Joseph R. (1930–), Minnesota state representative (1975–92), former IRRRB board member 38

Blandin Foundation, Grand Rapids, Minn. 95, 98–99

Blanton, David, Rock Falls Ill. mayor, (2005–13) 163, 165, 175, 176

Bloomberg, Michael (1942–), New York mayor (2002–13) and publisher 45

Blueberry/Art Festival, Ely, Minn. 89, 90, 193

214 *Index*

boosterism, US political tradition 5
Boundary Waters Canoe Area
    Wilderness (BWCA or BWCAW),
    Minnesota 83, 91, 109, 110; "portal
    zone" (former logging area) 110
branding as an economic development
    strategy, application in Hibbing,
    Minn. 122–123, 126, 148, 149
Butler, Ely, city administrator of Ely,
    Minn. (2005–07) 104–105

Candor, New York 64
Cannata, Rick, Hibbing, Minn., mayor
    (2011–) 127
capital flight, vulnerability to 12, 46, 50
Carter, James Earl "Jimmy" (1924–),
    Georgia governor (1971–75), US
    President (1977–81) 84
Cast Corporation, metal fabricator,
    Hibbing, Minn. 136, 145
Central Iron Range Initiative
    (CIRI) 135
Central Iron Range Sewer and Sanitary
    District (CIRSSD), joint powers
    board, Iron Range area, Minnesota
    134–135, 147
CGH Medical Center, Sterling, Ill. 174
Chicago and Northwestern Railway
    see Union Pacific
Chicago, Ill. 8, 13, 59, 89, 102,
    157, 164; connection with I-88
    West corridor 174; decline in
    manufacturing employment 44;
    historical avoidance of debt and
    relationship to state policy 76;
    history of railroad to Milwaukee 69;
    negative effects of local government
    fragmentation 54; political impact
    of death of mayors 200; pursuit of
    retail revenue 168; use of parking
    meter privatization to generate lump
    sum 205; use of sales tax-centered
    revenue strategy 72–73; vacant land
    left by railroad station closure 205
Chisholm-Hibbing Airport Authority
    (CHAA), joint powers board
    administering Range Regional
    Airport 127, 129, 130, 140, 150
cities' role in the national
    economy 70–71
city–county consolidation, as economic
    development tool 21–22
civic capacity, theory 23–25,
    54, 75–76

Cleveland-Cliffs, mining and steel
    firm 98; *see also* Hibbing Taconite;
    Northshore Mining
Clinton, Hillary (1947–), US Senator
    (2001–09), Secretary of State
    (2009–13), Democratic presidential
    nominee (2016) 10
Cohasset, Minn. 56–57
collective action problems, influence
    on policy and governance 21, 29, 65,
    134, 198
Colorado River Compact, as example
    of intergovernmental agreement 18
Community Development Block
    Grant (CDBG), federal program 37,
    67, 198
community development 2, 5, 12, 14,
    28–33, 46, 50–54; as definition of
    public policy 18–24; in Ely 100–102;
    in Hibbing 14, 123–127, 130–132;
    institutional frameworks for 64–77
Community Economic Development
    Joint Powers Board, Ely, Minn.
    31, 85, 95–101, 118, 204; and city
    defunding of 85, 92, 93, 106; funding
    of operations 85, 189; instability of
    agenda 186; and "steering", "driving"
    of policy 182, 206; use of to build
    area policy consensus 93, 108, 114
comparative methods in analyzing
    policy outcomes 29, 35–37, 75–77
constraints on local government *see*
    local government: constraints on
council-manager and mayor-council
    systems, convergence between
    "adapted city" 65
council-manager government 7, 15,
    129, 160–162, 181, 183, 194; conflict
    reduction 22–23, 160–161; effect on
    policy and administration 18–19, 54,
    65, 154; conflict over whether or not
    to adopt 93; history of adoption 65;
    public finances 7, 18–19
council-manager government
    compared with mayor-council 22,
    93, 105, 181–184, 205
Crisfield, Md. 64
CWTSatoTravel, formerly Sato Travel,
    corporate travel service and call
    center in Ely, Minn. 97, 98, 111, 114,
    118, 147, 186

Daley, Richard J. (1902–76), Chicago
    mayor (1955–76) 200

Index 215

Daley, Richard M. (1942–), Chicago mayor (1989–2011) 45

Dayton, Mark (1947–), Minnesota state auditor (1981–95), US senator (2001–07), Minnesota governor (2011–) 125, 149, 189, 202

Defenbaugh, William "Bill", Ely city attorney (during 1980s) 110

deindustrialization 50–51

Delta Air Lines reservations center in Chisholm, Minn. (formerly owned by Northwest Airlines) 135

demographics of US towns and cities 7, 14, 27, 34, 51, 53, 67, 86, 88–89, 124

Dicklich, Ronald (1951–), Minnesota state senator, Hibbing mayor, lobbyist 128, 138–139

Dicklich, Thomas (1978–), Hibbing city administrator (2011–) 127–128

Dill, David (1955–2015), Minnesota state representative (2003–15) 91

Dillon family of Sterling, Ill., manufacturers, philanthropists 153, 177

Dillon, John Forrest (1831–1914), Iowa and federal judge 4, 5

Dillon's Rule 4, 20, 69, 70, 72; and English common law 4, 69; state control over local government 4, 36

diversification of economy 8, 37–38, 50–53, 55, 139, 149, 192

Dixon, Ill. 168–169

DMR Electronics, subsidiary of Detroit Reman, engine re-manufacturer, Hibbing, Minn. 127, 145

Downey, Richard, Rock Falls city administrator (2003–11) 162

Duluth, Missabe and Iron Range Railway (DM&IR) 110

Ecklund, Rob, Minnesota state representative (2015–) and union official 91

economic development policy: "builder mayors" and 45; business assistance 14, 23, 30, 101, 105, 132, 188, 198; as conducted by local government 33, 53–57, 65; definition of public policy 18–19; "demand-side" versus "supply-side" policy 30; effect on policy of devolution of authority to local government 30, 33, 71–72, 158–159, 180–181; governance of 31–33; job creation (or "new jobs")

30, 67, 100, 125, 107, 158–160; policy delivery, dependence on established decision-making process 181, 199, 204; public services and infrastructure 30, 31, 70, 85, 114, 174–175; "supply-side" policies 14, 30, 97, 99, 105, 140

economic "imperatives", meme in economic development policy 1, 5, 45, 50–53, 55–57, 64–65, 71, 136

economic inequality: influence on economic development policy 5, 36, 43–44; influence on funding public services 4, 54

economic trends affecting municipal governments 14

electoral politics: 1978 general election, Minnesota ("Minnesota Massacre") 125, 149; 2002 election, Hibbing, Minn., and economic development 129, 139; 2004 election, Ely, and city administration issue 103; 2005 election, Rock Falls, Ill. 175; 2005 sales tax referendum, Dixon, Rock Falls and Sterling, Ill. 168–169; 2006 election, Ely 100, 104, 193, 196; 2008 election, Ely 109; 2010 election, Hibbing 123, 127, 140, 182, 184; 2010 elections, and voter revolt 117, 123, 140, 184; 2015 special legislative election, Ely, Minn. 91; 2016 election results, and populism 10, 16, 91, 162; 2017 election, Sterling, and populism 11; Ely, Minn. and school district funding 193, 194, 196; Minnesota Iron Range Democratic tradition 122

electoral politics and running for office, perception of vulnerability of businesspeople to 85

Ely Area Development Association (EADA), economic development forum in Ely, Minn. 95, 96, 98–101, 106, 118, 186

Ely-Bloomenson Hospital, Ely, Minn. 110, 121, 151

Ely Business Park 106–7, 110–113, 114, 121, 182; development of 91, 111, 186; expansion of infrastructure 101, 102; JOBZ designation 136; major tenants 97, 111–113; management of 94, 110, 189; politics on city council of 107, 110; restrictive covenants on retail/residential use 111–112, 114; siting on former railroad land 85–86

216 *Index*

Ely Chamber of Commerce, Ely, Minn.
31, 115, 193
Ely, Minn., city council 34, 92–95,
103–108, 110, 117, 180, 181,
183; authority over economic
development policy 14, 31, 34,
93, 97, 100–101, 106; controversy
over personnel issues 103–104;
controversy over tourism support
193; debate over city administration
85, 93, 104–106; financial support
for arts and tourism 90, 92, 193;
management of city infrastructure
94, 106–108; management of
covenants in business park 112–113;
political support for mining 91
Ely, Minn., city of 7, 8, 28, 29, 35,
91–95, 96, 192; conflict between
tourism and proposed copper-
nickel mining 90–91; development
of public infrastructure 85–86, 97,
121, 136, 182, 186, 189; Economic
Development Authority 93–94,
186; economy of 32, 86–92; Ely
Airport Commission 94; high
citizen participation in elections
and community affairs 92, 193;
investment in public infrastructure
8, 31, 85, 114; political relationship
with surrounding jurisdictions 8,
100–101; public buildings 101–102;
public finances 8, 16, 85, 93, 130,
190–191; public works garage
106–107, 114, 188; sewage treatment
plant project 85, 106–107, 114, 115,
120; utility infrastructure 108, 120
Ely public schools (Independent
School District 696) 96, 97
English common law: 1682 revocation
of London charter and relevance
to US law 4; influence on US and
Canadian local government law 4, 69
Enterprise Zone, Whiteside/
Carroll County, Ill. 8, 32, 165,
174, 179; as example of locally
led definition of operating area
158–159; development of Walmart
distribution center 173, 176;
improvements in relations between
Rock Falls and Sterling 159; land
availability within zone 172, 178;
role in business recruitment 154, 199;
role in coordinating local economic
development policy 159

Environmental Protection Agency,
US 178, 182; experiment to reverse
eutrophication of Shagawa Lake,
Minn. 115; funding of brownfield
reclamation, Rock Falls and Sterling
158, 162, 164–166; remediation of
Northwestern Steel and Wire site,
Sterling, Ill. 164

Fairview Range Medical Center,
Hibbing, Minn. 135, 145, 151, 152
Fall Lake, Town of (Minnesota local
government unit, also known as Fall
Lake Township) 7, 10, 16, 92, 96
federal direct spending on US local
government, cuts in 45, 64–67
federal intergovernmental aid
for economic and community
development 45, 67
Fedo, John, Minnesota politician,
consultant and property developer
112–113, 114
Feldman's department store, Hibbing,
Minn. 141
fire coverage, as measure of
intergovernmental relations 8, 22,
92, 101, 192
Fiscal Disparities Act, Minnesota 202
footloose capital (see capital flight) 1
form of local government, influence on
policy 19
Fort Wayne, Indiana, and local
government reorganization 22
fragmentation of government,
geographical, and influence on
policy 21, 27, 36–37, 54, 74, 92,
146–147
fragmentation of government,
institutions within units of
government 54, 77; impact on setting
policy agendas 93
Frantz Manufacturing, Sterling, Ill.
156, 177
free market policy tendency in economic
development 1, 24, 46, 71, 97
Fridley, Minn., as example of
interaction between local
government aid and tax base 202

Gardiner Trust, Ely, Minn., public arts
endowment 90
Garrity, Pat, Hibbing, Minn., city clerk
(1975–91, 1995–2003, 2007–) 133,
139, 183

Index 217

Glass Box, Duluth, Minn., former department store 141
Glencore, Swiss mining firm 91
globalization 14, 43–44; comparison with Gilded Age 43; free trade and impact on local economies 43, 47–48
Glumac, Anne, Iron Mining Association of Minnesota president 59
Grahek, J. P. "Doc" (1911–2001), Ely mayor (1956–80, 1987–90) 83–86, 102, 200; 1973 annexation agreement with Morse Township 186; aftermath of retirement of 84–86, 92–93; infrastructure projects 115; political influence 83–84; top-down governance style 93
Greater Sterling Development Corporation (GSDC) 31, 32, 161, 172; distribution and retail strategy 163; leadership 161; role in business recruitment 161, 163, 165, 172; role in reclamation of Northwestern Steel & Wire site 164–165
Grinnell, Iowa, as example of economic growth 53

Hansen, Bill, Tofte, Minn., resort owner and environmental advocate 91
Harvey, David, geographer 50–51
Harvey, Ill., as example of economic scarcity 202
Henderson, Pat, Minnesota community organizer and economic development official 98–100, 118
Henning, William "Bill", Ely economic development official 96–8, 102; broadband Internet 97–98; recruitment of Sato Travel 97; role in creation of Ely area Community Economic Development Joint Powers Board 96–97, 118
Henrekin, Sandy, economic development official, Rock Falls, Ill. 171
Herberger's, department store chain, and Hibbing 135, 141
Hibbing Airpark, business park in Hibbing, Minn. 96, 133, 136, 186; development of speculative office/industrial building ("Spec Building") 127, 132; IRRRB grant for 137
Hibbing, Minn., city of 7, 28, 29; influences of land area on economic development 27; large land area

133; negative past reputation in economic development 124–126, 134; public finance 129–130, 190–191; retail development strategy *see* Retail Market Analysis Study of Hibbing; shift to activist economic development policy 102, 126–132
Hibbing Community College 132, 136, 144–145
Hibbing "Down Winders", campaigners against regional sewage plant 134
Hibbing Economic Development Authority (HEDA) 96, 128–132, 143–147, 148–152; administration of 31; autonomy from city council 128–129, 132, 138–140; city administration 129; economic development, Economic Development Special Revenue Fund (EDSRF) 127, 129, 132; political stability of 128–131, 138–140; retail recruitment strategy 135, 140–141, 143–145; role in business finance 128, 132, 138, 141, 145–146; support for L&M Radiator 194
Hibbing Fabricators, manufacturer 138, 145, 151
Hibbing, Minn. 6, 8, 14, 35; in popular culture 122
Hibbing, Minn., city council 7, 134, 138–140, 150, 184; 1994 open meeting law case 126, 183; relations with neighboring governments 134–135
Hibbing Taconite (iron ore mine) 49, 122, 131, 137; as major employer 145, 151–152; as recipient of IRRRB funds 147
Highway 1 Corridor Task Force, Minnesota community and economic development group 99
Hull–Rust–Mahoning mine pit, Hibbing, Minn. 49, 122
Hummel, Greg, Chicago real estate lawyer 164–165
Huntsville, Ala., as example of analysis of economic development 52
Hutchinson, Minn., manufacturing job losses 53, 60

I-88 West, and Whiteside/Carroll County Enterprise Zone 174
I-88 West, economic development marketing in Sterling/Rock Falls 173–174

218 *Index*

Illinois 17th congressional district 10
Illinois American Water Company, commercial public utility 160, 173
Illinois Enterprise Zone Act, 1982 38, 71; enterprise zones and incentives for economic development 165
Illinois Environmental Protection Agency 165
Illinois Single-Family Owner-Occupied Rehabilitation program 167
Illinois, state of: causes of conflict among municipalities on economic development 188, 198; devolution to local government on economic development policy 197, 201; effect of fiscal system on economic development spending 189–191, 200; finance system and contrast with Minnesota 8–10; Illinois FIRST (capital bonding program) 173; implications of revenue system for tax poor cities 9; revenue sharing with local government 9, 28, 29, 158, 168, 200, 202; tax-raising power of local government 188
Incredible Ely, private economic development promotion group in Ely, Minn. 186
Indiana, state of, legislature and role in Indianapolis/Marion County Unigov consolidation 22
Indianapolis, Ind., as example of reforming city governance 21, 22; local government reorganization (Unigov) 21, 22
infrastructure spending, popularity of relative to business subsidies 30, 37
institutional capacity (definition of) 19–21, 25–30, 160; as preparedness and readiness 184–186; process and rules as component of 24–25; relationship to delivering policy 5, 20–21, 27, 71, 148, 181–184, 198, 208; theory 13, 15, 18–19
institutional organization and "venue-shopping" 110
institutional organization of government: bargaining power with business 54, 71–77; conflict reduction 30–31, 65; economic development policy 21–23, 148; governance 21, 22, 31, 54, 66, 74–75, 128–129, 131; impact on public policy 13, 54–55, 65, 66, 106–107, 126–127,

132; interaction with leadership 29; intergovernmental relations 52
institutional reform of local government 6, 65, 181–186; in Ely 93–106; in Hibbing 128–130, 138–140; in Rock Falls and Sterling 154, 162–163
institutionalization of policy making, influence on policy outcomes 19, 54
Inter-Community Cooperation Leadership Program (ICCLP), Minnesota 95–96
intergovernmental relations, links among local governments 134–136, 186–188
Internet and telecommunications: broadband city utility (Rock Falls, Ill.) 182, 190; as economic development policy 32, 134; IRRRB grant for fiber-to-the-premises, Hibbing, Minn. 137; rural broadband 86, 97–98, 118
Iowa, high manufacturing employment 48, 51, 58
Iowa, US state 4, 15, 141, 172, 177
Iracore International, pipeline manufacturer in Hibbing, Minn. 147, 150, 152; designation of JOBZ tax break 136; HEDA assistance to 146; IRRRB assistance to 145; support from Hibbing industrial loan fund 127
Iron Range culture, "Iron Range Alzheimer's" quote 84–85
Iron Range (Minnesota region) 14, 60, 91, 92, 95–96, 122, 141, 155–156, 197, 201; economic development efforts 56–57, 125, 136; economy of 49, 57, 83, 86–87, 98, 143–144; intergovernmental aid to municipalities in region 37, 68; location 8, 12; mining industry 48–49; patterns of governance 131, 136; politics 10, 105–106, 125
Iron Range Resources and Rehabilitation Board (IRRRB) 8, 27, 29, 32, 33, 56–57, 100, 112–115, 134–139, 201, 203; 2016 Legislative Auditor's report 32; compatibility of agenda with that of local governments in service area 94, 128, 131, 145–148; differences in agenda with smaller municipalities 27, 32; funding of local economic development 94, 95,

99, 137–138; negativity in reputation 56–57, 125–126; preemption of local government 114–115; role in economic development 94–95, 97, 99, 137–138, 145–148, 150, 184; role in public infrastructure and community development 85, 95–96, 99, 112–113, 198; state legislative domination of board 32, 94

Irresistible Ink, division of Hallmark Cards, Inc., Ely, Minn. and Two Harbors, Minn. 112

Johnson, Douglas J. "Doug" (1942–), Minnesota state senator (1977–2002) 112

Kess, Paul, Ely city council member 103, 104, 121
King Charles II (1630–85), 1682 *quo warranto* writ and local government authority 4
Klun, Larry (1952–2006), Ely city attorney (mostly during late 1970s, 1990s and 2000s) 110

L&M Fleet Supply (regional hardware store chain), expansion in Hibbing, Minn. 143, 184
L&M Radiator, manufacturer and servicer, Hibbing Minn. 145–146; assistance from IRRRB 147; designation of JOBZ tax break 136; financial assistance from HEDA 145–146, 150, 194; support from Hibbing industrial loan fund 127, 138
Lakewood Industries, Hibbing, Minn., chopsticks factory 125–126, 137
Lamppa, Gary, former commissioner of Iron Range Resources and Rehabilitation Board 125
land use policy: brownfield reclamation 34, 58, 157–168; Ely Business Park 110–113; as local government economic development tool 72–73, 109–110, 170–172; *see also* annexation
Larson, Nancy, Ely, Minn. economic and community development official 100, 118, 119
Laurentian Energy Authority, biofuels utility project, Minnesota 134–135
Lawrence, David L. (1889–1966), Pittsburgh, Pa., mayor (1946–59), Pennsylvania governor (1959–63) 77

Lawrence Hardware, closed manufacturer in Sterling, Ill. 156, 157
leadership: influence on policy outcomes 53, 64, 85, 114, 175–176; relationship with institutional organization 23, 85, 93, 95–97, 114, 127–128; role of in economic development policy formulation 29, 183, 93, 96–97, 126–127
Lee, Charles "Skip", Sterling Ill. mayor 192
Lees Rentals and Commercial Development, property developer, Hibbing, Minn. 141, 143, 144
Leggett & Platt, furniture manufacturer 164–165
Levy limits (state-mandated limitation on local property taxes) 21, 202, 208
local ancestry of community leaders and effect on politics 96, 127–128
local governance, agreements and arrangements among municipalities 8, 18, 31, 43, 54, 71, 76, 92, 120, 187
Local Government Aid (LGA), Minnesota revenue support program for local government 9, 52, 68–69, 88–89, 130, 160, 188, 201–202
local government constitutional standing *see* Dillon's Rule
local government: constraints on 5, 18, 55, 70, 72, 74, 130, 198, 205, 207; economic development policies by 53–54; how policy choices are exercised 5, 30, 46; intermediary between individual and state 3; potential to enable free exercise of choice according to local preferences 3; role in economic development policy 65, 69, 70; structural limitations on 5, 36, 64–71, 206; taxing authority, relationship to state law 3, 29, 71; theoretical freedom of businesses to leave jurisdiction at will 46
local government finances: concept of "permanent fiscal crisis" 68; debt and borrowing 70, 76–77, 97, 111, 129, 161; impact of economic trends on 45–47; retiree liabilities and impact on policy 68, 206; structural impact on public policy 45, 72, 130; tight finances and examples of consequences 205

220 *Index*

local option sales taxes 136, 140, 180, 184; impact on economic development policy 72–73, 140, 158–160, 190, 199–200; impact on local government revenue 10, 94–95, 171, 176, 191, 202; referenda 95, 158, 163, 168–169, 176, 178; role in triggering competition between neighboring cities 159–160, 176, 188; state role in 29, 52, 94–95, 136, 140, 203

London, England 4, 50, 70, 165, 205

Louisville and Jefferson County, Ky., as example of city–county consolidation 21

Lowe's, Inc. (home improvement and hardware store chain), Hibbing, Minn., store development 139, 143–144, 147, 184

LTV Steel Mining, Hoyt Lakes, Minn.: closure of (2001) 87, 98, 185; use of site for proposed new copper-nickel mine 91

Lynn Boulevard, Sterling, Ill., access road for business parks 190

manufacturing employment: 1980–2010 decline in US 47–50; distribution within US 48, 51; framed as "good paying jobs" 44–48, 86–87, 136; impact on employment from 2001 recession 157, 185; local dependence on 47, 124; local trends relative to US national average 44; trends in larger cities 44, 48; trends in smaller towns 44, 46, 48–50, 124

manufacturing, as economic development policy 27, 30, 54, 72, 98–99, 110, 127, 138, 145–146, 174

Massachusetts, local sales taxes *see* local option sales taxes, state role in

mayor-council systems of municipal government 15, 22, 54, 65, 93, 102, 128, 160–161, 199, 200, 205; reform with city administrator or chief operating officer 6, 7, 14, 104, 129, 162–163; transition to 208

Maytag, as example of offshored manufacturing 51

Metropolitan Council (regional government body for Minneapolis/ St. Paul metropolitan area, Minnesota) 202

microlending, as economic development strategy 98–99

Milwaukee, Wisc., subsidies to railroads for routes to Chicago 69

mining: copper-nickel, proposed in northeastern Minnesota 91, 101, 193, 105–106; iron ore, economic impact of 86–87, 124; as political issue 105–106

Minneapolis, Minn. 53, 55, 56, 60, 68, 98, 107, 143, 144, 202

Minneapolis/St. Paul, Minn. ("Twin Cities") 8, 68, 89, 102, 104, 125, 135, 149, 202

Minnesota 8th congressional district 10

Minnesota Department of Revenue, Minnesota Collection Enterprise (MCE), Ely, Minn. 85, 97, 98, 106, 111–112

Minnesota Miracle, tax reform from 1971 9, 52, 201, 202

Minnesota Power, electric utility, internet services, division of Allete, Inc. 56, 97

Minnesota, state of: centralization of economic development policy 32; Department of Employment and Economic Development 113, 117, 201; fiscal equalization of local government 9, 52, 88–89; Iron Range Resources and Rehabilitation Board (IRRRB) *see separate entry*; Job Opportunity Building Zones (JOBZ) program, 2003–15 27, 38, 115, 159, 204; JOBZ program, compared with Illinois enterprise zones 136; legislative vote required to authorize local option sales tax 29; politics 52, 107

Mondale, Walter (1928–), US senator (1966–76), US vice president (1977–81) 83, 84, 149

Morse, Town of (Minnesota local government unit, also known as Morse Township) 7, 8, 96, 101, 108

Mulvaney, Ed (1947–), former Rock Falls Ill. mayor 160, 162, 163, 165, 167, 175

Muncie, Ind., as example of analysis of economic development 52, 64

Nashville and Davidson County, Tenn., as example of city–county consolidation 21

National Manufacturing (division of Stanley Black & Decker), Sterling, Ill. 156, 157

Index 221

New Federalism (Reagan Administration policy), impact on local government 45

New York, city of 55, 64, 70, 76–77, 205; nature of employment in, compared with Rust Belt 51

Nixon, Richard (1911–94), US senator (1950–53), US vice president (1953–61), US president (1969–74), administration of 68

Nolan, Rick (1943–), US congressman, Minnesota 8th district (2013–) 10

Northagen, Duane, former Hibbing, Minn. economic developer 126, 148, 183

Northern Lakes Arts Association, Ely, Minn. area arts promotion and events group 90, 193

Northshore Mining, Babbitt, Minn., subsidiary of Cleveland-Cliffs 98

Northwestern Steel and Wire, Inc. (NWSW), Sterling Ill. 49, 173–175, 177, 185; declaration of bankruptcy 153; decline in employment before bankruptcy 59; impact of collapse on area employment 155, 157, 173; local political leadership after collapse 160–161; reclamation of site 162–165, 178; role in community 153

Novak, Chuck (1946–), Ely mayor (2007–09, 2015–) 100, 104, 105, 109

Obama, Barack (1961–), US senator (2005–08), US president (2009–17) 10

Oberstar, James L. "Jim", (1934–2014), US congressman (1975–2011) 107, 189

Parrish-Alford, closed manufacturer in Rock Falls, Ill. 155, 156, 185; involuntary possession of site by Rock Falls 166; reclamation of riverfront site 163, 165, 185, 190; reorganization of city government and effect on reclamation project 175

Paulucci, Luigino "Jeno" (1918–2011), Hibbing-raised entrepreneur and corporate executive 126

Pawlenty, Tim (1960–), Minnesota house speaker (1999–2002), Minnesota governor (2003–11) 120, 149, 160, 208; attempt to reduce local government aid through "unallotments" 201; citizen representatives on IRRRB 97, 102;

creation of JOBZ program 38, 136; cuts by Pawlenty Administration in local government aid 9, 130, 160, 188; withholding of funding for Highway 169 project near Ely, Minn. 189

Pena, Federico (1947–), Denver mayor (1983–91), US transportation secretary (1993–97), energy secretary (1997–98) 45

Perpich, Rudy (1928–95), Minnesota governor (1976–79, 1983–91) 122, 125

Peterson, Paul, political scientist 3

Pittsburgh, Pa., non-profit leadership of economic development policy 77

plant closings, examples of 51, 59, 87, 91, 98, 116, 153, 155–157, 160–161, 173, 185

policy formulation, "steering" and "driving", relationship between 19

political agency, definition 3, 13–14, 45

political culture of selected communities 10–12, 84–85, 92, 191–192; Ely 84–85, 92, 192–193; Rock Falls and Sterling, Ill. 168–169

political geography: annexation and relationship with policy 21, 27, 132–133; consolidation of municipalities and policy 21, 22, 133; impact on local leadership 133, 146, 183

PolyMet, proposed copper-nickel mine, Hoyt Lakes, Minn. 91

privatism, US political tradition 5

Project Firefly, economic development initiative in Ely, Minn. (2005–08) 98–100, 118

Quie, Al (1923–), US congressman (1958–79), Minnesota governor (1979–83) 125

"race to the bottom" 3, 8, 44, 45, 55

Range Regional Airport (formerly Chisholm-Hibbing Airport), Hibbing, Minn. 127, 129, 135–136

Reagan, Ronald (1911–2004), California governor (1967–75), US president (1981–89) 45, 67, 77; 1981 inaugural address regarding role of government 67

Redshaw, Brian, former city administrator, Hibbing, Minn. 128, 183

222   *Index*

regimes, urban theory, and applicability to institutional processes 23–25, 55, 70, 74–77

regionalism and regional cooperation 74, 135–136

Retail Market Analysis Study of Hibbing ("Retail-MASH"): citizen response to survey 140; economic development policy 150, 152; funding 132; inclusion of neighboring cities 135; outcomes 144

retail sales: impact on tax base of Illinois municipalities 202; role in Ely economy 83, 89, 115

retailing as economic development strategy 72; in Ely 98; in Hibbing 123, 126–127, 135, 140–145; in Rock Falls and Sterling, 169–173; edge of town development 170–171; potential impact on government finances 168, 171

retirement of community leaders, impact on policy and governance 24–25, 105, 199; Bill Henning, Ely 102, 118; Ed Mulvaney, Rock Falls 165; J. P. Grahek, Ely 83–84; Lee Tessier, Ely 93, 114

revenue-sharing: among local governments 108, 186; federal, with local government 68; state and federal, with local government 2, 29, 43, 45, 67–68, 71, 158

Rick Lees (property developer, Hibbing, Minn.) 141, 143, 144, 183

Ridley, Sam (1919–2003), Smyrna, Tenn., mayor (1947–87) 64

Rock Falls Community Development Corporation (RFCDC), economic development agency 15, 32, 154, 168, 172, 185, 190, 208; creation and governance 162–163; leadership of brownfield reclamation 165–167; role in property development and land use 31, 171; strategies 163, 172–173; winding up 154, 159, 176, 182

Rock Falls, Ill. 6, 8, 14, 15, 154–155; Eagle Country Markets bankruptcy 172

Rock Falls, Ill., city council 162–163, 169, 172, 175, 178; emergence of consensus on brownfield reclamation 165; vote to support Sterling expansion of enterprise zone 159

Rock Falls, Ill., city of 7, 8, 28, 32; commission form of government prior to 2002, 162; direct mayor/council control of economic development 159; public finances 189–191; public utilities, internet as economic development policy 32, 182, 190; transition from commission system to mayor-council government 154

Rock River Redevelopment Project, Sterling, Ill. 164, 190

Rubbermaid, as example of offshored manufacturing 52

Rukavina, Tom (1950–), county commissioner, St. Louis County, Minn. (2015–), state representative (1987–2013) 99

Russell, Burdsall & Ward (RB&W), closed manufacturer in Rock Falls, Ill. 155–156, 166; city reorganization and effect on site reclamation 175; closure 155–156, 185; development of Holiday Inn Express on site 166, 171; site reclamation 163, 165–166, 180, 190

Rust Belt 44, 48

Ryan, Jack (banker and investor, former IRRRB member, Hibbing, Minn.) 38, 183

Salerno, Frank (1930–2013), Ely mayor (1990–93, 1995, 2003–05) 102–104

sales tax statistics: Minnesota cities 142, 144; Illinois cities 191

Sanders, Bernie (1942–), Burlington, Vt., mayor (1981–89), US congressman (1991–2007), US senator (2007–) 10, 11

Santa Barbara, Calif., as example of analysis of economic development 52

Sassen, Saskia (1947–), sociologist 3

Sato Travel office in Ely, Minn. *see* CWTSatoTravel

Sauk Valley Chamber of Commerce, Sterling, Ill. 161, 182

Sauk Valley College, Sterling, Ill. 159

Schaumburg, Ill., as example of strong tax base 202

school enrollment, declines in, Ely, Minn. 88, 116

service sector employment, local dependence on 47–48

shared vision of community development, effect on local politics 30, 73

Sheffield, England, difficulty redeveloping industrial site 205

Shelley Robinson, health care executive and former IRRRB member 38

Skraba, Roger, Ely mayor (2005–07, 2009–13) 91, 102, 104, 109, 193; lobbying Twin Metals to take more visible community role 91

small towns and governance, disadvantages relative to major cities 29, 55; examples of governance 56, 64, 168–169

Smyrna, Tenn. 64

Somerset, Md. 64

Sotelo, Heather, chamber of commerce official and economic developer, Sterling, Ill. 161

St. Louis County, Minn. 89, 107, 110, 112, 124, 201; Board of Adjustment 89

St. Paul, Minn. 67, 125

Stassen, Harold (1907–2001), Minnesota governor (1939–43) 38

state budget deficits, impact on local government 9, 45, 68, 205

state centralization and effect on local policy 26, 29, 188, 197, 200, 203

state government: comparison between Minnesota and Illinois funding of local government 8–10, 197, 200–204; framework of rules over local government 2, 14, 66–73, 176; frameworks at state level for local government in Europe 36, 53, 74; local economic development policy 22, 57, 67, 72, 99–100, 136; role in funding public infrastructure 85; variations in policy as analogy for international comparisons 37

state influence on local spending, "flypaper effect" 33, 188

state law, local government as "creatures of the state" 72

state-level fiscal regimes, impact of: on economic development spending 189–190; local government revenue 10, 21, 28–29, 52, 71, 88, 176, 189–191; public policy 9, 20–21, 72–73; public spending 9, 28, 67–68, 71, 189–190; schools 9

Steger Mukluks (apparel manufacturer), as example of economic development 112–113, 147

Sterling city council 12, 154, 169, 181, 199; tax increment bond vote for Sterling Steel 165

Sterling, Ill., city of 7, 28, 32, 154–155; public finance 7, 161, 189–190

Sterling, Ill. 6, 8, 14, 15

Sterling Public Schools (Sterling Community Unit School District #5) 173

Sterling Steel, manufacturer in Sterling, Ill. 59, 157, 163–165, 177

Sterling Today, nonprofit group in Sterling, Ill. 182

Stone, Clarence (1935–), political scientist 23

Stonite, kitchen countertop product 56

survey interview methods 33–35; interview selection 34–35

Taconite Assistance Area (IRRRB service area and taxing district, Minn.) 29, 32

tax increment financing (TIF) 143, 201; as component of Hibbing economic development spending 146; declined by Walmart for Sterling distribution center 173, 176, 189; differences in levels of use among local governments 189–190; fall from favor among local governments 189; Sterling Steel 165

Technimar, as example of economic development failure 56–57

Tessier, Lee (1938–), Ely, Minn. city clerk (1986–2000) 93, 114

Thompson, James R. (1936–), Illinois governor (1977–91) 38

Tiebout, Charles (1924–68), economist, theory of tax competitiveness of local jurisdictions 3

tourism and economic development 6, 53, 72–73, 86, 91, 100–101, 148; Ely area townships' concern about overdevelopment 109; impact on Ely of changes in travel market 89–90, 114

Tourville, John, public official and consultant, former Hibbing and Ely city clerk 98, 102–104, 117, 119

Trump, Donald J. (1946–), US president (2017–) 10, 91, 194

224 *Index*

trust in politics by public, and impact on policy 193

Tscheschlok, Christian, economic development official, Rock Falls CDC director (2002–07) 162, 165, 171

Twin Metals, proposed copper-nickel mine, southeast of Ely, Minn. 91, 113

two-level case study design 35–37; applicability of to larger cities and other countries 36

United Kingdom, local government 36, 71

Urban Development Action Grant (UDAG), former US program for community development 66

US Constitution, Compact Clause 18

US Department of Agriculture, role in local government infrastructure 107; US Forest Service 97, 108, 110

US presidential election, 2016, results in selected communities 10, 194

US trade and impact on local economies 5, 43–44, 47–48, 50, 55

US trade statistics 58–59

utility infrastructure as economic development strategy 159–160; historic US lead in 69–70

Ventura, Jesse (1951–), Minnesota governor (1999–2003) 9, 149

Vermilion Community College, Ely, Minn. 85, 97, 193, 195–196

viability of community, maintenance through organization or policy 21–22, 55

Wahl Clipper, manufacturer in Sterling, Ill. 156, 174, 177

Walgreens, US drugstore chain: as example of retail development 143, 144, 147; Hibbing, Minn., rezoning to allow store 184, 194; new store cited as positive sign for Rock Falls, Ill. 171

Walmart Distribution Center, Sterling Township, Ill. 30, 59, 172–174, 177, 178; extension of utility lines to 159; pay rates 59, 174; recruitment of 157, 192, 199; rejection of TIF 173, 176, 189; tax abatements for 186, 201

Walmart: development of Supercenter in Hibbing, Minn. 139, 143, 151; impact on manufacturing 51; Rock Falls, Ill., store as example of older store 170, 172; Supercenter in Sterling, Ill. 171

Waterloo, Iowa, plant closings in 51

Welliver, David, Minnesota banker and lobbyist 56, 60

Wescott, William "Bill", Rock Falls, Ill., mayor (2013–) 176

Whiteside/Carroll County Enterprise Zone *see* Enterprise Zone, Whiteside/Carroll County

Wieland, Jay, former city manager in Sterling, Ill. 160, 164

Wisconsin Dells, as counterpoint to Ely, Minn., economic development, tourism 109

Wisconsin, US state 48, 51, 58, 69

Wolff, Rick (1951–2013), Hibbing Minn., mayor (2003–11) 127, 129, 139, 183

worker training as economic development strategy 3, 6, 19, 20, 145, 159

Wyss, Thomas (1942–), state senator, Indiana legislature 22